Christmas: 1940-1959

A Collector's Guide to Decorations and Customs

Revised 2nd Edition

Schiffer Publishing
80 Lower Valley Road, Atglen, PA

Dedication

This book is dedicated to everyone born after 1940. You were born into a period of history that has seen rapid technological changes, world-wide global concerns and partnership, and unbelievable changes in both Christmas decorations and in decorating customs. You have witnessed the advent of motion lights, musical tree lights, fiber optic trees, and glow-in-the dark novelties. It is this generation that has seen Christmas come to the World Wide Web, be it web sites devoted to holiday history, various action sites which bring Christmas items into homes across the world, or email communications taking place between collectors across this continent and the European continent as well. World War II had a profound effect upon our Christmas history in that we sought our own identity; then, in the later part of the Millennium, we once again returned to our European roots.

It is to my favorite person born in 1949, my wife Sharon, that I personally dedicate this book. Without her love for Christmas, and for others, the world would be far less rich. Born into a wonderful German family steeped in German traditions, she passes these traditions on to her nieces and nephews. Sharon has spent her time in the pursuit of helping others, be they students, relatives, friends, or even almost total strangers. She indeed is "The Spirit of Christmas."

Sharon Thiel underneath her Christmas tree in the 1950s holding her favorite Christmas present that year. $Priceless.

Library of Congress Cataloging-in-Publication Data

Brenner, Robert.
Christmas, 1940-1959: a collector's guide to decorations and customs/ by Robert Brenner.
p. cm.
ISBN 0-7643-1899-3 (pbk.)
1. Christmas—Collectibles. 2. Christmas decorations—Collectors and collecting. I. Title.
NK4696.4.B688 2004
394.2663'0973'075—dc22

2003021846

Designed by John P. Cheek
Type set in Goudy OlSt XBd BT/Goudy OlSt BT

ISBN: 0-7643-1899-3
Printed in China
1 2 3 4

Published by Schiffer Publishing Ltd.
4880 Lower Valley Road
Atglen, PA 19310
Phone: (610) 593-1777; Fax: (610) 593-2002
E-mail: Info@schifferbooks.com
Please visit our web site catalog at **www.schifferbooks.com**
We are always looking for people to write books on new and related subjects. If you have an idea for a book please contact us at the above address.

This book may be purchased from the publisher.
Include $3.95 for shipping.
Please try your bookstore first.
You may write for a free catalog.

In Europe, Schiffer books are distributed by
Bushwood Books
6 Marksbury Ave.
Kew Gardens
Surrey TW9 4JF England
Phone: 44 (0) 20 8392-8585; Fax: 44 (0) 20 8392-9876
E-mail: info@bushwoodbooks.co.uk
Free postage in the U.K., Europe; air mail at cost.

Contents

Acknowledgments 4
Introduction—Our European Past
- 1850-1859 5
- 1860-1869 5
- 1870-1879 5
- 1880-1889 5
- 1890-1899 6
- 1900-1909 6
- 1910-1919 6
- 1920-1929 6
- 1930-1939 6

Chapter I. The 1940s—A New Beginning and Identity 7
- An Historical Perspective of this Decade—Dramatic Changes in Christmas 7
- Our Greeting Cards, Advertising, and Paper Memorabilia 14
- Our Trees 19
- How We Decorated Our Homes 21
- American Influences on Glass Tree Decorations 23
- European Influences on Glass Tree Decorations 26
- A Closer Look at Other Tree Decorations of the Decade 30
- Under Our Trees 43
- Indoor Electric Lighting of Our Trees and Homes 53
- Outdoor Electric Lighting 67

Chapter II. The 1950s—The Industrial Age Molds Our Christmas Traditions 69
- Historical Perspectives—Radical Changes Take Place 69
- Cards, Wrapping Paper, and Paper 80
- Our Trees 89
- How We Decorated Our Homes 93
- How We Decorated Our Trees 98
- European Influences on Our Glass Ornaments 98
- American Influences on Our Glass Ornaments 115
- A Closer Look at Other Tree Decorations of This Decade 117
- Under Our Trees 136
- Indoor Electric Lighting of Our Trees and Homes 154
- Outdoor Electric Lighting 171

References Cited 174
Index 175

Acknowledgments

Without the generous help, motivation, and understanding of countless individuals, this book would have never been possible. I especially wish to thank Bruce Waters for his photography expertise, which is evident throughout. Hours upon hours of careful handling and delicate maneuvering were necessary to photograph the hundreds of Christmas items contained herein. His patience is beyond belief. Special thanks go also to Fred Studach, a close personal friend who spent countless hours helping Bruce with the intricacies of photographic work here on site in Princeton. Eric Stensrud also helped with sorting, categorizing, and even providing Italian light sets to be photographed for this project. Thanks go to Jeff Snyder, "editor extraordinaire," who spent hours upon hours working with me on the editing of this book and John Cheek who also spent countless hours doing a magnificent job of creatively planning the layout of this book.

Equally important is my wife Sharon, who spent hours upon hours helping with various aspects of this book as well as picking up other household duties when I was writing. As usual, her editorial skills and suggestions were of tremendous help in this project. Special thanks to my first mom, Jeanette, and my second mom, Carmen, who help manage our collection. They sorted, categorized, and cataloged the many Christmas items photographed from our collection for this project. Moms are the best! Sharon and I are so lucky to have such loving families.

Certain individuals from Europe were extremely instrumental in helping me with information and wonderful images. First of all, I wish to thank Ulrike Bohm-Beck of Lauscha, who served as a translator of never-before read material on the period in Germany between World War II and the Reunification of Germany. Lutz Nauman was the expert photographer who copied the marvelous images from the archives of the glass museum in Lauscha. His expertise in photography and Ulrike's marvelous command of German and English helped to enrich this portion of the book. Of special help in Germany was Helena Horn, the director of the marvelous glass museum in Lauscha. What a wonderful gift to Germany this museum curator is. Ms. Horn has transformed this museum into a spectacular display of Christmas tree ornaments and interpretative exhibits revolving around their manufacturing and a stupendous display of German glass blown in this region. Also of great help in Germany were Helmut Krebs, Harald Wohlfahrt, Sandra Brehm, and Michael Krebs.

From Italy, I would like to acknowledge the unselfish contributions of time, research material, and photographs from Enrico Scaletti and Luca Terruzzi.

From Czechloslovakia, I would like to thank Filip Brogowski. From Poland, I would like to thank Marek Palowski, Glen Lewis, and Patricia and Eric Breen.

Where would the world be without qualified and gifted librarians? Once again a project of this magnitude would be impossible without the help of so many different librarians. Even though Princeton is rural and somewhat isolated geographically, our very qualified staff goes far in bridging this gap. Thanks go to Vicki Duhr, our new competent head librarian, who spends countless hours helping everyone who asks for her assistance. Thanks also go to other staff and volunteers who helped with the many requests filled to complete this book: Shirley Hamaishi, Ruby Keller, Dawn Wianecki, Nelson Marvin, and Marge Philbrick.

Thanks go to the following friends and associates who provided so much help in many different ways: Jim and Roberta Fiene, Laura and Craig Beane, Mike Makurat, Mike Garvey, and Eric Stensrud. Eric has been instrumental in helping with our collection. Having been a Christmas collector since the age of ten, at twenty-three, Eric has been our main-stay in helping to decorate and undecorated at Christmas and has built an unbelievable collection of those items which fit into these decades.

Finally, I wish to thank all those who have gone before us who have produced these creative and colorful Christmas items for so many years. But most of all, we all need to thank those people who cared enough to save these Christmas works of art so that our generation might appreciate their beauty. Thanks also go to the countless collectors like you who collect these items, serving as caretakers so future generations might continue to enjoy their beauty.

Introduction—
Our European Past

Lauscha, Germany—the birthplace of the Christmas tree ornament industry, circa 1900.

For anyone living before World War II, Germany was the principal supplier of all Christmas tree ornaments for the United States. Germany had enjoyed a rich heritage, originating back to the early 1820s when the first glass ornaments were produced in Lauscha in the Thuringian area of Germany. Gradually, by the 1880s, Germany had developed the skill of blowing thin glass figural ornaments, the likes of which garnered the attention of nearly every American when they sought new decorations for their tree. These are the decorations that grandmothers and grandfathers all over the United States once hung on their trees.

World War I brought a brief interruption to this rich history of glass production. Immediately After the war, Americans once again returned to Germany for their glass ornaments. Other European countries, including Poland and Czechoslovakia, also produced ornaments. There is no doubt that the period between World War I and World War II was the "Golden Age of Glass Ornaments" as thousands of different figural ornaments in multitudes of different styles graced our trees. In order to gain perspective of what preceded World War II in terms of decorating customs, a quick and concise listing of the different decades is provided.

1850-1859

Our very first trees were decorated with edible, perishable ornaments. Pastry, confectionery, red-cheeked apples, and nuts were the most essential Christmas decorations. Decorated on Christmas Eve, the tree was undecorated and consumed on January 1st. Therefore, popcorn and cranberry chains, simple cookies, molded pastry ornaments, and candles attached by placing pins through branches appeared on this tree. Note also the use of lanterns. Many families would place oil in these glass tumblers, place a wick inside, and then light their trees. This practice of using edibles on trees continued until the birth of glass Christmas tree ornament making in the 1830s. The very wealthy continued to decorate with edibles while the poor started to decorate with glass ornaments since they could be recycled year after year and they were extremely affordable. Our very first ornaments emulated edibles: plums, apples, pears, nuts, and candy. Very few documented references to decorated trees are recorded since the Christmas tree was not yet a widely accepted practice in America.

1860-1869

In this period, the majority of trees continued to be small and were placed on tables. In 1861, the *American Agriculturalist* depicted a tabletop tree decorated with flags, fruit, candy containers, and candles. Paper decorations of all sorts were used, including gilt paper folded into various shapes and paper containers for holding edibles. But most popular were flat Dresden ornaments flashed with gold, red, and green lacquers. Heavy glass ornaments were blown since German glass blowers had not yet perfected the art of blowing the thin-walled ornaments with which we are familiar today. Most kugels were blown into round spheres. Kugels are the early, heavy glass ornaments that were the first glass decorations for the Christmas tree. Originally they were used as decorations in glass blowers cottages; eventually, they found their way to the tree, no doubt due to their brightness and color, which so beautifully reflected candles lit on these early trees. Clay ball weighted candleholders patented in 1867 were used to hold the candles that illuminated these early trees. Feather trees, artificial trees made from green dyed turkey and goose feathers and wired around branches and finished off on each branch with a red composition berry or a candleholder, were used as early as 1841, but were not commonplace in Germany until the 1860s.

1870-1879

Lavishly decorated tabletop trees were the order of the day. However, many of the decorations were home-crafted. As early as the mid-1870s, people complained that Christmas was becoming too commercial and we needed to return to creating our own ornaments. Therefore, note the variety of home-crafted paper decorations and cornucopias on this period tree. Most of these were home-crafted by women and children based upon directions found in various magazines of the day. Grape-shaped kugels made their appearance in this decade, along with other very rare fruit shapes. But these heavy ornaments were soon to be replaced with lighter-weight ornaments. In the early 1870s, Germans had perfected the art of blowing thin glass figural ornaments. Some of these early examples are found on this tree. Very simple in nature, these glass creations were their first attempt in developing the art of glass blowing. Counterweighted candleholders with tin and lead alloy balances created by the toy makers of Nuremberg, Germany, appealed to those who wished to have some decorations with their candles. We also decorated our homes with crepe paper roping, paper decorations, and lots of natural greens and materials.

1880-1889

Thin glass figurals continued to be perfected in this decade and some very elegant examples are seen on these trees. The tradition of using glass beading on the tree becomes somewhat commonplace as families attempted to fill in the large empty spaces with ornamentation. Paper decorations continued to be favorites. Produced by a 24-color plate process, these ornaments took on a three-dimensional effect, especially when embossed by machines. Glass ornaments continued to gain more recognition as tree decorations. Especially favored were those early wire-wrapped ornaments embellished with tinsel, cellophane, cotton, and even crepe paper. Tin and lead candy baskets also made their debut. Often times they were filled with candy . . . other times with tiny gifts. In this period, it was also quite common to hang some of the presents on the tree as decorations. Note the development of candleholders: patented in 1887, clip-on candleholders permitted people to place candles on the far tips of the branches, making it somewhat safer to light the tree. Most of these early holders were lithographed with various designs and were often cut and formed in the shapes of angels, clowns, and even Father Christmas.

1890-1899

During the Victorian period of the late 1800s, lavishly decorated trees were the order of the day. Tabletop trees were now replaced with huge floor-to-ceiling trees in homes with high ceilings. These full-length trees were decorated with huge quantities of ornaments made from many materials: glass, wax, paper, wood, cardboard, and even metal. The more the Victorians could place on their tree, the better it was. Glass figurals continued in popularity, with birds, pinecones, St. Nicholas figures, and other comic figures of the day being produced from glass. Those heavily wire-wrapped ornaments also continued in popularity, especially at the height of the Victorian period. Wax angels, cardboard Dresden ornaments (often candy containers as evidenced on this tree), and even small wooden ornaments were used to decorate trees. Also, it should be noted that the placement of the tinsel roping on the tree was somewhat haphazard. Our Victorian homes reflected this extravagant decorating technique: the more, the better! Note that E-shaped candle holders, patented in the United States, allowed us to more "safely" place lit candles on our trees. Natural greens, dried flowers, paper roping, tinsel sprays, and even plates with Christmas themes were employed.

1900-1909

In reaction to the gaudy and extravagant decorating style of the Victorian period, families sought to return to a more "natural" tree decorating approach. Rather than crowd the tree with loads of edibles and various brightly colored decorations, artists and writers of the time suggested that no color be put on the tree. They recommended only glittering cotton, angel hair, tinsel, clear or silver glass ornaments, imitation snow, pinecones, and only white candles. This style was very popular, as seen by photographs from this period. This "white tree" prevailed up to the start of World War I. Gradually, all the beloved items of earlier days snuck back in, but many times not in their original forms. Santas, bells, birds, and other figural ornaments were used on trees, but they were all white. Many shrewd families saved money by washing the lacquer off the ornaments they had previously purchased. Frugal Americans would strip the needles off their trees and then use them for many years after. Cotton was employed to simulate snow on an evergreen. Thus, an inexpensive artificial tree was quite simple to obtain.

1910-1919

Following the white fashion, trees returned back to brilliant, colorful ornamentation in many forms. Czechoslovakian beaded ornaments in a variety of shapes and paper ornaments added a profusion of color to the tree. Glass figurals continued to be perfected, many of them actually being representations of various comic characters found in newspapers' comic strips. Happy Hooligan, Foxy Grandpa, and Flip appeared on our trees. However, World War I prevented the importation of European ornaments into America. Thus, we had to resort to a few seasons with some very heavy, undesirable ornaments. During this period, Americans, with the aid of German glass blowers brought into New York State, blew glass ornaments. But they were not very successful. We quickly turned to Europe After the war once again for our decorations. Electric lighting began to be employed more and more as Americans sought a new look for their trees. European figural lights were the rage.

1920-1929

This decade marks the start of the "Golden Age of Glass Ornaments," as by now the decorated tree was a now a widely accepted focal point of our American celebration of Christmas. Almost every home now had a tree. Paper, cardboard, wood, and metal ornaments were abandoned and replaced with countless wonderful, brightly colored glass spheres, indents, and figural ornaments of all sorts. Americans especially loved the red, white, and blue painting styles. American society is reflected in ornaments: our love for baseball, our love for transportation, and even our fascination with Indians. Electric lights were the mainstay of the tree. Now more than ever, Americans electrified their trees as the cost of electric lights came ever more within the reach of the "Average American Family." Milk glass lights from Japan became very cheap; thus, we started the trend of adding some variety to our lighting as well. Of course, the end of this decade brought some very impoverished times, but we still sought to decorate our trees as best we could, even if we could purchase only a few glass ornaments or a single string of electric lights. We were not going to have a "sad" Christmas tree.

1930-1939

"The Golden Age of Glass Ornaments" continued in this decade with a profusion of different figural shapes created for the American market. Bells, Santas, fish, pinecones, and horns abounded as we went to Woolworth's and our local "Five and Dime" stores to pick glass ornaments out of bins to take home. Cotton fruit, waxed angels, and some simple small paper ornaments found their way to our trees, but they were scarce in comparison to glass ornaments. Japanese and Czechoslovakian fashioned decorations also found their way to our trees. Especially popular were the cardboard buildings flocked with tiny glass beads. After the British Blockade in October 1939, no more ornaments could be imported from Europe. Then Corning Glass Company took over and produced over 400,000 glass ornaments for the 1939 Christmas season. However, American manufacturers began to experiment with lighting, creating Mickey Mouse lights in 1938 as well as those marvelous Whirl-Glo shades we placed over our lights to add motion to the tree. We imported fancy metal and glass lights from Japan, manufactured wonderful Matchless Stars with cut glass prisms in the United States, and put plastic covers over our lights. This period, more than any other, started the trend of Americans seeking innovative ways to light our trees.

Christmas through the Decades, the first book I authored on the decade by decade approach to Christmas decorating, will give the reader a detailed perspective into these early decades, with many historical photos, color pictures of decorations from each of these decades, and a detailed text elaborating on the quick bullets of information contained above. If you have not read this first book, I feel you would enjoy it immensely. For those of you who are searching for a basic book which covers the different periods of glass Christmas ornament manufacturing; wood, cotton, wax, paper, and metal ornaments; and the lighting of the tree by candles and electricity, *Christmas Past* would be of particular interest. Those interested in advertising; crèche scenes; Santa figures; and different glass decorations for the tree—including tree tops, bead garlands, and Italian ornaments, would find *Christmas Revisited* of interest as well.

Regardless of your collecting interests, knowledge through research and reading will help you gain perspective on what there is to collect, information regarding the pricing, and valuable insights into the reproduction history of these highly sought decorative items.

Chapter I. The 1940s—A New Beginning and Identity

An Historical Perspective of this Decade—Dramatic Changes in Christmas

This decade, more than any other decade of the twentieth century, changed America's Christmas decorating customs and themes. The war years were ones of mixed emotions, but when it came to Christmas there were scant few who felt this holiday should not be decorated. In fact, adults attempted to create that "perfect" Christmas for the children so that the war's negative effects would not take hold of our children. Most certainly, the war created a shortage of materials necessary for Christmas ornament and light manufacturing. But, we were industrious and found our ways around this by reverting to creating many of our decorations from scraps in our homes and did with much less when it came to electric lighting for our trees and homes. Tin cans, string, and magazine pictures were regularly recycled as tree ornaments. Americans went back to the home-crafted look of past decades in an attempt to create ornaments when commercial ones were scarce due to the war effort. All-in-all, everyone seemed to agree that the tradition of Christmas needed to be maintained for both the youth and for those who needed something to cling to in a time of true uncertainty.

While we celebrated at home, thousands of men of the Army and Navy bravely sang around government Christmas trees, wondering what they would do when the last orange and carton of cigarettes had been handed out by the grimly cheerful officer. No doubt, afterwards, they strolled to their tents and barracks to study well-worn maps of the cities and towns they knew so well. The war caused not only servicemen, but those people left at home as well, to be a bit more thoughtful than usual and to be wide open to memories in a period when memories meant our survival in harsh and severe times. Certain traditions were not abandoned, in part, simply because these traditions triggered memories and helped us to carry on as best we could.

Christmas 1941. Elegant setting in a Jamaica, New York City home with an elaborate crèche doll scene in front of ornament laden tree. $140-150.

In 1940, the National Christmas Tree, a 30-foot red cedar from Virginia that stood on the Ellipse, was lit in 10,000 watts of brilliance. Most of the world was at war while Americans carried on the Yule tradition, church choirs sang, festive tables bore heavy loads, and children laughed with joy. We needed to carry on for the sake of our children.

House Beautiful in 1940 seemed to sum up the feelings of most Americans in its December Christmas editorial: "It is Christmas Day and the year is 1940. Nearly two thousand years ago, with peaceful wings unfurled, angels bent down to earth where the quiet sheep and the marveling shepherds watched. It is Christmas Day and there is no peace except the peace, which is in our hearts as we gather around our beloved Christmas tree. Let us make this the most beautiful Christmas America has ever seen. Not blindly forgetting. But as a pledge to our children that there will be peace again some day, a peace for which men and women and children today are dying. Christmas came to us across the ocean. It is packed full of old memories from many lands. But Christmas, like the people of America, has gone into the melting pot. It is our own. Where else would you see fireworks on Christmas Day except in our own South? Where else than in California would you hang wreaths of wild cherry in your window and on your front door? Grim reality comes early to children now. But you can offset the cruelty and tragedy by making this Christmas shine like the holy star which led three kings to Bethlehem long ago. To the alien children who share the warmth of our firesides, you can offer toys and faith, gaiety, and beauty. Put aside heavy heartedness for this day. Look deep into your heart to rediscover the eternal verities which are challenged. Read again the story of what happened in a stable in other troubled times.

"Christmas has always been for children. They are still innocent and trusting. Make them happy. It takes so little. Teddy bears and popcorn, wreaths and garlands and trees, winking candles and the sound of the old carols. A house where, without cynicism or doubt of the ultimate dignity of man, of the individual, the Child of Bethlehem is still deeply loved. Over the snowy hills and valleys of America, in the clear air be born the brave old melody: O come all ye faithful joyful and triumphant. . ."

In 1940, Americans decided to "forget the War." Stores hailed all-time highs in volume of Christmas trade. Americans bought big, expensive things like automobiles, refrigerators, and radios. The mood that Christmas contrasted significantly with Christmases of past years. There was a hectic flush in which streamlined, mass-produced, mechanical Santas of identical image grinned and nodded in department stores windows from coast to coast. California vintners reported a boom in vintage wine sales. Decorators performed tricks with electricity and plastics. This strange new mood is not difficult to understand, taking into consideration that Americans had lived on its nerves for the past fifteen months. Americans spent because few could foresee any future surety for which to save.

Interestingly enough, Santa Claus continued to advertise so very much for Christmas. In 1939, a California State senator, disturbed by the sight of Santa Claus selling everything from bottled beer to automobiles, introduced a bill to restrict the use of Santa's image. However, this bill gained very little support and Santa continued to advertise whatever was necessary for merchants to sell.

Another popular Christmas character arrived. Intended to be a character in a story, Rudolph the Red-Nosed Reindeer played his part in a story written by Robert L. May, an advertising copywriter for Montgomery Ward, written for his daughter Barbara in 1938. May's wife was very ill and would soon pass away, just before Christmas. When May made his tale of Rudolph into an illustrated poem, Barbara loved the story. After reading it at a company employees' party, he was encouraged to use it in the next year's advertising campaign. May created a give-away storybook and over two million copies were given away. In 1940, three million copies were printed and distributed. The story captured the hearts of Americans. However, during World War II, the materials needed to print these books were in short supply and Rudolph ceased to be promoted.

Christmas 1941 was more shocking than even imagined, but we carried on as best as we could. Seventeen days after the Pearl Harbor incident, the evening we lit our National Christmas Tree, we continued our tradition, but with sober reflection and prayer. Sir Winston Churchill, who had crossed the Atlantic secretly to confer with President Roosevelt, was on the platform and joined the President in extending Christmas greetings to the American people. In his brief remarks on this historic occasion, Sir Winston said, "Let the children have their night of fun and laughter. By our sacrifice and daring, these children shall not be robbed of their inheritance or denied the right to live in a free and decent world."

Tree and Putz scene of George and Beatrice Moe in Milwaukee, Wisconsin. Circa 1942. $8-12.

"God Bless the Soldiers, Sailors, and the Marines."
The McKinleys, '42

Christmas in Kellogg, Idaho, in 1942—a patriotic card sent that Christmas in special recognition of those fighting for our country. $15-20.

During the 1940s, a radical departure from trees of the past decades took place in America. No longer were Europeans considered providers of tradition when it came to Christmas. The bitter feelings caused by the war helped to develop in America a sense of independence when it came to buying consumable products. Americans turned to American manufacturers for their decorations. They rushed to buy American-made Visca artificial Christmas trees and decorated them with commercially made ornaments that were available in boxed sets.

There was even a Santa Claus shortage during the war when young actors were overseas and oldsters had to return to the Broadway stage and other theaters to take the places of those in combat. Since the typical age was 45-75 for those not in the armed forces, this shortage of males was acute and women were substituted at Saks Fifth Avenue in New York City. The most zealous crusader for the profession of Santa Claus was Charles W. Howard of Albion New York, who spent a lifetime in the study of Santa Claus. He began by selling his services to a local store, devoting himself to the profession, and became so competent that he opened the Santa Claus School. Cost of matriculation in 1947 was $150. His school, located in Santa Claus, Indiana, covered such subjects as the origin and history of Santa Claus, the art of make-up, showmanship, salesmanship, child psychology, and the economics of the toy industry. The majority of his students in 1947 were young married men between the ages of 25 and 35.

Christmas play in Sheboygan, Wisconsin. Circa 1943. $20-25.

Dearborn, Michigan, marked its 1941 Christmas season with an almost life-size outdoor nativity scene set up on the City Hall grounds. These Masonic figures were cut out in silhouette and illuminated by indirect lighting. Carols and singing programs were presented on the three evenings before Christmas Eve.

America's second wartime Christmas in 1942 found Rockefeller Plaza placing three trees, one decorated in red, one decorated in blue, and one decorated in white. In accordance with wartime restrictions on electricity, no electric lights were used.

Christmas 1944 found Americans spending money, increasing their spending by 10 percent over 1943. Christmas 1945 found Americans on their first Christmas without war since 1938. As families were reunited after years of separation, joy reigned across our country, but countless memories flooded back, especially for those families who lost a loved one fighting for freedom across the seas. Even Rockefeller Plaza commemorated this peacetime Christmas, once again using electric lights on their trees. The tree was trimmed with fluorescent globes that glowed when a black light was focused on them.

Life Magazine, in their December 24th issue, captured in photographs and recounted the Christmas of the Irwin family of Neosho Rapids, Kansas, who celebrated Christmas early with their entire family reunited at the close of the war. A cedar tree resplendent with electric lights and ornaments served as the focal point as the family enjoyed a Christmas dinner together for the first time in years.

Rudolph the Red-Nosed Reindeer appeared once again at the close of the war, now that supplies were available to once again print his story. At the end of the war, Montgomery Ward turned over all rights to Robert L. May. Rudolph was revived and became so popular that businesses rushed to contact Mr. May for the rights to manufacture novelties and various goods to commemorate this famous reindeer. Puzzles, booklets, school bags, cups, cereal bowls, snow globes, pens, watches, games, and countless other memorabilia came to the market. In 1947, six million copies of Rudolph's story were sold. Even cartoons immortalized Rudolph.

Christmas 1947, Jimmy and Tommy playing with their new toys in front of a tree decorated with C-6 and C-7½ bulbs as well as American and European manufactured glass ornaments. $85-90.

After the war, Americans sought a new identity when decorating for Christmas. The trend is easily summed up in the words of *Recreation* magazine in 1946 when they stated, "Well, those days of simplicity are gone, swept away by science and mass production and crowded living and gadgets. We are living in the brave new world of industry. . . . It's a world of new materials, of new knowledge about ways to use old materials."

The economic boom After the war was most certainly evident in our Christmas purchasing. Christmas sales hit a new high in 1947, surpassing by 10% the amount spent the previous year. Now more than ever, all Americans decorated a tree. Roy Barclay Hodges in *American Magazine* estimated that over two million people decorated their first tree in 1946 and five million more in 1947. Most certainly that figure was boosted by the fact that there were over 47% more children under five years old than before. For first Christmas trees, Americans averaged about $10 on tree ornaments and lights, and $2-3 dollars each year after for replacements and additions.

America's personalities and their decorated homes attracted media attention. Marian Anderson decorated her mantle with old musical instruments, sprayed white, on ribbons. Margaret O'Brien decorated her tree with only home-crafted ornaments which she herself created. Beatrice Little hung her tree simply with cards, which each guest was invited to sign and mail with a check for $10 to CARE. Thomas Mann trimmed his tree with just one thing: tiny white candles. Helena Rubenstein wove green roping down her staircase with clusters of glass ornaments spaced about twelve inches apart.

In 1948, a member of the Boston city council complained that there was a Santa on every street corner and children were beginning to wonder. The council formally asked the mayor to permit only one Santa in the city and to station him on the historic Boston common.

Dressed for Christmas, this family poses by the tree. Underneath that tree can be found elegant examples of wrapped presents from this period. Circa 1947. $80-85.

Cautious buyers avoided purchasing some luxury items in 1949; however, television sets sold extremely well as Americans embraced this new technology. Toys, especially electric trains and educational toys, also enjoyed great sales. This year, the Rockefeller Plaza sprayed their famous decorated tree with silver, causing quite a sensation and some "not so pleasant" comments from traditionalists.

In 1949, Max Fleischer's Technicolor movie cartoon featuring Rudolph the Red-Nosed Reindeer premiered in movie theaters across America at Christmas. His film spurred renewed interest in Rudolph items. Montgomery Ward, who originally introduced this lovable character, sold numerous items including a girls' snowsuit, watch, tree ornaments, storybooks, records, banks, and even jigsaw puzzles. Many lucky youngsters that Christmas received a three-piece feeding set which included a 7-¾-inch plate, a 6-½-oz. cup, and a 6-½-inch cereal bowl. Even "Mukluks," moccasin-socks, and slippers kept their little toes warm. Other gifts included a school bag, bank, and game. Christmas 1949 is another memorable date in Rudolph's life. Johnny Marks wrote a song about Rudolph and Gene Autry sang the hit tune of that Christmas, "Rudolph the Red-Nosed Reindeer." The sheet music, published by St. Nicholas Music, Inc. in 1950, is extremely collectible today. Also desirable is the original 1939 Montgomery Ward give-away.

Christmas Crackers were designed for but one brief moment of glory as part of the Christmas scene; however, crackers appeared at parties, celebrations, and other special occasions at any time of the year in England. Termed "crackers" by the English, we as Americans *favored* the term "favors."

Christmas Crackers were an indispensable part of holiday celebrations in Britain. They came in a variety of shiny colors; some had bits of holly, tiny silver bells, or paper flowers attached. The ends were either plain or made of lacy paper. They were usually small, but one could find giant crackers, too, that were several feet long. Tucked inside were silly paper hats and crowns, little toys, and strips of paper with funny riddles (mottoes) printed on them. Grown-ups as well as children enjoyed popping them, putting on the hats, and reading the mottoes. Most British families would be disappointed if crackers were not part of their holiday celebrations. They became popular in America with families who brought this tradition from England to the United States.

In the 1940s, the *Utility Cracker* appeared. It was not much to look at, with not much inside, but was bright and cheerful. There were some novelty gifts enclosed inside such as snowmen. However, war-themes prevailed with such designs as "Sailor Girl," "Rations," "Nurse," and "Soldier Boy."

Betty Lou with Doll by her Christmas tree. Circa 1948. $15-20.

Anne Holderfield at the age of 9 on December 20, 1947, posing in her Christmas finery. $25-30.

Christmas 1949, with fine examples of beaded chains and cardboard reflectors behind each light. $20-25.

John and Dick with Uncle Bobby, together for Christmas 1947 with a tinsel laden tree. $20-25.

Christmas 1949 at the Grunfields. Wonderful examples of toys from that year. $30-35.

Christmas 1943 with a lavishly decorated tree and countless examples of wonderful toys for good little children. Note the village scene underneath the tree. $180-190.

Lu Paulson, Christmas 1943 in La Crosse, Wisconsin. $20-25.

Rau Lorenzo at one year of age, Christmas 1947. $25-30.

Christmas during World War II. Note the use of cardboard hangers to attach the clear glass ornaments to the tree and the use of real candy canes. $30-40.

An elaborate village scene constructed on a platform in a living room. Note the milk glass light bulbs strung above in the garland and the Visca tree in its ceramic base by the window. Lots of beautiful animals and houses. $80-90.

Christmas during the 1940s. Note the tinsel, electric lights, and wreath on the fireplace. $30-40.

Christmas 1945, with lots of clear Corning glass ornaments combined with old-fashioned lead tinsel. $30-35.

What a lavish Christmas! Hobby horse with cowboy and other toys indicate Santa was especially good to this one little girl. $70-75.

Christmas 1942. Two Views: tree and mantle. $20-25 each

Christmas tree illustrating a 1940s spun glass tree top and celluloid animals and brush trees underneath the tree on cotton batting sheets. $50-60.

Christmas 1949 in a rural Wisconsin church showing the tall balsam tree decked with lots of electric lights and lead tinsel. $20-25.

Christmas party for the Women's Club in Sheboygan, Wisconsin, after World War II. Note the use of both American and pre-World War II German ornaments. $45-55.

Christmas card sent to mark the end of World War II. $40-50.

Christmas 1946. Note the use of waxed paper stars made when commercial ornaments were hard to obtain. $25-30.

Our Greeting Cards, Advertising, and Paper Memorabilia

Interestingly enough, greeting cards enjoyed their greatest growth during the war years. Thirty million in sales in 1935 rose to fifty-three million spent on greeting cards in 1943. Per capita purchases of cards reached eighteen in 1943. Early war cards were somber and patriotic in theme. Many incorporated religious themes with the American flag and soldiers. There was a growing demand for spiritual and romantic-themed cards. By 1943, however, whimsical verses were substituted. Americans realized that only their sense of humor could save them in times filled with death and despair. Therefore, cards began to change drastically in their approach.

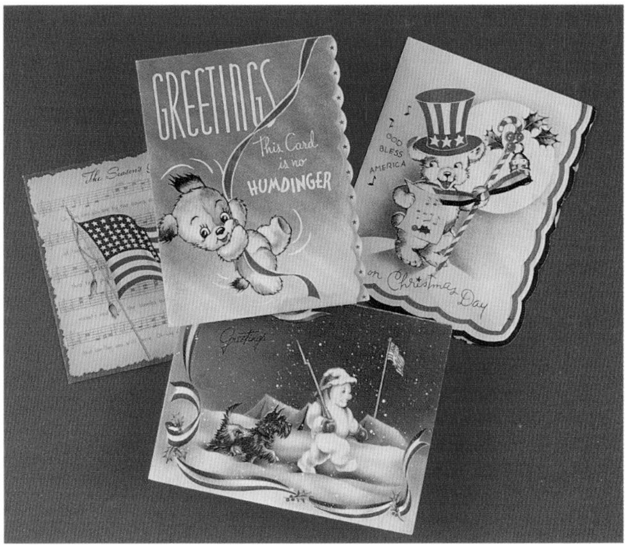

Patriotic themed cards from early years of war. $10-15 each.

The War Production Board considered curtailing the numbers of cards manufactured in the United States. In 1940, with more than fifty-three million dollars expended on cards, Hallmark Cards (which employed 3,000 persons) operated their presses around the clock in order to fulfill the demand for cards. The average household was purchasing eighteen cards by 1943, and retailers looked to a steady increase as the war intensified. Cards did change in that ribbon ties and French folds used prior to the war were still employed, but gold and silver ink work, along with familiar foil overlays, became war causalities. While the flag and patriotic themes abounded in 1940, Americans preferred lighter and more whimsical-themed cards.

Spurred by wartime sales, greeting card companies scrambled to provide countless brightly-colored boxed assortments of Christmas cards. Especially popular were the more expensive cards available with the senders' names imprinted in black ink, eliminating the need for personally signing each card. Popular themes in 1949 included winter scenes, family-themed scenes, Mr. and Mrs. Snowman illustrations, and religious-themes. Cards with flocked silky rayon, the "Touch-Me" assortments, also proved to be quite popular.

Large Patriotic card with a flag and patriotic theme. $25-30.

One development helped the entire industry in some very competitive times. The Greeting Card Association of America was founded in 1941 to help out the industry, including the companies who produced Christmas cards. Earlier it was known as "The National Association of Greeting Card Manufacturers," which consisted of almost ninety percent of the firms that produced cards in the United States. When reformed in 1941, it consisted of sixty different firms. The association was composed of three groups: one served the retail stores, one served the wholesalers, and the last one served those whose products were purchased by sales representatives selling directly to the consumer.

Parchment paper was a favorite in this decade, upon which some very Art Deco type designs were imprinted. One decorative novelty of this period involved cut out part of the front of the card and placing silver or gold foil behind it (or upon occasion, thin plastic upon which a lace design was printed), reminiscent of the fancy cards sent in earlier decades. Stylistic ladies wearing huge hoop skirts and carrying open parasols reflected the womens' fashions of days gone by.

The Fairfield Line appears to begin in the 1940s from the style of the cards found. These cards often have cut open designs revealing lined or full foil Christmas trees, bells, and holly designs with printed greetings and the use of ribbons, which was revitalized as a part of card designs in the early part of this decade. Trinkets, keepsakes, and charms such as plastic wishbones, spoons, and medals were often added in an attempt to produce cards which would attract peoples' attention.

Whimsical assortment of cards from the late 1940s. $6-8 each.

Boxed assortments of mid to late 1940s greeting cards. $15-20 for box complete with cards.

Assortment of children's cards from mid to late 1940s. $4-5 each.

Advertising blotters are among the more interesting collectibles of this decade. Even though they originated in the early 1870s with advertising imprinted on them, their popularity stems from their incorporation of images of Santa Claus, many of which are quite well done. Bulova advertised its watches with Santa faces; so many banks advertised their saving programs with Santa Claus and childrens' themes that the artistic creations of this decade are outstanding. Also, it became a mainstay of department stores to illustrate their stores decorated at Christmas on advertising blotters. Also very popular during this decade were paper ornaments of Santa Claus, one side richly illustrated with Santa and the other side containing advertising of savings rates for banks and other such savings institutions.

Array of advertising matches and covers from the 1940s. $15-20 each.

Early 1940s advertising cards and ornaments. $15-20 each.

Santa Claus ornaments which doubled as advertising for banks' Christmas Club Savings plans. $7-10 each.

Store advertising banner from a grocery store in Endeavor, Wisconsin. Late 1940s. $60-70.

A 1947 advertising calendar for a garage in Crivitz, Wisconsin. $20-25.

Calendar tops. On the bottoms were tiny pads of the months. Once finished, these were then recycled as wall decorations in subsequent years. Late 1940s. West Germany. $30-40 each.

A 1949 Czechoslovakian fold-out book. Front view, unopened. $125-130.

The 1949 Czechoslovakian fold-out book. Front view, opened, illustrating intricate layers of this Santa's workshop. $125-130.

Children's books from the late 1940s. American printed. $35-40 each.

A 1949 children's card which reveals the date and verses of "The Night Before Christmas" through the open window. $90-100.

East German Advent calendar. Late 1940s. $12-18.

Assortment of sheet music from the 1940s. $10-15 each.

Assortment of 78 rpm records in long play from the 1940s including Mario Lanza and "Rudolph the Red-nosed Reindeer" lyrics. $5-15 each.

This wrapping paper from the 1940s illustrates gift wrapping trends of the decade. $4-8 for a complete sheet.

Wrapping paper from the 1940s in bright colors and patterns evident of this almost Art Deco period. $4-8 for a complete sheet.

Two children's records, typical of the red vinyl so popular in holiday records for kids. $6-10 each.

String and ribbon from the late 1940s used to wrap presents. Ribbon package, $4-5 each. String roll, $5-6 each.

Wrapped boxes with authentic wrapping and ribbon from this period. All are original gift boxes. $10-40 each, depending on size and wrapping paper design.

Gift tags and greeting cards which doubled as ornaments for the Christmas tree. $3-5 each.

More elaborate gift tags and greeting cards which doubled as ornaments. $4-8 each.

Our Trees

By the 1940s the trade in Christmas trees and other greens amounted to $25 million a year for the country as a whole. Franklin D. Roosevelt grew trees for the Christmas market at Hyde Park while he was governor of New York, and continued in the business after he became President of the United States. Raising trees had become profitable with the development of "stump culture," a technique whereby the tree is cut above the "live-branch whorls," so that they once again can grow into trees for a subsequent season. However, fire hazards, the increased emphasis on conservation, and rising prices dampened the market.

Practically every live tree imaginable was used somewhere in America for decorating at Christmas time: not only evergreens, but oaks, maples, and other deciduous growths. Over 15 million trees were cut, representing some 20 million dollars worth of profit for a little-known industry. About two to five million people set up their first tree each year After the war. The number increased dramatically because there were 47 percent more children under the age of five than ever before. Most popular, according to *Travel* in December 1941, was the five-foot version retailing for 75 cents. In the early 1940s, the balsam fir comprised more than sixty percent of the East Coast's cut Christmas trees. Next in popularity was spruce, which comprised twenty-five percent. Douglas fir, pine, cedar, holly, and such made up the remainder. The Frasier fir was the South's favorite while the Douglas fir was the Pacific coast's favorite. The evergreen forests in Maine and the Adirondacks had as many as 100,000 seedling trees to the acre.

A large number of our trees were imported from Canada. But, by 1943, there was a shortage of trees due to the lack of available labor to harvest them and the short freight space available on railroads. About twenty-five percent fewer trees were available. The great bulk of Canadian balsam trees were grown in Nova Scotia, New Brunswick, and Quebec. Therefore, many turned to some ingenious devices. One family took a board and nailed spruce boughs to it in the conical shape of a tree. Lights plugged into a wall bracket and attached to the boughs quickly electrified this tree. A few home-crafted ornaments and lead tinsel completed their alternative to a live freestanding tree.

After the war, Christmas tree farms were once again promoted as a means of agricultural survival; in fact, some government agencies suggested that ex-GIs could make a very tidy income by growing trees. Poor timberland, which never supported good saw-timber growth, was good for Christmas trees because these trees grew slowly, acquiring the ample covering of branches and well-balanced form the market demanded.

The trees were again grown under the previously mentioned "stump culture" system. After two or three thinnings, the trees remaining became the permanent crop. The heart of a tree was cut out first and sold, but the lower branches were left. Two or three of these lower branches then developed themselves to become well-shaped trees. The stump could survive many cuttings, the later trees maturing faster as the root system developed. Ten years was required to get such a system established, during which the growers had to meet expenses by selling twining and other byproducts.

Selling prices for trees for 1946 at the shipping point were around 20 cents for a two-foot tree, 25 cents for a four-foot, 40 cents for a six-foot, and on up to $1.50 for a twelve-foot. One very unique product of this period was the prepackaged Christmas tree, cut in the Pacific Northwest in December and shipped forest-fresh in an individual moisture-sealed container. Pacific Evergreens of Seattle, Washington, marketed the "Gifttree." Before shipment, each tree butt was fitted with a metal canister filled with wet peat moss containing a chemical to help absorb water. The technique was developed before the war, but its use was delayed until 1947. Douglas fir was the choice of tree, due to the fact that it was exceptionally supple, allowing it to be pressed into a small-sized carton and still spring into shape on unloading. Conservationists heralded this new product because it avoided the waste of cutting for markets where normally many trees remained unsold on Christmas day.

In 1947, prices for live trees ranged from 75 cents for a small one to $50 for a large and perfect 15 foot. specimen. Six foot trees retailed at $3. Perhaps the largest cut live tree in our country was formally lit and decorated each year at Rockefeller Center in New York City. The tree averaged between 75 and 90 feet, and weighed around 12 tons. In 1947, it was decorated with 8,000 lights and over 8,000 ornaments.

Christmas tree plantations soared in number. Fred Musser, of Indiana, Pennsylvania, operated one such plantation. Musser was reputed to be the largest grower of cultivated trees in the entire world in 1946. By cutting them back and pruning his trees, he produced a stronger, shapelier tree than could be grown wild. It was in this period that tree plantations began actively pruning and shearing trees to produce trees which had little space for hanging branches and were extremely thick with green branches.

Returning to the "gifttrees," Pacific Evergreen, Inc. of Seattle, headed by Milo W. Morris, marketed those first American pre-packaged trees. As previously stated, the idea was delayed by the war, but in 1947 these trees were shipped forest-fresh in individual moisture-seal containers. Supple Douglas Fir in three to six foot sizes, ranging in price from $4.50 to $7.50 prepaid, were shipped anywhere in the country. With each tree went an assortment of fresh-cut greens, sprigs of colorful native huckleberry, Oregon shrubs, and a piece of mistletoe. Also included were four pieces of plywood that locked together, without nails or screws, to form a stand.

In 1948, *Colliers* gave the title "Christmas Tree Capital of the Nation" to Eureka, Montana, whose population of only 1,400 had shipped about 1.8 million trees—about 300 freight car loads. Every one got involved during tree cutting season, including farmers, storeowners, and even the judge when he was not hearing cases. The owner of the land received half of the revenue from the trees, with the cutter making the one-half profit. A good cutter made between $30-40 a day.

Spruce was a popular choice for a live tree toward the end of this decade. The common spruce (Picea abies) is a native of Europe, widely found from the mountains of Southern Russia westward. Not a native of this country, it has been cultivated since early settlement days.

Artificial trees primarily were made of Visca, but some "American-produced" feather trees were still sold in the early 1940s. However, it is believed that these trees were manufactured before the war. Artificial feather trees all but disappeared due to the scarcity of paper and wire. Any artificial trees, which appeared for sale during the early years of the war, were left over from previous years. These trees were often advertised as American-made so consumers would purchase them. Often storeowners would sand off "Made in Germany," which appeared on the bases of these feather trees.

Straw-like viscose was the material of choice for artificial trees in 1949. Montgomery Ward sold trees in 36, 52, and 96-inch sizes. Sears Roebuck sold trees in 30, 40, 55, 60, and 72-inch heights with the number of branches varying from 24 on the smallest trees to 75 for the tallest models. Prices ranged from 49 cents to $4.53 for the largest available size. Flame-resistant, these American-made trees folded flat for storage.

A 24-inch feather tree manufactured before World War II, but sold after the war by a Wisconsin rural country store. $200-250.

Sparsely branched viscose tree manufactured in the mid-1940s, but missing its low red rectangular stand. With stand, complete. $40-50.

How We Decorated Our Homes

With so many wartime restrictions, it was difficult for many Americans to conceive of ideas for decorating their homes. However, various manufacturers were seeking alternatives to glass and metal ornaments. Many magazine writers and illustrators quickly published decorating ideas employing paper scraps, string, and other such items commonly found in peoples' homes. The most noticeably absent were those marvelous thin glass spheres made in Germany which were used by so many Americans in table and fireplace mantle arrangements.

Experiments were also run to see if glass could be replaced by something more durable and unbreakable. Plastic was thought to be the answer. In 1941, plastic ornaments manufactured from nonflammable cellulose acetate powder were produced by Freeman, Taylor and Stanley of New York. Woolworth, Kresge's, and like chains stocked these ornaments. J. M. Gordon & Co. produced fluorescent ornaments of celluloid. Best effects with fluorescent ornaments could be obtained by lighting them with "black lighting" units (near ultraviolet light). These units were made by General Electric, Westinghouse, and others, and distributed by Gordon along with the "Fluor-Glo" ornaments. But the hitch was the cost: $30 for the 100 watt black-lighting unit. But OPM's ban on cellophane and other cellulose materials ended these experiments. However, so many were manufactured in 1941 that lots were available yet in 1942.

Early celluloid ornaments produced by Freeman, Taylor and Stanley of New York. $10-15 each.

Foresight on the part of American industrialists accounted for the liberal supply of tinsel tinfoil and metal reflectors in stock. Lead became the major component of foil, reducing the use of aluminum and tin. Consequently, small amounts of strategic metals now needed were released. Since the shredded cellophane was banned in 1942, many families went back to stringing cranberries and popcorn balls.

The years 1942 to 1944 were years of restrictions, including the use of lights on the National Christmas Tree in 1942. In his message to all Americans, the President uttered some stirring thoughts when he said, "Loving our neighbor as we love ourselves is not enough. We as a Nation and as individuals will please God best by showing regard for the laws of God. There is no better way of fostering our goodwill toward man than by first fostering good will toward God. If we love Him, we will keep his commandments." In 1943, the President's address came from Hyde Park and was piped to a crowd of 15,000 waiting on the South Lawn, by means of a special cable running from the White House down into the tree.

During the war, designers suggested Americans return to using what only seemed perfectly natural: evergreens from outside. From New England to California, Americans went outside and found laurel, rhododendron, Oregon huckleberry, or any of the myriad varieties of pine and balsam. The fresh scent of Christmas greens on tables, fireplaces, and even above pictures and mirrors was complemented with only a few simple glass American-made Christmas spheres. Replacing artificial wreaths were wreaths made from ground pine, holly, boxwood, and laurel since they lasted much longer inside than pine, spruce, cedar, balsam fir, hemlock, or other narrow-leaf evergreens. Balls of evergreens were also fashioned and suspended from ceilings and balconies. Candles were placed in fresh evergreen arrangements and helped to compensate for the absent electric lights, so difficult to purchase during the war years.

We brightened our doors with gay red crochet shopping bags bulging with intriguing packages. Odd squares of colored wrappings, filled with candies, nuts, and raisins were tied up in little balls and strung together to hang like a bunch of grapes with a big bow at the top, and were used over fireplaces or as table centerpieces.

After the war, we once again turned to using commercially produced ornaments. Cellophane was used as a medium for window pictures. Electric lights were often run between the glass window and its painted cellophane scene.

Red cellophane wreaths with cardboard candles and inserted electric lights appeared in windows along with "Candoliers" in two, three, and eight-lights. These early examples had wood bases, cardboard candles, red lights, and transparent halos to reflect light. Also popular were crosses into which sockets were wired with red bulbs and "Glolite" metal crosses with red glass points through which bright light would glow in windows across this country.

Nine-inch cellophane wreath from the late 1940s. $20-30.

Mid-1940s chenille-wrapped cross from Japan. $15-20.

Also popular immediately After the war were "Glolite" trees. These non-fading green trees contained a bulb inside which lit up tiny, bulb-shaped glass rods. They were sold in 10-inch, 14-inch, and 15-inch sizes. One of the more intriguing table decorations was a star-shaped lighting set with four-star reflector lights posed with a poinsettia-leafed decoration at the base. Each of the curved rods is covered with a red silver-foil based wrapping to make this a most desirable 1940s decoration.

Flame-resistant bubble light tabletop trees with nine vari-colored bubble lights sold in white and green colors in 1949. For the price of $7.75, Americans could have an 18-inch tree, made of thick straw-like viscose mounted on an Ivory finished aluminum base. Electric bell clusters, made of 5-inch red plastic trimmed with silver leaves, appeared on many doors and in windows.

Also popular house decorations were paper, cardboard, and honeycomb decorations made by the Beistle Company of Shippensburg, Pennsylvania. Honeycomb is layers of tissue paper glued together in such a way that it can be opened, accordion-like, into a three-dimensional shape. World War II interrupted Beistle's production of paper decorations temporarily, since they involved themselves in producing parachutes and watertight wraps for military supplies. H. E. Luhrs, who came to work for Beistle in 1924 as a sales manager in the New York office, and then became active manager of operations in Shippensburg, became president of Beistle in 1941. Most of the very intriguing Christmas items copyrighted "H. E. Luhrs" are Beistle products that were developed by Luhrs and copyrighted in his name.

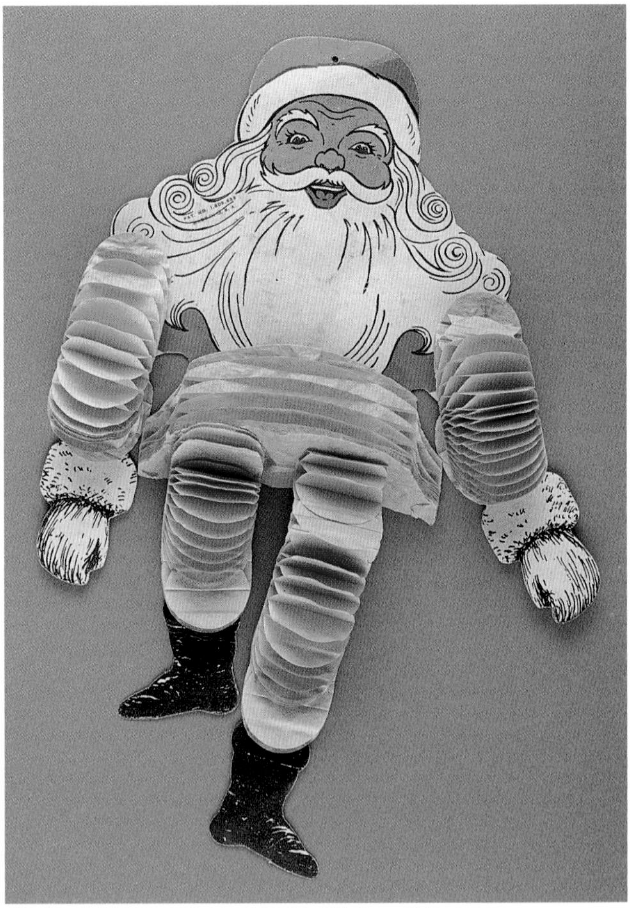

Beistle Santa from 1948. $50-60.

Also quite involved in providing paper decorations for our homes was the Dennison Manufacturing Company of Framingham, Maine. It was one of the largest producers of crepes, table covers, borders and festoons, gummed stickers, and cardboard cutouts. Their little holiday party books contained suggestions for house decorating themes as well as providing illustrations of their products.

"Glolite" tree in green, 12-inch including metal base. $45-55.

"Glolite" tree in white, 24-inch including plaster base. $50-60.

American Influences on Glass Tree Decorations

On December 9, 1940, *Life Magazine* reported to Americans that "The War has reached long tentacles into the coziest corners of U.S. industry, and, as a result, the U.S. this year for the first time in history will be self-sufficient in the matter of Christmas-tree ornaments." In the years immediately preceding the war, America had imported from 50,000,000 to 80,000,000 ornaments a year from Europe, primarily from Germany and Czechoslovakia. When our supply was cut off in 1939 when the British Blockade prevented European ornaments from reaching our shores. America suffered a severe ornament shortage. However, it was to be short-lived as American industrialists quickly moved in to fill the void. These companies also saw this as an opportunity to wrest a significant portion of a lucrative industry from European hands permanently.

In 1940, imports dropped $124,000, and Japan, instead of Germany, was the principal supplier. Yet, in 1942, Americans purchased 120,000,000 ornaments for tree decorating. Cash outlay for these ornaments had risen to between three and four million dollars. Before the war, in 1937, our total value was over $1,250,000, of which about 90% was amounted for by Germany and Czechoslovakia.

American-made indents and balls were the only glass ornaments available in 1940. In 1940, a 20-piece set complete with a 9" decorated tree top sold for 69 cents and was available from Sears Roebuck. This set included 5" solid color balls, five reflector type balls, four bells, three oval ornaments, and two lanterns. Inexpensive clear ornaments with a tinsel spray inside were sold along with the more expensive silvered ornaments. Many different Christmas motifs were silk screened onto these American-made ornaments. Toys, animals, Santas, stars, and stripes were the most common. During this period, bells, oblongs, pyramids, lanterns, diamonds, reflectors, pinecones, and acorns were manufactured.

Representative examples of silvered ornaments sold in the early years of the war. American-blown shapes by Corning. $4-7 each.

It is interesting to note the development of American ornaments through the war years. The first wartime American ornaments were made from glass, but were not silvered on the inside due to war restrictions. Quickly they were decorated with a tinsel spray inside to give a bit of a "sparkling effect" to an otherwise dull-appearing ornament. Americans complained because these unsilvered ornaments did not reflect electric lights as the European decorations did. As the war effort intensified, American ornament manufacturers abandoned this practice because metal was needed for the war effort and could be scarcely wasted in such a frivolous manner. So, the next year we found ornaments with thin metal caps. But, in 1942, even metal caps disappeared when all metal was diverted to the war. In this year, paper and cardboard tops were employed. Some companies even used a piece of wood to which a string had been attached and placed this into the neck of the glass ornament.

Some 1940 American ornaments in more common shapes with tinsel spray inside. $3-7 each.

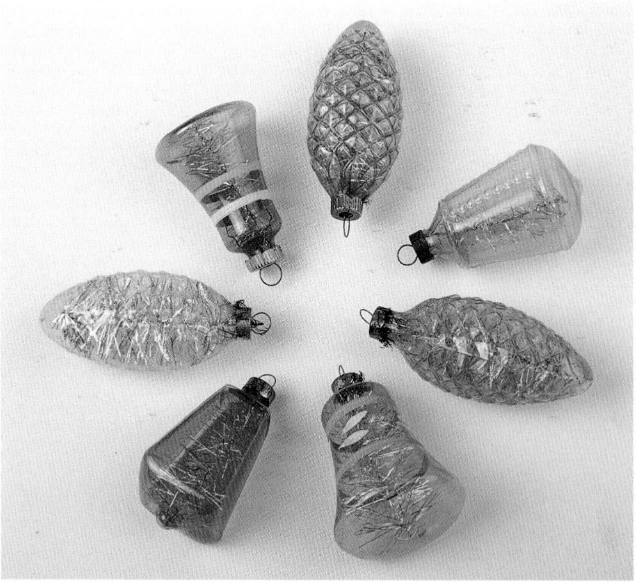

Some 1940 American ornaments in more unusual shapes. $5-7 each.

Several 1941 American ornaments. No tinsel inside, but still with metal caps. $3-7 each.

American industry quickly became involved in the manufacturing of glass tree ornaments both for necessity and profit. With the war in its full intensity in 1940, only $124,000 in Christmas decoration and lights were imported from Japan. Thus it was up to the American industrialists to carry on the manufacturing of items previously imported from Europe.

Corning Glass Company of New York was the primary manufacturer with 40,000,000 America ornaments turned out for Christmas of 1940. In peak production, Corning produced 300,000 ornaments (about 400 a minute) in a day compared with around 600 a day turned out by a typical German glassblower before the war.

Max Eckardt, an importer of German ornaments since 1907, foresaw the events of Germany dictating an end to his business, as it had during World War I. He knew of Corning's "ribbon" glass blowing machine for electric light bulbs. He knew this machine could produce almost 2,000 lights a minute. Eckardt reasoned that if Corning could make a light bulb, it should be able to produce a glass ornament as well. Thus he began negotiations with Corning. In the late summer of 1939, as a result of inquiries from Bill Thompson of F. W. Woolworth Company, planning started in earnest. It took these two individuals to propel Corning Glass ahead in its new venture.

The Steuben design staff submitted several designs for ornaments. Of these designs, a dozen were chosen. They were called "molded fancies." Fancies were bells, pinecones, tree tops, teardrops in solid colors—red, blue, gold, green, and silver. Plain balls also came in these colors. A Santa Claus figure was manufactured on an experimental basis, but was discovered to be too expensive to be made and to decorate. The ornaments were distributed through jobbers, decorators, and directly to stores. Catalogs illustrating their product lines were not produced in the early years.

By 1940, 120,000,000 colored glass balls and ornaments were sold, with 3-4 million dollars being spent on ornaments which sold for two to five to ten cents each. These were all simple glass spheres produced at Corning's Wellsboro plant. During the war years, Corning had 100% of the domestic market.

Six months of intensive work by Corning engineers made possible the ingenious machines which turned a pound of glass into thirty average-size ornaments. It took about three weeks to change a batch of raw material into usable glass, which was of almost the same kind as that used for electric light bulbs. Heated to 2,800 degrees, the mixture entered the ribbon machine. The mixture continued along between rollers horizontally, clinging to the underside of a moving belt.

Puffs of compressed air blew through it from above to form bubbles that grew in size until each was plucked off between the halves of a mold moving up to meet it. Clamped inside the mold, the bubble of glass was blown up to the desired shape. Asbestos heads on a rotary transfer mechanism took the hot, shaped bulbs from the molds of the ribbon machine. Then, turning from a horizontal to a vertical position, they laid them on a belt which carried them to the "lehr" for cooling.

It took the globes about twenty minutes to pass through this forty-foot machine, where the temperature was lowered gradually to prevent strains. Emerging from the lehr, the bulbs were carried by a moving belt past girls who removed broken pieces and inspected them for imperfections. At this stage the clear glass spheres resembled soap bubbles. The bubbles then passed through a polarized-light testing instrument, a polariscope, to show lines of stress or tension which might make them break easily.

Then the bulbs were placed on racks in a machine for silvering and coloring. First, chemicals were sprayed up through the necks to give a mirror surface inside. Then they were dyed the color desired. After, the dye has been dried quickly, an automatic machine cut off the necks. At the end of the long production line, the globes were sorted, broken ones removed, and the acceptable sorted globes packed in partitioned cardboard boxes. Close to one-fourth of them were rejected for flaws.

Because of the machine method of production, the domestic ornament differed from, and was superior to, the imported ornaments in three ways. It was absolutely spherical, hence stronger. The long, slender neck was shortened and made larger. This also made the ornament less fragile. Last of

A number of 1943-1945 American ornaments with cardboard and paper tops. $7-10 each.

all, the metal caps were fastened on a great deal more securely, whereas the imported article habitually fell apart or broke, often while being placed on the tree. In 1940, new ornaments were furnished in five different colors and two sizes. The two-inch size weighed approximately two grams and the three-inch size twelve grams. In thickness, they were about the same size as their European counterparts, but they contained more glass.

Other companies to which Corning supplied these blanks produced decorated ornaments. Two-thirds of ornaments produced were sold to decorators. These hand-decorated ornaments were made by Marks Bros., Boston; K & W Glass Works, North Bergen, New Jersey; and U.S. Manufacturing Co., Brooklyn, New York.

At its peak, Corning produced over 500,000 ornaments a day. Corning's employees enjoyed their vacations between December 20th and January 8th each year. They made about two-thirds of the 125 million glass ornaments sold in the country. K & W Glass Works of North Bergen, New Jersey, reported that 40% of their volume in glass ornaments was in decorated round balls, with the other 60% of the round spheres being made in solid colors. In the South, people preferred stripes and designs on the glass bulbs. In the Pennsylvania region, the favorite color was red. Red was the favorite throughout the country, for that matter, silver and blue tying for second, green in third place, and gold taking fourth.

In 1946, Kurt S. Adler established Kurt S. Adler, Inc./Santa's World, commencing what would become a major contributor in creating and developing the trim-a-tree and Christmas collectibles industries. Although he had never owner or operated a retail store, he had always moved merchandise. "When I came back from the army, I didn't want to take orders any more," Adler said. Quite soft-spoken and unassuming, Adler was gifted with an uncanny design savvy and a keen eye for style. Capturing the imagination of well-heeled, post-war customers, he brought a European flavor and sense of fashion and integrated it extremely well with American tastes at affordable prices. When he wasn't purchasing and designing new products, he traveled, learning what the collectors desired. Adler then took prototypes of his ideas overseas to create some very high quality products. Ornaments were primarily sold in toy and department stores only during the Christmas season. Alder imported European products for the Christmas season. As his list of customers expanded, so did his number of suppliers. Ornaments were the mainstay of his line. Kurt S. Adler was the first to design, develop, import, and distribute ornaments crafted of high-quality materials including better woods, ceramics, stained 'glass, resin, fabric-mâché, and mouth-blown glass. "It was a one-man operation when I started," Adler reminisced about his business.

Late 1940s American silvered ornaments in the same shapes as those in clear glass. $2-3 each.

By the end of the decade, another major producer of glass ornaments was Harry Heim, Sr. and Harry Jr. of Savage, Maryland. Before the war, they were interior decorators in Baltimore. The decorating business usually fell off during the holiday season. To take up the slack, the Heims began trimming Christmas trees for commercial firms. But the war cut off their best supply of high-quality glass ornaments, so the Heims began making their own. In *Popular Science*, their story was recorded. In 1949 they had 400 employees busy producing seventy million ornaments a year. It was a machine process like that used by Corning Glass.

However, the Heims did their own hand decorating with a silk-screen stencil method. The fancier, higher priced ornaments were hand decorated by skilled craftsmen who thought up their own designs. One interesting mechanization was the finish decorating applied to Christmas tree tops. Red spheres were placed on a striping machine. The operator held a multiple-tip brush against the revolving ornament. Up to five stripes in as many different colors could be applied in one operation.

Late 1940s American clear ornaments with smooth metal caps. These are more rare since they did not sell well and were soon discontinued. $5-7 each.

Heim decorated glass ornaments illustrate stenciling techniques employed by this glass company. $2-5 each.

Richly molded American ornaments from the late 1940s. $3-5 each.

Fluorescent finished glass ornaments. $35-40 for the boxed set.

European Influences on Glass Tree Decorations

In the period between 1939 and 1945, no glass ornaments were produced in Germany due to the restriction and prohibition of production. Glass blowers were brought into war industries to utilize their glass blowing skills in providing items needed for the war effort. Until 1945, glass blowers were home workers who were registered as small enterprises. In 1947, the production of glass ornaments resumed in home workshops, utilizing bottled gas since the piping infrastructure had been destroyed during the war time bombings. In 1948, cooperatives were formed for purchasing and delivering supplies to these home workers, with materials then being centrally ordered and located. In these beginnings after World War II, much relearning of the glass blowing, painting, and decorating process was necessary as much was forgotten in the war period.

At the end of the hostilities, the allied powers divided Germany into four sectors: the American sector in South Germany; the British in North Germany; the French in Southwest Germany; and the Russian in East Germany. In 1949, the Russian power founded a new state, the German Democratic Republik (GDR), in the eastern part of Germany, which included the Thuringian forest. The western powers founded the National Republik of Germany (FRG), which included the three western sectors. Following the war, the major part of the glass Christmas tree ornament industry found itself behind the "Iron Curtain." Lauscha was then in East Germany while Coburg was in West Germany, less than twenty miles apart.

The first shipments to the United States After the war came from East German exporters Cuno and Otto Dressel, Max Eckardt and Sons (owners of Shiny Brite, New York), Bernhard Matthai, Elias Greiner Vetter Sohn, Bechmann, Steinheid, Kuhnert and Egli, and a few small firms. It has been generally believed that most of the East German ornaments of the late1940s had been smuggled by Thuringian East German glassblowers by nightfall over the border to Neustadt in the Western sector. However, only a comparatively small number of the ornaments were brought to the West. Fritz Rempel of Neustadt purchased ornaments from the East and paid money, or more importantly, chocolate, coffee, cigarettes, or other supplies unobtainable in the Eastern Zone.

World War II devastated Lauscha, the birthplace of the glass Christmas tree ornament. It was never a wealthy village and it depended greatly on its exports to the United States. Heinz Muller-Blech played an integral part of the revival of glass ornaments After the war. His great-grandfather invented the metal cap commonly used to hang ornaments. To eliminate confusion with all the Mullers in Lauscha, his great-grandfather changed the family name to Muller-Blech (metal or tin). Heinz lost his father in the war. This left Heinz alone with his mother, a brother, and the skill to produce ornaments. At the conclusion of the war, Lauscha was vacated by the Americans and turned over to the Russians. To survive in these very difficult economic times, Heinz blew ornaments during the day and slipped across the border from the Russian Zone to the American zone and traded these ornaments for anything that he could use to barter in Lauscha. His journeys in the dark were long and quite dangerous as he had to evade the Russian soldiers patrolling the forests.

Early West German imports from the late 1940s. Santa and human figures, $20-25 each. Dog on ball, $45-55. Other assorted figurals, $15-40.

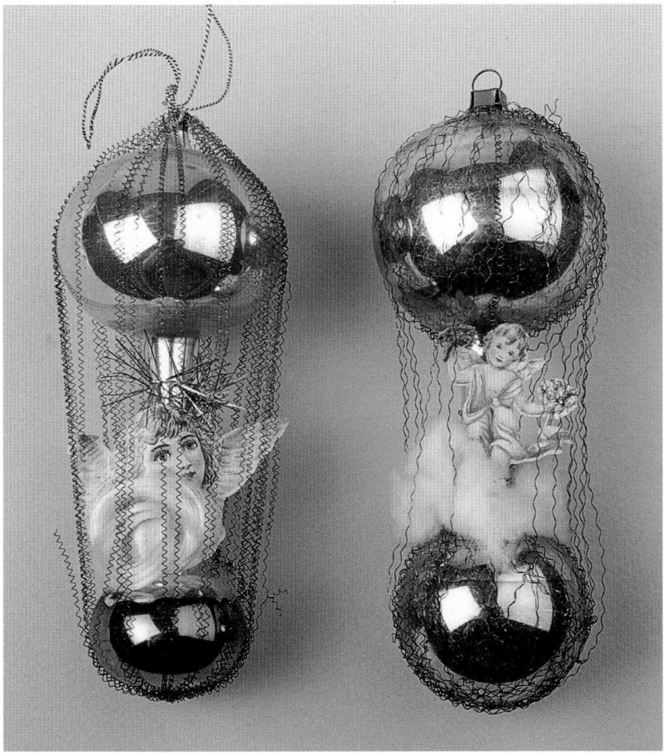

Late 1940s wire-wrapped balloons made in Lauscha, but transported to West Germany to avoid high tariffs. $55-65 each.

However, there were individuals in the United States who had a great influence upon the re-importation of European ornaments After the war. Whitehurst Imports began back in 1947 when Olga Whitehurst (a native of Lithuania in the Baltic states of eastern Europe), and Morris Whitehurst traveled to Lauscha. At that time, Lauscha was in Russian controlled Eastern Germany. Travel was extremely difficult in postwar Germany with virtually no hotels and little gasoline and food. Because they wished to import only the finest of European goods, they brought ornament-making supplies (which were not readily available in war-torn regions) such as ribbons and wire caps to the blowers so the artisans could continue production as they had prior to the war. Demand for these glass ornaments once again boomed, and Morris, then an attorney, gave up his practice to take up ornament sales.

For the Christmas of 1945, glass ornaments once again appeared with silver nitrate inside to return to the pre-war look of glittering silver glimmering through the lacquered glass ornaments. However, distributors who had an ample supply of these ornaments left in stock pushed clear glass ornaments. Silver tinsel was placed in the inside to help give a glittering effect to these ornaments. A dozen simple glass bells sold for $1.39 in 1949 while one dozen fancy reflector glass ornaments with single or double reflectors sold for $1.75. Leaf, frost, and scenic designs were popular stencils for glass ornaments in 1949.

Starting in 1947, Japan began once again to export Christmas items to this country, but with the label "Made in Occupied Japan." In 1947, Poland started to once again manufacture glass ornaments, and, in spite of many economic and social problems, managed to regain a lot of its market strength with the beautiful and delicate glass ornaments. Many of the Polish ornaments were indented to reflect the electric lights used on American Christmas trees.

During World War II, Prussia and the German nation once again occupied Poland and took over their factories. They left behind additional ornament molds in their hurried escape from the Russian army at the end of the war. Under communist rule in 1947, most Polish factories were centralized and nationalized. The predictable result was a drop in quality. While Polish ornaments continued to be bright and quite colorfully painted, they lacked the quality of pre-war ornaments.

"Occupied Japan" blown ornaments. $12-18 each.

"Occupied Japan" miniature ornaments with original boxes. $10-15 for box and ornaments.

"Occupied Japan" figural ornaments. All one to two-inches. $3-5 each.

Medium-sized Polish-blown ornaments. $2-3 each.

"Occupied Japan" and Japan-blown pine cones. $3-7 each.

Large four to five-inch hand-painted Polish ornaments from the late 1940s. $5-10 each.

1947 Polish-blown ornaments. One to two-inches. $1-2 each.

Czechoslovakian beaded ornaments imported in 1948 in various star and geometric shapes. $12-18 each.

Czechoslovakian beaded ornaments imported in 1949 with original paper labels. $12-18 each.

Japanese counterparts of the Czech beaded ornaments. Primarily, these were manufactured in star shapes. $7-10 each.

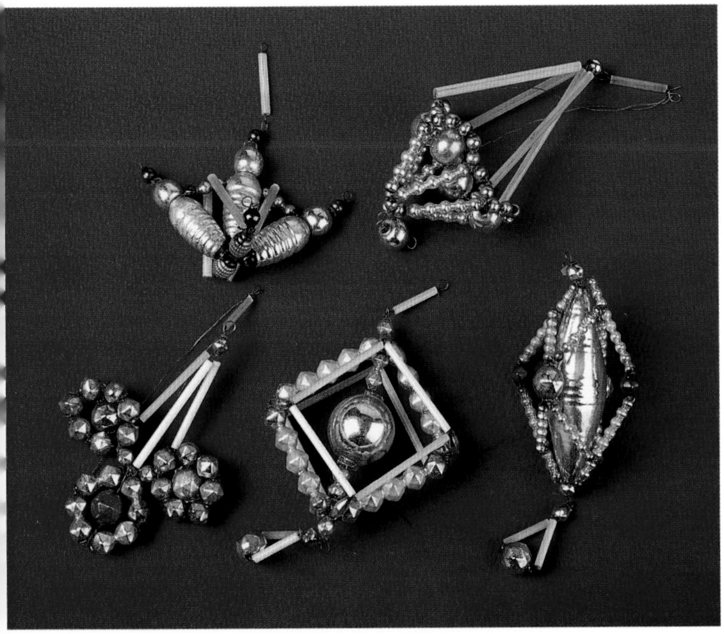

Czechoslovakian beaded ornaments imported in 1949 in various shapes, but with the characteristic silver color of this period. $15-20 each.

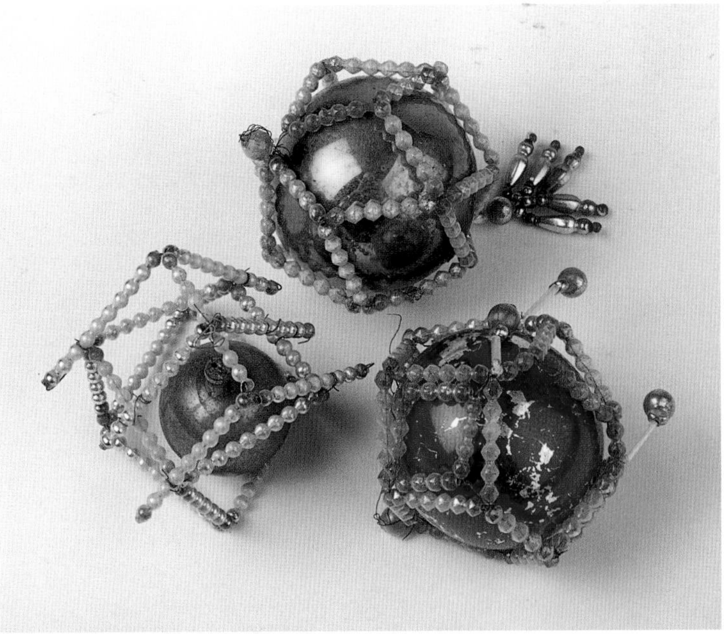

Japanese beaded ornaments with a large blown sphere in center of each. The rarest is the house-shaped ornament. $8-12 each.

A Closer Look at Other Tree Decorations of the Decade

During these war years, there were many individuals who suggested that the tree should be abandoned in a time of extreme war shortages. However, how could we live without the almost universal symbol of a Christmas celebration? Even the nationally distributed *Better Homes and Gardens* stated that the easy thing to do was to decide to give up the tree this year, and the wreath on the door as well. "But, think carefully. After all, in spite of battle, murder, and sudden death, war and separation, Christmas is special and demands a special garb. So make homemade decorations . . . clothespin angels, peanuts, popcorn, cranberries, paper dolls, pine cones, tin cans cut into icicles and various paper shapes, paper chains, etc."

It was the patriotic thing to do. Rather than purchase ornaments, craft and ladies' magazines encouraged home-crafted decorations for the tree like those created in earlier times. "Pipe cleaner dreams" were suggested as one possibility. A package of 24 cleaners was tied together in a bunch around the middle. Then the ends were opened to form a circle until the desired shape was achieved. One of the hooks was turned over to produce a clip and an ornament was created. There was a revival of paper ornaments cut from scraps of paper. Patterns for flat, one-dimensional butterflies, birds, fish, horses, flowers and fruit were among the most common. Three-dimensional patterns were available for those who desired the more extraordinary. In 1943, *American Home* offered patterns for cardboard churches, surprise balls with toys enclosed, nut men, peppermint-stick ladies, angels, candles, clowns, lambs, and Santa Claus—all of which were designed to be wartime tree ornaments made out of non-priority war items.

Recreation in December 1942, suggested home-crafted ornaments in colors of red, white, and blue. One of many novelty ideas that year for a patriotic tree was the paper chain cut from these colors. Christmas cookies, scenes cut from last year's Christmas cards, metallic paper cornucopias, white popcorn balls, and English walnuts in dyed colors were other suggestions.

Americans returned to creating their own decorations. They found that Christmas trees could be gay even if tinsel and lots of the familiar glitter were not available. Designers suggested that odd bits of ribbon, net, paper, lace, and colored papers that were usually thrown away could easily be recycled into decorations. Popcorn and peanut strings were suggested, dyed in bright color with red gelatin. Christmas balls from eggshells were once again made. Family members removed the white and yolk through a hole in one end and painted them in bright colors to use on their trees. Cornucopias and little satchels were formed from saved Christmas wrapping paper.

Even burned-out light bulbs were recycled. These bulbs were decorated as fruit with fresh leaves added. They also were used to make tree decorations. The bulbs were coated with poster or oil paint, facial details were added, and cotton was glued to created hair and beards, and then finished with paper trim as hats, collars, and other details.

In the early 1940s, candles and simple tin candleholders were sold in rural areas where families still clung to the tradition of using candles on their trees. Some very remote families did not yet have access to electricity, either through poverty or their own design.

By 1944, commercially-produced supplies of Christmas decorations and ornaments were extremely low. *Recreation* in their December issue stated, "There's a special reason why this Christmas of 1944 is a good time to start a new Christmas tradition, the tradition of making things together. Reports from the shopping front don't look very rosy for Christmas decorations, 1944." Therefore, now more than ever, Americans made their own decorations. Paper lanterns, cookies, paper chains, paper cornucopias, popcorn balls, peanuts in the shell, and even halved walnuts with inserted scenes cut from Christmas cards were made based upon directions found in many magazines, including *House Beautiful*. Directions appeared for making paper birds and fish, reindeer, angels, and Santa Claus figures. Tin can tops were cut into corkscrew shapes and even used to create tin icicles for the tree.

"Make 'em Yourself" ornaments, all die cut, ready to be folded and pasted, came in the shapes of cornucopias, stars, balls, lanterns, and icicles in 1940. Made of "mirro-metal," they came in red, green, or orange, all combined with silver metallic paper.

Novelty additions, such as foil icicles and bubble lights, were especially popular. Americans, in increasingly large numbers, started to purchase artificial trees.

After the war, cookie ornaments had another revival, but this time they were cut and lavishly decorated with gumdrops, cereal, M & M's, and other candies. In December 1945, *House Beautiful* provided cookie recipes, outlines of shapes for cutting, instructions for decorating, and listed paraphernalia needed for assembling these ornaments.

Home-crafted ornaments continued to be popular After the war. For, as *Recreation* stated in December 1946, Americans were living in a brave new world of industry. "It's a world where toy dolls walk and talk and drink their milk when 'mother' tells them and toy trucks move under their own power." It was a world where gas stations grew live trees overnight, decorations for the tree were set in bins so you could take your choice, and a world of new materials developed as a result of World War II. Therefore, Americans needed to buck the industrial hassles and make their own creative decorations for the tree.

After the war, we once again enjoyed the electric beauty of a National Christmas Tree. New lights adorned the tree in 1945, signaling a rebirth of the colorful festival begun in 1923.

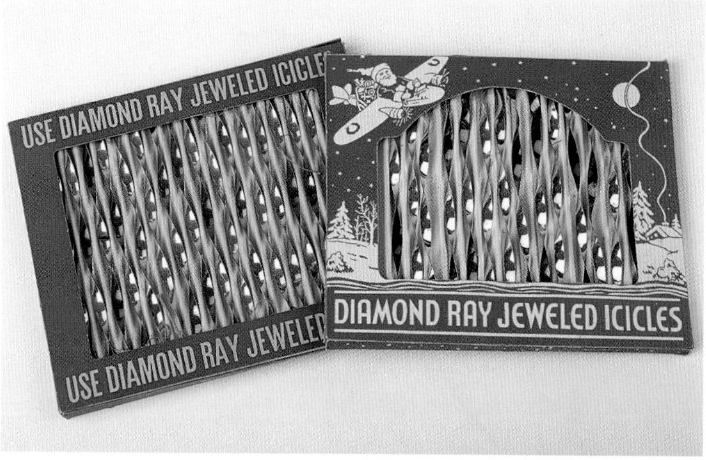

Metal spiral icicles. Manufactured once again after World War II in the late 1940s. $20-25 for a boxed set. $1-2 each.

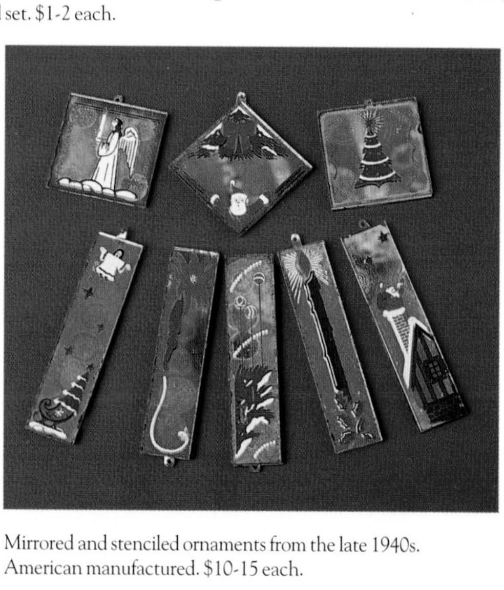

Mirrored and stenciled ornaments from the late 1940s. American manufactured. $10-15 each.

Late 1940s metal bells with metal clappers. American manufactured. $2-3 each.

Boxes of tree hooks used in the 1940s. $3-5 each.

Tree Tops

The electric-lighted tree top Angel was the most popular top after World War II, perhaps because this angel heralded a period of peace for all. Silvery white, she appeared with a real-looking mohair and rayon wig, wings of gleaming silver color, and a dress of glistening rayon brocade. The bulb behind her head helped to cast a glowing halo of light from behind the composition head. Other Snowmen and Star-shaped tops were also electrically lit. Also popular were the NOMA metal tops which contained five candelabra bulbs. Metal Star, "GloLite Illuminated Christmas Star Tops," 7-½-inches in height, were inexpensive tops which brightened the top of a tree when lit. National Tinsel also marketed many different sizes and styles of foil stars, into the centers of which an electric light was inserted. If anything were the norm for the period just After the war, it was "an electrically lit tree top." No doubt this was due to the strict wartime restrictions on lighting as well as the unavailability of electric tree tops and lights during these war years.

Blue and white-robed Angel tree tops from the late 1940s. $35-40 each.

National Tinsel spun glass Angel tree top from 1948. $50-60.

American tree top. Metal center with prism-cut glass points which reflected the color of the inserted electric light. 1949. $25-30.

Later Noma version of star top made from plastic and metal with the original box. $15-18.

Earlier Noma metal star tree top with the original box. $10-15.

1948 Noma plastic lighted Angel topped with a mohair wig. In the original box. $35-45.

Paper and Cardboard Ornaments

Also continuing their popularity were those metallic paper and cardboard ornaments in the shapes of the Jack-in-the-box, baby buggy, horsy rocker, soldier boy, gun, wagon, plane, drum, clown, and others. All made in America, they were thin cardboard, but covered with very bright foil paper and colors, somewhat reminiscent of those German-manufactured Dresden ornaments before World War II. Also continuing in popularity were those Japanese paper bells covered with foil. Sometimes hung on the tree, they were also used as window and wall decorations.

Mirror-like metal foil pom-poms sold with many crinkly surfaces to catch the brilliance of the electric lights. These were silver with varying colors of red, green, blue, and gold. Many other foldout foil ornaments in the shapes of bells and stars were sold.

Japanese-manufactured wreaths in 4" to 5" sizes with foil covered bells and glass beaded chains. $15-20 each.

Foil-crinkled ornaments from mid to late 1940s. $2-3 each.

Japanese-manufactured bells and wreaths in the 12" to 15" larger sizes. $20-25 each.

Japanese-manufactured wall decorations and tree ornaments in medium lengths. $15-20 each.

Lead Tinsel Icicles and Tinsel Garlands

Cellophane roping in green and red colors was the roping of choice for tree and house decorating. Sold in 30-foot lengths, the prices ranged from 29 to 39 cents. Sparkling metal foil icicles in 18 to 20-inch lengths appeared in silver and two tone colors, which included a combination of silver with red, green, or blue. Silk chenille roping was a popular choice in the early 1940s since it was inexpensive and American-produced. Sold in 54-foot lengths, and 7/16th-inch thick, it sold in red and green colors for 23 cents. Tinsel garlands were still available in the early war years due to a large accumulation of stock. It was sold in silver or in a combination of silver with red, green, or blue.

Tinsel manufacturers used 1,500,000 pounds of copper (in the form of fine wire) and platted it with silver or gold, some drawn as fine as .0022 of an inch thick, then flattened out, and woven into ropes or garlands for the tree. Candy-striped rayon canes and white spun rayon icicles were sold along with thick-woven rayon ornaments in the shapes of wreaths, flowers, crosses, and stars. Over seven million pounds of lead were used yearly for icicles.

American-made fiberglass garlands of silvery white or white with blue began to be sold with the Japanese fiber roping. Cellophane roping in red and green was also introduced.

Crystal garlands manufactured from fiberglass yarn in white or white mixed with blue sold for 29 cents in 18-foot lengths. Tinsel garlands in widths of 1/2" to 1 1/4" were silver coated on a metal base. Cellophane roping in red and green in lengths of 30-feet, as well as Japanese rayon chenille roping in green, was also sold. Red and green honeycomb tissue paper bells, with garlands to stretch to the corners of rooms, also made a comeback in the 1940s.

Red and blue cellophane woven with rayon feather-like roping was very popular in the mid-1940s. $10-15 for a three-foot length.

Late 1940s cellophane woven roping made in Japan. $10-12 for a four-foot length.

Red and green fiber chenille roping from Japan. Late 1940s. $5-7 for a five-foot length.

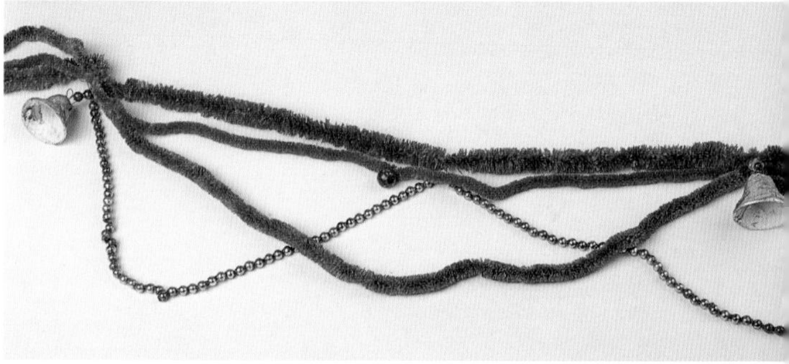

Rarer chenille roping which combines glass, paper foil bells, and other decorative effects from the late 1940s. Often used across doors. $20-25 for a complete length of eight feet.

"Merry Xmas" chenille roping and decorative wall hanging. Late 1940s. $35-40.

Boxed lead icicles from the late 1940s. $5-8 per box.

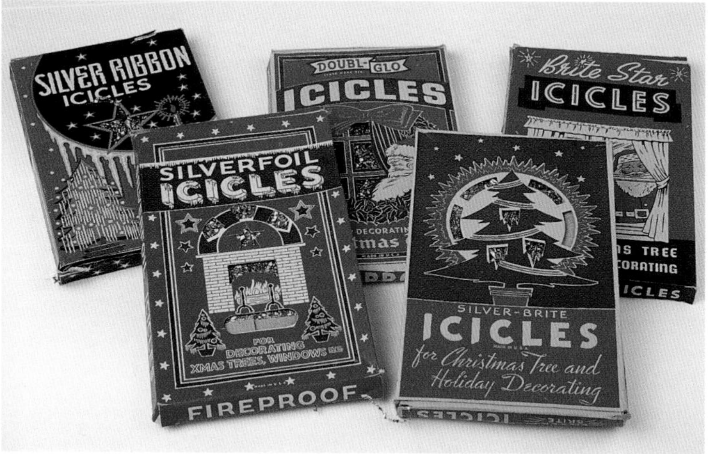

Assortment of lead icicles from the late 1940s. $5-8 per box.

Wooden Ornaments

Those Americans who were first generation Germans and Austrians remembered their pyramids, nutcrackers, and wooden ornaments made in Seiffen, Germany. While they were almost impossible to obtain, they were still being produced in Europe. Many of these nutcrackers and wooden ornaments reached the market when servicemen brought them home as souvenirs. The Erzgebirge area was the source of some of the most beautiful wooden articles in the world. There was an abundant supply of wood, lots of waterpower, and a rich, historical tradition, related to the centuries-old occupation of the area, the mining of metals. This area lies just north of the Czech Republic, then Czechoslovakia. It rises from the Elbe River to the highest altitude of 4,000-feet.

By 1945, following the occupation of the Seiffen region by the Red Army, they were ready to start running a modern factory. As they were already a workers' cooperative, the Soviet officials regarded them with favor, using their activities as a living piece of public relations for the "Socialist Way." By the time that the control had been passed to the German authorities in the 1950s, the Seiffen cooperative was somewhat of a Socialist darling. The established export market for their pyramids was a welcome source of negotiable currency for this newly emerged state. Also produced in large quantities were nutcrackers, also of great interest to Americans who remembered these figures from their youth.

A set of early wooden ornaments exported by West Germany but, in actuality, made in Seiffen, East Germany. $10-15 each.

Candy Containers

By the mid-1940s, thousands upon thousands of candy containers could be made in one day. Paper and cardboard replaced tin during the war years, which never returned. J. H. Millstein Co. of Jeanette, Pennsylvania, started a new trend in candy container design. Their containers were larger, and thus more expensive. Some were all glass and others combined glass and plastic, including a Santa Claus figure and a lantern. Their Santa was marked on the bottom of the glass with a keystone with an "O" in its center. Santa had a plastic head with red hat, round mouth, and black dot eyes. Red arms, black belt and boots, and white fur finished the glass portion of the body. Sears Roebuck advertised this Santa in their 1947 Christmas catalog.

In 1945, Sears Roebuck sold a set of five glass candy-filled toys in the shapes of a battleship, locomotive, tank, mug, and telephone for 49 cents. Other glass candy-filled toys included airplanes, trucks, U.S. bomber planes, and station wagons. A very elaborate set of four consisted of a 7" horn, 5" lantern, 6" roly-poly Santa, and 6" candy pump. The pump had a hose and crank that actually turned out candy when cranked. This set of four was hard plastic and glass combined. Also available were the "Candy Town Boxes" with decorated village scenes and cutout fronts. Less elaborate cardboard boxes with Christmas-themed illustrations were sold. Each would hold about a half pound of candy. In 1949, toffee-filled red net stockings in 9 and 13-inch sizes were sold by Montgomery Ward for use as tree or mantle decorations. Santa candy pops and "Bunte Santas," which were chocolate covered figures filled with chocolate pudding, sold by the thousands. They were to be used as tree decorations first, and candy treats later, if they were not "stolen" off the tree by hungry youngsters.

American-produced glass candy containers from the late 1940s era. $45-55 each.

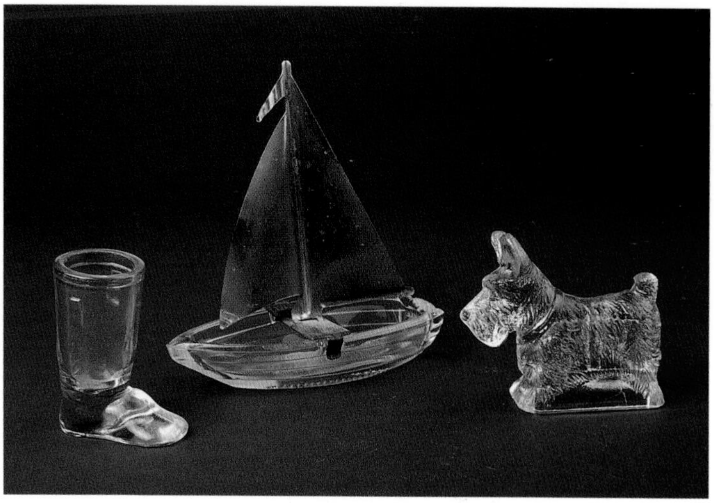

More common American-produced glass candy containers from the late1940s. $20-25 each.

Plastic candy containers, most often in the shapes of boots, snowmen, and Santas, became another popular choice immediately after World War II. Often times, these plastic containers were sold as a set. In 1948, Sears Roebuck sold an assortment which included a white Trojan horse with four lollipops astride it. Candy came out of a secret opening in the underside on the horse. On wheels, the horse was 5-½" high and 5" long. Also included was a jolly fat Santa on skis with ten lollipops in his pack. This red and white Santa stood 4-½" high on green skis. A white plastic snowman, 5" in height, with a coal black stovepipe hat, buttons, and pipe, carrying ten lollipops on his back was another container. Priced at 98 cents, the set was completed with a Santa Claus boot, 3" in height, filled with ten lollipops.

E. Rosen Company of Providence, Rhode Island, manufactured the all plastic red and white Santa with an open bag on his back for candy and green skis glued to his feet. The more rare version had white snowshoes for feet. Advertised in 1947 by Sears Roebuck, it came filled with lollipops, jellybeans, or Maybelle creams. Also quite popular was the 5-¾" tall Santa blowing a yellow trumpet mounted on a cardboard circle decorated with a wreath. He also had a pouch on the back for candy. Printed on the paper bottom was, "Ingredients: sugar, corn, syrup, citric acid, artificial color, and artificial flavor."

Late 1940s candy boxes lithographed and manufactured in the U.S.A. $15-20 each.

Late 1940s village houses, the backs of which each had a rectangular box for candy. $12-18 each.

Late 1940s foil covered cardboard candy boxes made in the U.S.A. $25-30 each.

Each 1940s house was shipped flat, with the teacher or pastor assembling and filling the boxes for distribution at Christmas. $12-18 each.

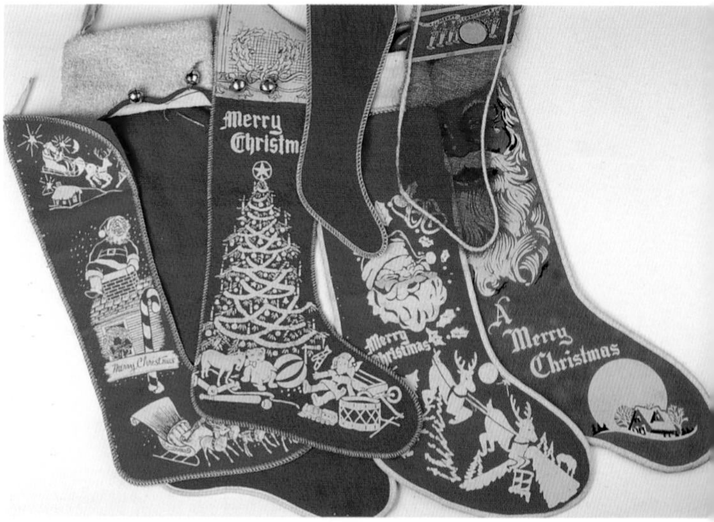

Felt, net, and paper stockings from the mid to late 1940s. $40-60 each.

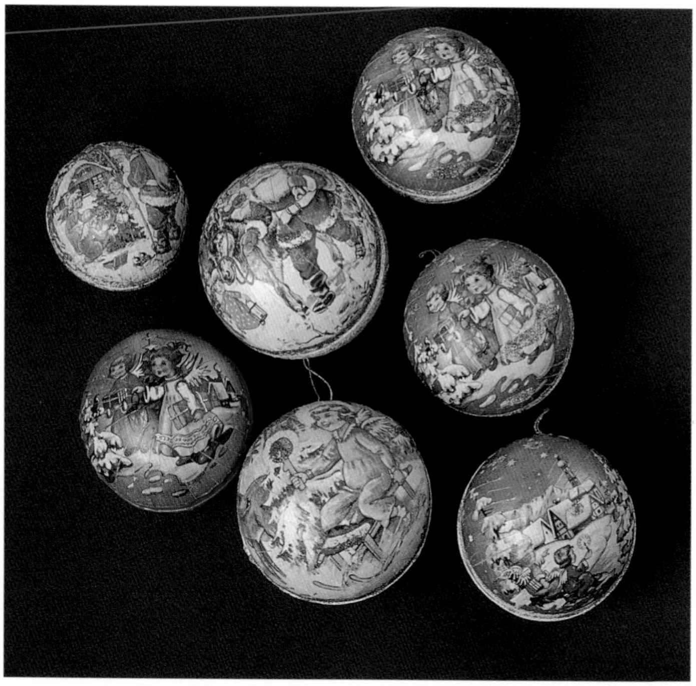

Assorted candy containers (that separate in the middle) from the late 1940s to the early 1950s. West German. $55-65 each.

Rosen Santa containers. The example on the right has the original paper disk. $45-55 each.

Rosen Santa containers on snow shoes. More rare. $40-50 each.

Metal tins from this period, which originally held candy, but were then recycled as Christmas cookie gift containers. $35-45 each

Rosen Santa containers on skis. Suckers were placed in the back. More common. $20-25 each.

1940s containers for "Oblaten" for Christmas Eve dinner and lebkuchen for Christmas eating. $25-30 each.

Plastic Decorations

Our first plastic decorations were manufactured from celluloid, actually cellulose nitrate, and were extremely flammable. In an effort to solve that dilemma, cellulose acetate was born in 1911. The Tennessee Eastman Corporation was one of the early pioneers of this plastic and, in 1932, developed the first cellulose acetate molding material which could be compression molded, extrusion molded, and injection molded. "Tenite" was its trade name with the Celanese Corporation soon following with its similar product, "Lumarith." These materials revolutionized the plastics industry because now millions of identical plastic items could be swiftly created with little finishing required. Compression molding dominated the plastics industry in the late 1930s, according to Bill Hanlon. In compression molding both a predetermined amount of plastic powder (in bullet form) was loaded by hand directly into an open mold cavity. The mold was closed and the material squeezed into the desired shape by heat and pressure. Finally, the mold was cooled and the finished ornament removed. Injection molding, however, is what propelled the plastics industry forward and Bill Hanlon, in *Plastic Toys,* details the process. In this process, a metered charge of molding powder, usually in granule form, was gravity fed into a horizontal heated cylinder in each machine cycle. There it was liquefied and compressed. It was then forced at a high speed into a closed cold mold by a plunger or screw. The liquid plastic entered the mold by means of a "sprue" or channel which led into the mold. Once inside, "runners" feeding off the "sprue" moved the plastic into the individual cavities. There it entered the cavity through a "gate." As soon as the thermoplastic hit the cold metal, cooled by water, it solidified to the molded shape. Then the mold opened and the ornament or object was ejected. These well-molded ornaments were extremely durable, almost impossible to break when dropped, and never fractured easily as did the glass ornaments.

Cambridge Plastics Company of Cambridge, Massachusetts, pioneered the marketing of plastic balls and other tree ornaments in 1945. Ornaments made of nonflammable cellulose acetate also appeared in this decade. Freeman, Taylor & Stanley of New York distributed several million balls manufactured from cellulose acetate powder, which were blown by a process similar to that used in making ornaments and were competitive on a price basis. Woolworth, Kresge's, and other variety stores immediately stocked these very popular ornaments. The New York display firm of J. M. Gordon & Company made fluorescent ornaments of Celluloid Corporation's Lumarith, treated with special dies to give a double pigmentation. Only larger department stores east of the Mississippi River carried these ornaments. Retail prices ranged from 5 cents to $1.50 for an elaborate encrusted ball, six-inches in diameter. Retailers suggested that black lights made by General Electric, Westinghouse, and others be employed with these "Fluor-Glo" ornaments. However, the price of a 100-watt black unit being about $30 prevented the average American from purchasing these new novelties.

Cellulose acetate houses and trees. $30-35 each.

Cellulose acetate Santa figures. $30-35 each.

In 1941, an Office of Precious Metals (OPM) order allowed a 60-days grace period for using up cellulose on hand, and since production for the next Christmas customarily started well before the holiday at hand has been celebrated, manufacturers put aside some materials for 1942.

According to *Business Week*, on December 13, 1941, the ornament industry's foresightedness in the matter of production accounted for the liberal supply of tinsel, tinfoil, and metal reflectors in stock that year. Manufacturers changed their formulae to made lead the major component of foil and reduced the use of aluminum and tin. Therefore, it was thought at that time that the OPM would release small amounts of strategic metals needed to continue to produce Christmas decorations and ornaments. However, in subsequent years that hope was squashed as we could spare no metal in the manufacturing of any Christmas items.

The E. Rosen Candy Company of Providence, Rhode Island, provided the sweets and Rosbro Plastics, also of Rhode Island, provided the novelty ornaments and toys. The Rosen family owned both companies. E. Rosen bought out the Tico Toys Novelty Company in 1946, which made many of the unmarked plastic ornaments found today. Sears, The Miller Electric Company, and the Royal Light Company bought novelties in this Rhode Island area. Tico and Rosen used mostly the same molds. Their wonderful pieces include cycles, automobiles, skis, snow shoes, and evens rockets, appearing with Santa Claus and, sometimes, his elves. One of the more collectible sets includes four pieces, a snowman, Santa on skis, Trojan horse, and a red boot, all of which came complete with hard sucker "pops" and came attractively boxed in a richly lithographed cardboard container. Many of the platform toys on wheels included Santa holding a tree, a "Merry Christmas" sign, or a plastic tool such as hammer or chisel. One such set of eight different colored Santas included a different color coordinated tool for each figure. All of these decorations were intended for use as tree ornaments. Blue, green, red, purple, and yellow were the representative colors used in this late 1940s and early 1950s set.

Rudolph tree ornaments from Rosbro Plastics were made of hard-to-break plastic, fawn-colored bodies and molded bright red ribbons around the neck. A plastic loop for hanging the ornament on the tree completed this 3-½-inch decoration. Plastic tree birds were also available in yellow, brown, blue, and red natural color combinations. Their feet formed clips to hold the birds erect on the tree. Santa Claus and Snow Man ornaments were sold in sets of five each. The red plastic Santa was painted with white while the white plastic snowman was painted with black features. Plastic bells finished in a plated metallic, mirror-like finish were advertised as sturdy, attractive, and economical, as a set of 10 sold for 95 cents. Plastic birds and Santa Claus sets contained: five birds (6-½-inches long with spun glass tails in red and blue colors) and three Santa Clauses (3-¼-inches high in red and silver outfits). Foreshadowing a trend to appear in the 1950s, crinkle foil tree balls in vivid red, blue, silver, and gold appeared for sale in the late 1940s.

The Irwin Corporation, originally founded in 1922 by Irwin Cohn, also produced many of these early plastic decorations. The Irwin Corporation gradually became one of the most successful toy companies in the world, moving from Leominster, Massachusetts, to Fitchburg, Massachusetts, to Nashua, New Hampshire. The corporation had two large toy-molding factories, one was at 85 Factory St. in Nashua, the other was in Leominster. Great American Plastics Company, an affiliate of the Irwin Corporation at these two locations, made the ornaments and toys.

Late 1940s Angel tree ornaments. $6-8 each.

Late 1940s Art Deco reindeer. $4-6 each.

Late 1940s hard plastic Santa ornaments with red boot. $15-20 each.

Array of late 1940s hard plastic ornaments. $8-12 each.

Rudolph the Red Nosed Reindeer figures (with Robert L. May patent imprinted on the side). $15-20 each.

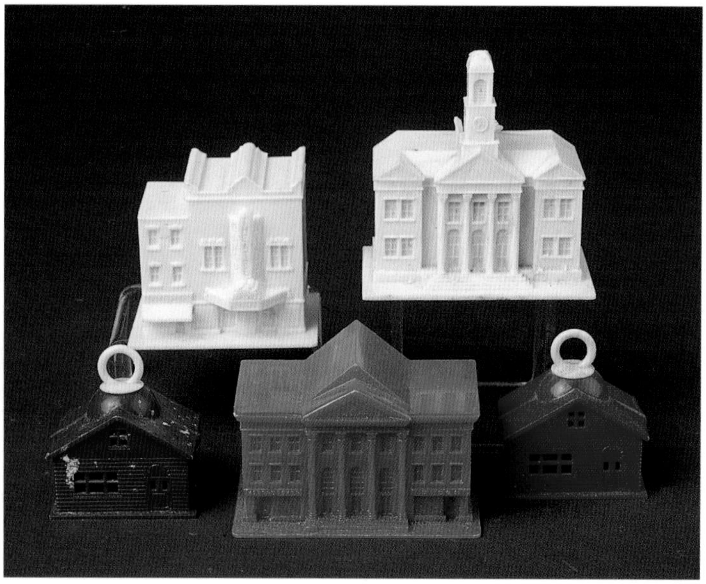

Assortment of plastic houses, the smaller of which are ornaments while the two large examples clipped over electric lights. $3-5 each.

Red, green, and blue silver finished plastic Santa ornaments from the late 1940s. $15-20 each.

A new idea, fluorescent acetate ornaments which emitted a soft glow when exposed to ultraviolet light, was marketed in 1949 by Magic-Glow Corporation of Chicago, Illinois. These were the outgrowth of several years of experimentation by Peter Pullman, president of the company. They die-cut angels, stars, bells, snowflakes, and animals from flat sheets of fluorescent cellulose acetate material supplied by the Monsanto Optical Co. and Celanese Corp. These items were made available in the following colors: red, blue, yellow, and green.

The ornaments were simply hung on the tree and a specially designed ultraviolet lamp, which as part of the set, was placed so that its rays were directed toward them. The standard set of ornaments, including eleven which were of three-dimensional construction with two sheets of acetate at right angles, came packed with the special lamp and holder, in a combination shipping box, container, and storage unit. It retailed at $12.95.

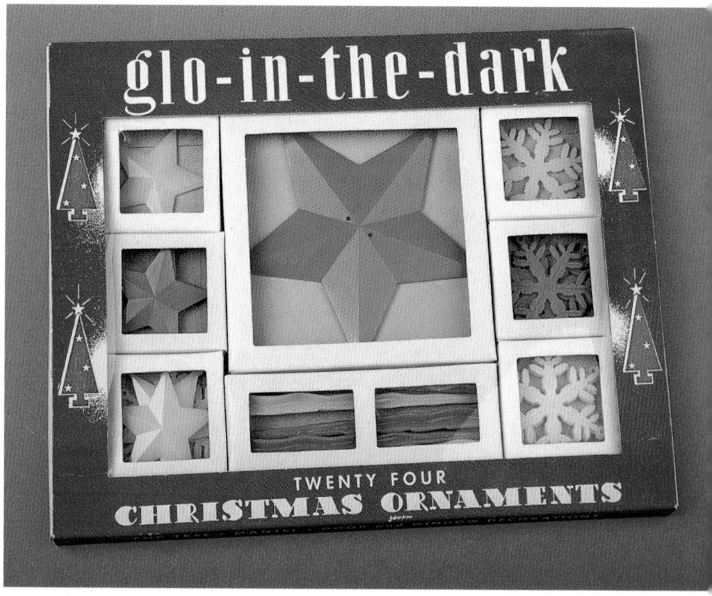

Set of 24 "Glow in the Dark" ornaments in the original box. $20-25.

Plastic continued to be a popular alternative to glass for ornaments After the war. Fluorescent snowflakes were injection molded of styrene by Design Center, Inc. These thin flat snowflakes were produced in very fine detail with all the minute crystallization of the real fakes. Available in a broad range of colors, they were lit once again by black light which caused the fluorescent pigmentations to give off a gleam, sparkle, and fire that was breathtaking.

The Plax Corporation of Hartford, Connecticut, produced blown acetate tree balls, ranging in colors from whites and pastels to the deep greens and reds. Also prominent among the decorations available were the formed fluorescent acetate pieces manufactured by the Vio-Glo Plastic Corporation. Formed bells of various sizes, artificial candles, and balls covered with chips of fluorescent materials, and feathered strips to replace the tinsel or "black light" decorations were manufactured. The Union Novelty Co. of New York City also marketed fluorescent ornaments kits which included tree top stars, bells, feathered ribbons, balls, candles, small double stars, icicles, snowflakes, pine sprays and "snow powder," or chips of fluorescent acetate. The Bo-Jo Molded Products Co. of Hollywood, California, also produced such ornaments, the molding of which was done by Southern California Plastic Co. of Glendale, Artcraft Plastics Corp. of Culver City, Aljac Plastic Co. of Ingewod, and Plastic Die and Tool Corp. of Los Angeles.

Entirely different were snow-like stars, crescents, and bells produced from styrene foam by Maharam Fabric Corp. of New York City. They had the advantage of being extremely light in weight and were available in gold, silver, and white. The year 1946 truly marked the entry of plastics into the Christmas decorations field on any large-scale basis.

Wax Ornaments

Figural candles were extremely popular as home decorations during this decade. Made completely of wax, they were sold in a variety of sizes and shapes. Santa Claus figures, choirboys and girls, reindeer, little children, angels, snowmen, and trees were the primary shapes employed by such manufacturers as the Gurley Company of Buffalo, New York, originally founded in 1926. Also known as the W & F Manufacturing Company, they originally intended to produce chocolate figures. Technical manufacturing difficulties led to candle manufacturing instead. Prior to their entry into the candle business, they were well known for those hollow wax liquid-filled soda bottles candies and wax lips. In the late 1940s, they signed an agreement with Socony-Vacuum Oil Company to create a colored line of figural candies. Their candles were primarily solid-core figures made from paraffin wax. Woolworths and W. T. Grant stores, among over five-and-dime stores, featured these candles for sale, at typically 20 to 60 cents each. Many of these candles are found with the prices still intact at the bottoms. Some of the most rare are black choirboys produced in very limited numbers. Candles produced by Gurley generally have a cardboard circle bottom which reads, "Gurley Novelty Co., Buffalo, N.Y., USA." Of interest are the safety directions found with the label on the bottom of the candle. Look for pricing information on dated tags and on boxed sets which invariably contained the copyright date. Another manufacturer of these candles was Emkay Candle Company of Syracuse, New York.

Wax boot candy containers for the tree. $3-5 each.

Waxed paper stars covered with glitter. Home-crafted during World War II when commercial ornaments were scarce. $2-5 each.

Original boxed set of wax figural ornaments. $80-90 for the box. $3-5 for each individual figure.

Large nine-inch Santa with original box. $20-25.

Original boxed set, complete with figures and fireplace. $35-45 for boxed set.

Original boxed set of Christmas candles. $50-60 for complete set and box. $2-3 for each figure.

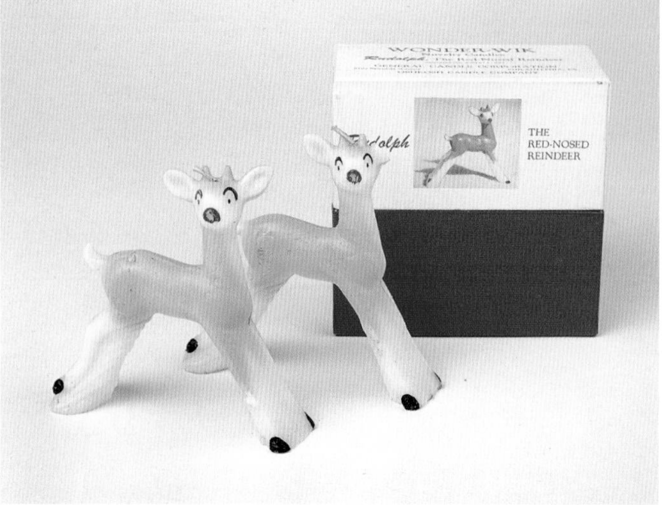

Rudolph the Red Nosed Reindeer candles with original box. Late 1940s. $25-30 for boxed set. $3-5 for individual deer.

1946 Santa and tree candles. $10-15 for Santa, $5-8 for tree.

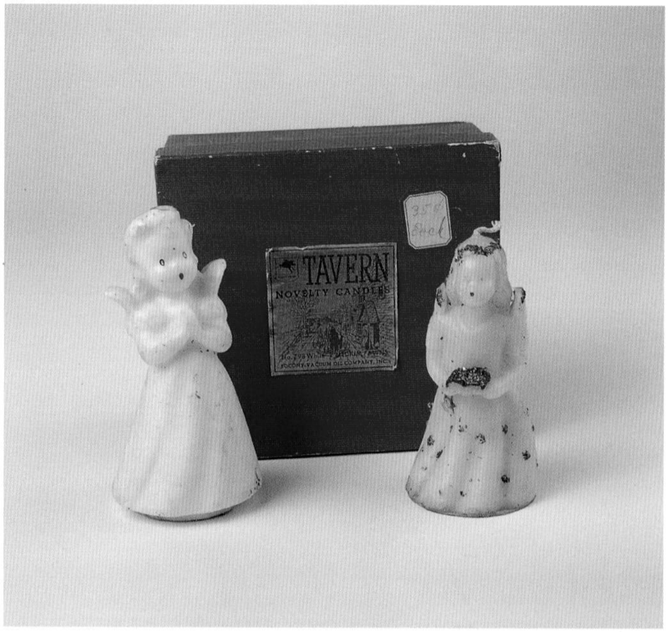

Two angels with original box. $12-15 for set in box.

Under Our Trees

It still was a popular practice to place a cotton batting sheet under trees and place on this sheet either a crèche scene or a simple setting of a few village houses and some Christmas figures. However, it was much more simple than those before World War II. Perhaps, people just did not find the time to create such elaborate scenes in an economy which demanded much more work from our Americans. So the custom of a scene under the tree was continued, but with some modifications.

Ground mica, some which was mined in the United States and some of which came from India, was packed into boxes so that Christmas snow could be sprinkled on the white cotton batting sheets placed under the tree. This white, glistening snow look extremely realistic, especially with the lights lit on the tree. "Christmas Mica Snow" was labeled as a product of the Geo. Frank Sons Co., a Baltimore, Maryland. This snow was prepared for them and sold under their name as they were primarily concerned with selling and producing glass ornaments as well as other decorations for the tree. "Double-Glow" was sold by Paper Novelty MFG, Co., Stamford, Connecticut, but the mica was produced by National Tinsel and sold under the Double-Glow" trademark. B. Wilmsen, Incorporated, Philadelphia, PA, was listed in *Nation's Business*, December 1950, as a manufacturer of artificial mica or plastic snow, tinsel, and tree hooks. At that time they had about 140 employees and produced different labels for different wholesalers and retailers.

Assortment of different snow products used under the tree, on fireplaces, and even on tables in the late 1940s. $5-8 for box.

Box of mica for under the tree. Note "asbestos" label on the box. $8-10 for box.

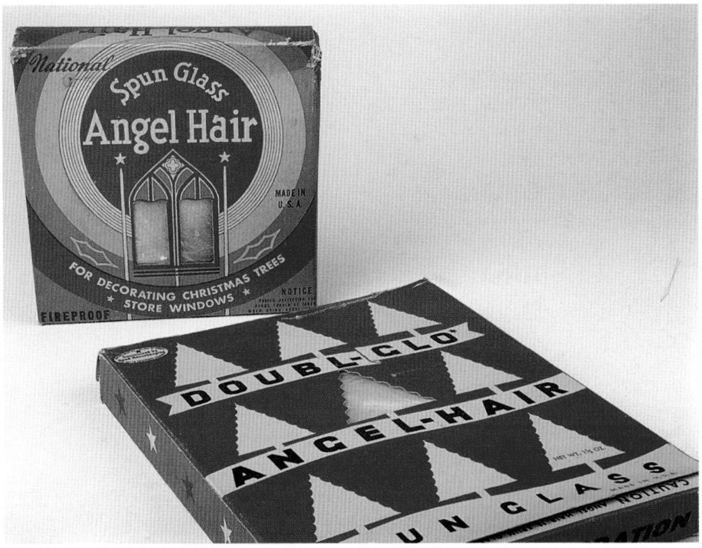

Angel hair was used on the top of white sheets and mica snow for snowdrift effects in Christmas scenes. $5-8 a box.

Nativity Scenes

In 1949 Montgomery Ward illustrated a 15-piece nativity set with figures of durable composition (actually plaster was the real medium) made in the United States for $2.98. These airbrushed figures were of low quality when compared to the Italian and German pieces produced before World War II. There were some early plastic sets available just After the war, being manufactured by American companies who also produced plastic ornaments and decorations for our trees, but they were not popular with families who sought the more traditional crèche scene.

Some very detailed crèche scenes were manufactured in Japan just after World War II. These included not only the basic figures, but a 7-inch palm tree and large wooden stable as well. Two angels in reverent positions, shepherd, three kings, and a beggar accompanied the four sheep, camel herd, cow, and donkey in worshiping the holy family.

But the very best sets were made in Italy and began to appear in the late 1940s. Their figures were extremely detailed in molding and exquisitely painted with painstaking detail. Most sets were small, but some larger 12-inch sets were available for those who really wished to create an elaborate scene in their homes.

Japanese-manufactured nativity stable and scene with figures glued to the base. Late 1940s. $25-30.

West German fold-out Christmas crèche scene. Late 1940s. $75-85.

Fences

In this decade, the most popular fences were red and green wood, manufactured in many different sizes and by many different manufacturers. One such manufacturer was the Valley Novelty Works of Bloomsburg, Pennsylvania, who produced a flat rail wooden fence, in an 18-inch square. Most sets fit in the 18-inch to 22-inch square or rectangular size. Most contained red center posts into which green-wood sections were inserted.

Village Houses

Village houses once again made an appearance After the war, but they were much simpler, with less detail. A set of eight brightly colored buildings, about 3-½" high, came with roofs sprinkled with glistening mica "snow," windows of transparent colored cellophane, and mounted on cardboard bases. These houses were primarily made in Japan, with a few sets (larger sizes) being manufactured in the eastern United States. White plastic fences appeared around these village scenes. A set of interlocking fence sections, 2-½" high, came with a gate section and 15 interlocking sections, creating a 24" square.

Boxed set, American-lithographed cardboard nativity stable and figures. Late 1940s. $40-45.

West German wooden houses with moss and detailed features. Late 1940s. $65-75 each.

West German houses, churches, and mill with moving wheel. Buildings electrified. Late 1940s. $70-85 each.

Japanese manufactured cardboard, snow flocked churches. $35-45 each.

Assortment of Japanese houses for use in Christmas scenes underneath the tree. Late 1940s. $20-30 each.

Brush Trees

Brush trees were the most popular trees for use under the tree and even in mantel and tabletop decorating scenes. Manufactured by the same process used to make bottle brushes for cleaning glass containers, these trees wove green fibers into a wire base which was cone shaped. Then the trees were flecked with white paint and plaster to give them a winter effect and placed in red wooden bases. Most brush trees were made in Japan, with a few of them being manufactured in the United States. Japanese trees were much less expensive, so the American versions often went unpurchased in the stores. Sizes of brush trees ranged from 1-inch up to 14-inches.

One to seven-inch brush trees in different color variations from Japan. $5-15 each.

One to eight-inch green, brush trees from Japan. $5-15 each.

Unusual brush trees marked "Occupied Japan." $3-6 each.

Animals and Figures

After the war, the Japanese immediately resumed production of celluloid reindeer and other animals and human figures for Putz scenes. "Putz scenes" or "Christmas Tree Gardens" were an outgrowth of the Moravian custom of creating a Nativity scene under the Christmas tree employing animals, human figures, trees, and a manger with Jesus, Mary, and Joseph as the focal point of the display. Made of cellulose nitrate, they were flammable. All of them are marked at some spot, usually in the back or on the boots. They are easily distinguishable from their earlier counterparts because the 1940s items were almost entirely airbrushed red with only white trim on Santa's coat and face with black dots for eyes. Americans also produced celluloid figures, but the were made of cellulose acetate, and were more safe to use. Multitudes of cows, donkeys, sheep, horses, pigs, and every imaginable animal were produced for children as toys and also for use in village scenes under the tree.

Five to six-inch celluloid reindeer from Japan with glass eyes. $35-45 each.

Nine-inch celluloid reindeer from Japan with glass eyes. $55-65.

More common celluloid reindeer from Japan with silver glitter trim. $10-15 each.

One to four-inch celluloid reindeer, all manufactured in Japan. $5-10 each.

Assortment of American-made celluloid animals. $10-15 each.

Array of two-inch celluloid animals (USA). $10-15 each.

Large six-inch celluloid "Occupied Japan" marked animals with glass eyes. $25-30 each.

Assortment of Japanese manufactured celluloid figures. $10-15 each.

The Japanese also produced composition-faced Santa figures in multitudes of styles and sizes just After the war. However, they lacked the detail of their earlier counterparts. Made more from paper than from fabric, they lacked the quality of those produced before the war. Their pants were no longer made from flannel, but from paper. Their faces took on a more "reddish" complexion as the careful detailing of cheek flushes and eyes were lacking in these post World War II Santas.

Array of five-inch Japanese composition Santa figures from the late 1940s. Note the composition heads. $65-75.

Five-inch Japanese Santa in wooden sleigh with wrapped presents. $75-95.

Large nine-inch Japanese composition Santa. $100-110.

Celluloid Santa with sleigh on flocked cardboard base. Late 1940s. $55-65.

"Occupied Japan" Santa nodder from the late 1940s. $120-135.

Squeaker Santa made from celluloid and plastic (squeeze noise box underneath jacket). When his head was pushed down, he made a squeaky sound. Japan. $190-210.

American plaster Santa covered with flocking and then hand-painted. 8" high. $45-55.

Papier-mâché Santa figures were produced for use under Christmas trees in a time when the Putz scene was not as popular. They came in varying sizes and most of them were either a simple white or red color with air brushed bodies. Details such as eyes were minimal. Generally, collectors refer to these as "egg carton" Santas because the papier-mâché, when viewed from the inside (through bottoms or tops, which were open since these figures often served as candy containers) appeared to look like the familiar egg cartons. American papier-mâché, later pressed millboard (similar to fiberboard or layers of paper saturated with paper) was pressed into molds, then heated, dipped into a mixture of linseed oil and tar, and baked again. The figures were then varnished, lacquered, and painted. Some items were not varnished and lacquered. Thus they have a dull finish. In the 1940s, American papier-mâché was produced by Milwaukee Pulp Products for a company named "Wisconsin Pulp, which later became "Pulp Reproductions," that later became "Carry-lite." Carry-lite did the finishing and merchandising of these Santa Claus figures. As well as Santa figures, snowmen and Santa boots of varying sizes were produced.

American egg-carton Santa figures. Six to ten-inches. Late 1940s. $70-80 each.

Japanese table decorations typical of this period. Foil and plaster berry beads in many different combinations were produced in the latter part of the 1940s. Poinsettia pot, $5-7. Berry trees in wooden pots, $5-6 each.

American egg-carton snowmen figures. Often doubled as candy containers as well as decorations. $75-85 each.

Plaster of Paris bank. 14-inches. $75-85.

This particular figure was a re-released, post-war, late 1940s version of the egg carton Santa figure that had been extremely popular in the mid-1930s.
$135-145.

Plaster of Paris bank. 26-inches. $100-125.

Late 1940s banks featuring Santa in an easy chair. Six to nine-inches. $75-85.

American hard plastic roly-poly from the late 1940s. $90-100.

American printed Santa and sleigh. Doubled as a candy container or a card holder. 15-inches. $95-105.

Originally pencil sharpeners, these two Santa figures were discovered in a collection of Putz items for use under the tree. Made of plaster, the black Santa is the most rare. Black Santa sharpener, $85-95. White Santa sharpener, $30-35.

American printed Santa and sleigh. Doubled as a candy container and a table decoration. 22-inches. $100-110.

Indoor Electric Lighting of Our Trees and Homes

In the 1940s, candles were not abandoned, especially in many rural parts of our country, which not only clung to tradition, but many times did not have the electrical power available in their homes to electrify their trees. In fact, many reverted to using candles during the war in an effort to conserve energy which could be better used in the war effort. Little hints, such as blowing out the flames of the candle upward so as to not cause smoke and removing candle drippings by immersing a cloth into cold water to facilitate the removal of such meddlesome drippings, were welcome. If candles were too large, they were not to be cut down. Softened under hot water, they were then pinched and pressed into the holder.

One interesting addition was the imitation metal candle with tinsel "flame," sold in assorted colors of red, blue, green, gold, and fuchsia, which fit into standard-sized candleholders for those who wanted candles, but didn't want the danger of a lit flame.

At the start of the war, Americans still clung to the notion that lights were essential to their Christmas celebrating and American-produced lighting was available. *House Beautiful*, in December 1940, described miniature candelabra and intermediate lamps which were wired in series, parallel, or multiple. Series lamps continued to be most popular in strings of eight lamps, wired so that each lamp was dependent on the other for its supply of current. Therefore, we continued the practice of searching for the one burned-out lamp on the entire darkened string. Series lamps (miniature) were available in the familiar tapered end, a larger one which resembled a candle, and a tiny one about the size of a flashlight bulb. All of these series lamps were rated at 15 volts, could be used interchangeably in the same string, and operated on any 110-220 volt lighting circuit.

Candelabra, the next sized lamp, was used in indoor parallel or multiple strings. Rated at 120 volts and operating on 110-220 volt lighting circuits, they were attached to parallel strings along which the current flowed without interruption. Quite simply, that meant that each lamp burned independently; when one lamp burned out, the others stayed lit. Tapered or candle-shaped lamps were available for strings which range from 7 to 25 lamps.

The last size, intermediate, was designed primarily for outside use. This tapered lamp, which consumed 10 watts, had an intermediate base and was attached to a heavier and more durable wire. Weatherproof, the bulbs were inside-colored for protection against rain and snow (a practice later abandoned). Easily recognized by its candle-flame shape, this bulb was the best of its time and is still considered by collectors to be valuable today due to its inside painting.

Boxed set of late 1940s candelabra-base lights. If one went out, the rest stayed lit. $30-35.

Boxed set of late 1940s intermediate-base lights. If one went out, the rest stayed lit. $30-35.

Boxed set of late 1940s miniature-base lights. If one went out, they all went out. $20-25 for boxed set.

Boxed set, late 1940s, intermediate based lights. Includes directions for finding burned out bulbs. $35-40.

Safety was an important factor and *House Beautiful* suggested that consumers check for sets carrying the Underwriters' Laboratories label testifying to their fire-safeness. Rubber washers were recommended for added safety. Clipping the lights to the branches was made easy by the use of beads which slid along the wires, clips attached to the socket, and even alligator clips used to keep bulbs upright (especially important when using bubble lights).

Interestingly enough, our later mania for trees decorated in one color had its roots in 1940s lighting. Americans striving for their own special dramatic effects searched for some different ways to light their trees. Design decorators suggested all white lamps for sparkle and crispness while white and orange were suggested for mellow brilliance. All blue lamps gave a soft, hushed appearance and all green lamps increased the greenness of the tree. Red was discouraged as it would create a brown tree. Multi-colored lights were suggested for a bright, cheerful tree when a particular effect was not desired. Other effects with lights were achieved by bringing the light strings down in straight lines from the top. A barber-pole design was suggested for tall trees or even a lively candy-stick pattern was proposed by inserting "pin-type" sockets at 6" intervals along the wires between the regular sockets. Floodlights were used with 150-watt projector lamps with colored lenses. Reflectors behind the lamps were promoted (probably in the interest of saving electricity in a time of war-frugality), which not only added color, but also added increased light, thereby possibly decreasing the number of bulbs required.

Since lighting was a problem, many innovative ideas were fostered and promoted. Arnold Radtke, in the 1940 issue of *Industrial Arts and Vocational Education,* suggested that shop teachers teach their students to decorate the school tree with ornaments cut from tin cans and old aluminum kettles. These ornaments were to be in the shapes of stars, squares circles, and even twisted spirals. Five spotlights (having red, blue, and green colors) were to be positioned with the blue spots centered one on each side, above, and a little toward the front of the tree. The green spots were to be placed on the floor about five feet or a little more in front and to the side of the tree, and the red was to be suspended that the light might fall on the front of the tree down the center. Properly disguised, these lights would provide a multi-colored effect when directed on the tin and aluminum decorations.

However, World War II had an effect upon the electric lighting of our trees, and in general, diminished our use of even outdoor lights at Christmas. In 1942, the Office of Civilian Defense (OCD) Director James M. Landis stated that OCD policy discouraged the use of elaborate or potentially dangerous lighting and of any extra outdoor lighting at all in all coastal levels. The OCD's position was based not alone on the potential dangers of enemy attack, but also upon concerns about the materials and electric power involved and the potential fire hazard at a time when any waste of resources was considered *sabotage*. From the security standpoint, Christmas lighting in dim-out areas was prohibited to protect shipping at sea. Landis urged that no new equipment or wiring involving critical materials be purchased for Christmas decorating. "We do not intend that individual stores and homes may not decorate their windows modestly as in previous years, so long as the lighting conforms to any dim-out regulations in their localities," Mr. Landis stated. "But such lights should burn only when the occupants are available to put them out promptly in the event of an air raid alarm."

Eight-light reflector sets of the period contained 15-volt miniature lamps. Behind each lamp was a star-shaped cardboard reflector to which was glued silvered glass mirror pieces. Thus, when lit, these lights were most spectacular indeed. Silver-colored metal "Kristolite" reflectors, sold in sets of eight, also added brilliance to the tree.

Mid to late 1940s cardboard reflectors with mirrored glass points glued to cardboard stars. $5-6 each.

Assortment of "Kristolite" reflectors flashed with color to add brilliance to lighting effects. Late 1940s. $2-3 each.

Assortment of "Kristolite" silver reflectors. Late 1940s. $2-3 each.

Wonder-Star Christmas lights were made in several sizes:

Series	Points	Size	Lamp
100	single	1 15/16"	miniature
200	single	1 1/16"	miniature
400	single	2 ¾"	candelabra
410	single	2 ¾"	intermediate
420	single	2 ¾"	standard
500	double	2 1/16"	miniature
700	double	2 9/16"	miniature
900	double	3 1/8"	standard
910	double	3 1/8"	intermediate

Assortment of smaller sized Matchless Stars. Glass crystals cut in Czechoslovakia. $75-85 each.

While Matchless Stars, first advertised as "Wonder Stars," were first patented by Paul Dittman in 1927, they were still advertised for sale in the 1940s, and many were sold up to the 1950s. P. C. Dittman took out his last patent on June 3, 1941. Sold primarily through Montgomery Ward catalogs and various hardware catalogs, these stars were absolutely elegant and bright when lit. The miniature lamps were 15-volts wired in series. The candelabra, intermediate, and standard base lamps were 110-120 volts. A small, clear, round lamp was surrounded by one, two, or three rows of colored cut glass prisms, imported from Czechoslovakia, wired together, and surrounding a round center prism of another color. Some were even dipped in acid to give them a frosted appearance. They were made in miniature, candelabra, and standard sizes. Colors included ruby-red, crystal-clear, topaz-amber, sapphire-dark blue, rose pink, emerald-green, and aquamarine-light blue. Matchless Electric Company of Chicago, Illinois, produced these stars, both for indoor and outdoor lighting. The name "Matchless" and "Made in USA Pat. Pending" is molded into each brown Bakelite plastic base. The most rare in this category is the Matchless Tree-Top Star (No. 300, miniature lamp) which was molded with five points.

Wonder-Stars were expensive. Prior to the war, the smallest ones sold for 18 to 20 cents each. The series 500 double row stars sold for 32 to 35 cents each. This is especially notable when historians record a boxed set of Paramount lights selling for 60 to 80 cents with a cord. The Matchless Electric Company was dissolved as a corporation in 1954, but continued their business through the 1950s.

Large lit standard-based Matchless Star. $500-600.

Another popular choice in the early part of this decade was the electric star, measuring 2-inches in diameter, colored in tones of red, blue, green, amber, and crystal, and made of translucent plastic. Produced in the USA by The Matchless Electric Company, each light was equipped with a 15-volt bulb. These were the new counterpart to "Wonder-Stars," being more expensive to manufacture, employing plastic, but so much easier to market due to their durability (no more glass points to crack and chip; the plastic resisted breakage when dropped).

Plastic "Wonder-Stars." Late 1940s. $50-60 each.

As early as 1940, wholesalers and retailers were advertising new sets for indoor tree lighting in which every socket was individually wired. When one light went out, the rest stayed lit. For the additional price of about fifty cents, consumers now could avoid the dreaded search for "dead" bulbs on their trees.

After the war, Americans now more than ever started to decorate outside in a very lavish fashion. Two leading Christmas-oriented cities, Allentown and Bethlehem, Pennsylvania, created unbelievably elaborate displays each Christmas. Garlands of 25-watt bulbs in solid settings of red, green, gold, and blue astonished many who saw the display for the first time. Bridge displays, lighted trees, and life-size lighted nativity scenes helped draw thousands to the city at Christmas to view its magnificence. Led by cities that set the trend, homeowners competed with one another to see who could create the most sparkling nighttime display.

In 1946, Noma Electric Corporation, best-know maker of tree lights, expanded into the year-round market with the acquisition of numerous subsidiaries. Henri Sadacca stated, "Noma was born from a little Christmas tree light, just as General Electric Co. was born from a small incandescent bulb." Noma was a familiar name to many Americans as that name was usually on the box which contained the string of Christmas tree lights used from year to year to light their trees. Before the war, however, these lights did become a great irritant – if one light went out, the whole set went out since they were wired in a series. Nevertheless, Noma played a major role in developing the dependable Christmas tree string and also the circuit of lights durable enough to use outside.

When Sadacca first went to Noma (he became vice president in 1927), its business was entirely seasonal. Sadacca had begun manufacturing lights in 1911, and had also begun his career as an electrical inventor. In the trade, light strings were termed "outfits." Competition was fierce, pitting one company against another in efforts to stay afloat. In 1925, firms in the business attempted to thwart this "war" by forming the National Outfit Manufacturers Association (NOMA). This was the start of Noma, which got its name from the association's initials. Failing as a stabilizer, Noma finally bought out the manufacturing companies and went into production itself.

Its original fourteen members included all but a few of the principal manufacturers. There was competition, but Noma was by far the principal producer of lights in the United States. On the average year, Noma produced between seven and ten million strings of lights to be hung on over twenty-five million trees sold. In excess of 100 million light bulbs were produced. Noma was the only manufacturer of such lights in Canada and Britain.

Sadacca did leave the company in 1932 for independent ventures. He purchased Monowatt Electric Corporation and Whitney-Blade Company, makers of wiring and accessories, and quickly created a market by selling low priced items to five-and-dime stores. Gradually, he sold out his ventures and returned to Noma, in 1938, as president. His mission included broadening the company's sales base. He added decorative and religious items to the lights then marketed. War interrupted his plans, and by 1942, his regular lines were out. However, he obtained permission to manufacture toys by locating plants in areas where labor and facilities were not involved in war production. Between 1943 and 1945, he sold twenty million toys.

Peerless boxed set of miniature-based bulbs. Late 1940s. $30-35.

Peerless boxed set of miniature-based bulbs from just after World War II. $35-45.

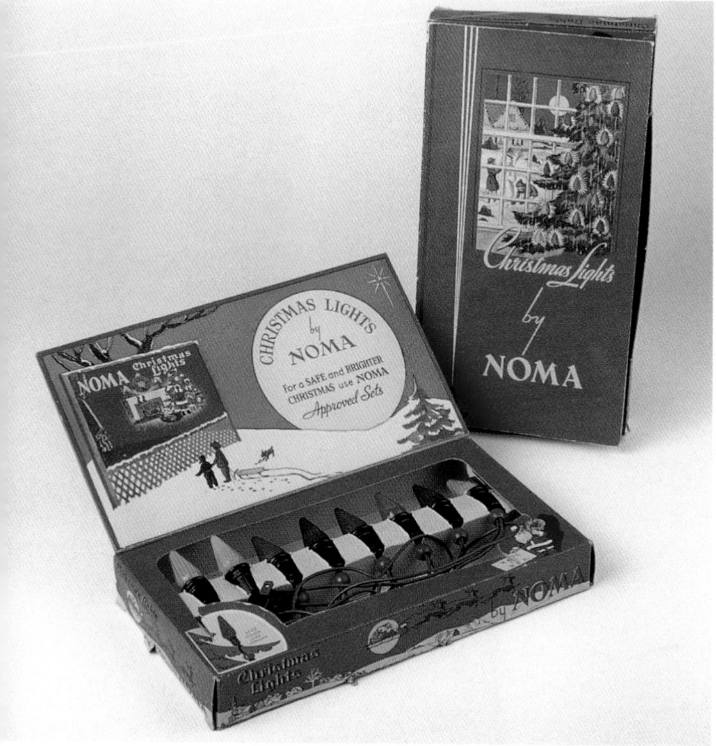

Common box of NOMA miniature-based bulbs. Late 1940s. $10-12.

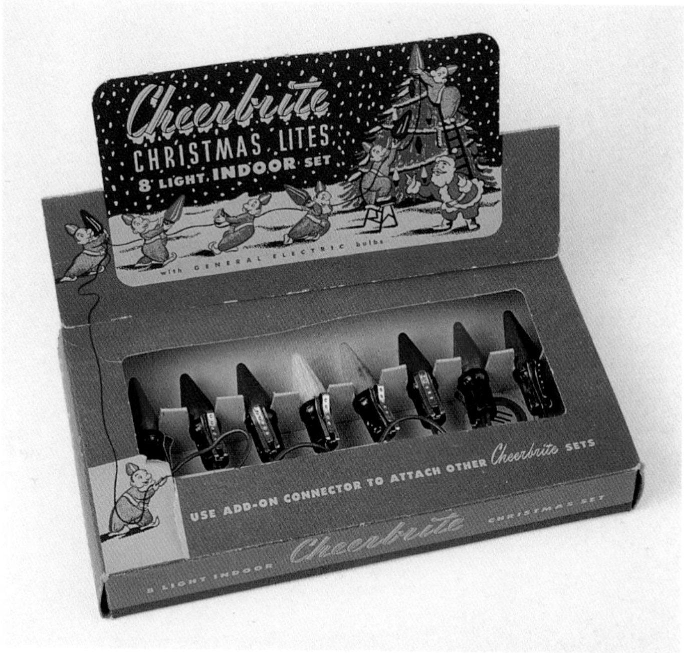

Cheerbrite boxed set of miniature-based bulbs. Just after World War II. $15-20.

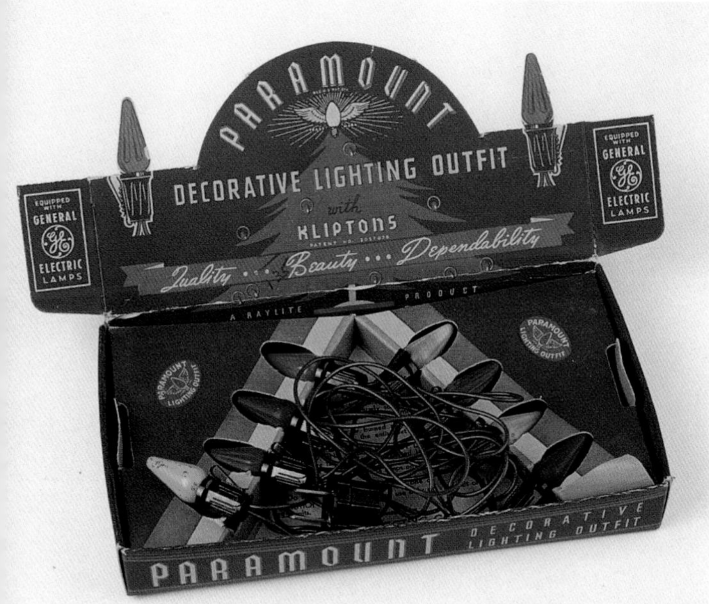

Paramount boxed set of miniature-based bulbs. Late 1940s. $20-25.

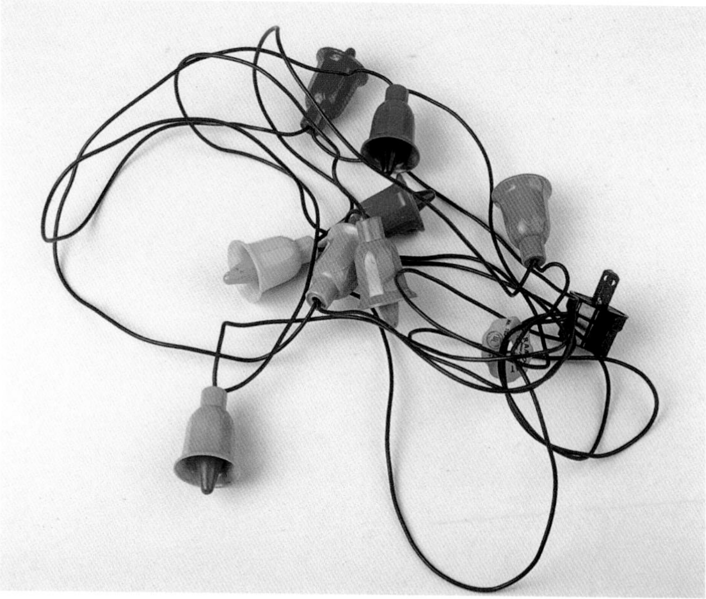

String of miniature-based bulbs with plastic bells over bulbs. $15.00 for string and bulbs.

Henri Sadacca displayed great foresight in scouting for new products near the end of the war. "Bubblelite" Christmas lighting was one of those products which profited greatly. Demand for the Christmas of 1946 was so great that Noma was only able to deliver 20% of its orders for lights and ornaments, and only 30% of its orders for toys!

Consumer's Research Bulletin, in December 1947, evaluated the electric lights available for sale that year. They bemoaned the fact that the lights made in China and Japan were of poor quality and short life—and priced quite high at 20 to 25 cents each. Given an "A" Recommended rating were Miller Outdoor-Indoor No. 100 and Noma 15-Light Decorative Outfit No. 3415. Given the "B" Intermediate rating were Amico, No. A; Amico, No. 701; Clemco, No. 505; Gem, Glolite No. 186C; Good-lite No. 40; Goodlite, Montgomery Ward's Catalog. No. 48-150; Noma No. 110; Park No. 707; Paramount No. 1301K; Reliance, St. Nick No. 68; Sterling No. 11000K; Timco No. 101; and Reliance No. 117. Given a "C" Not Recommended rating was Royal No. 102KA. This set was rated such as tinsel could make electrical contact with socket shells and the wire insulation easily loosened to expose bare wire at the sockets in sets examined.

Cheerful plastic Glo-Bird lights came in a set of four and were realistically molded of hard-to-break plastic in green, yellow, blue, and red. The bulbs inside came with a metal base protruding. These were interchangeable with standard miniature (series-type) bulbs. A set of four sold for 97 cents in 1948 and did not include the cords and sockets.

Garrison Wagner, a wholesaler for florists and gift shops, advertised both hand-operated and automatic color wheel floodlights for display purposes. While the hand-operated model came with a four-color wheel, the automatic model contained six assorted colors of the finest gelatine. They were available in 1,000 watt and 400 watt sizes. Most certainly, these early models were the forerunners of what Americans were to use in the next decade to light the ever-revolutionary aluminum trees.

"Watch them Bubble," "Glamour Light your Christmas Tree with Paramount Bubbling Lights," and "Watch them rise, watch them fall." These are only a few of the slogans used to help sell this phenomenon of the mid-1940s: "Bubble Lights!" For a brief period in history, there was hardly a home that did not have at least one string of these lights on their Christmas tree. Perhaps much of their charm lay in the action of the bubbles, for not since the use of candles was there such motion on the decorated tree.

It is this mystery of motion that causes many admirers to question the components of bubble lights. The basic elements of the bubble light are a light bulb, a tube partially filled with a special liquid, and a plastic base to house both items. Most bubble lights were made in the miniature base format, though many were made in the candelabra base, and, recently, in the midget variety, with both push-in and screw-in bases. The bulbs in most are flat-topped, which allows the liquid to rest on top, thus gathering as much heat as possible from the lamp. In nearly all cases, the base is comprised of two halves of plastic, either glued together or held together by interlocking teeth (as in the case of a Paramount brand). The bases were of colored plastic in red, green, blue, yellow, orange, pink, white, purple, and several variations on the shades of each color.

The tube of liquid is what sets the bubble light into its own unique category. The liquid is a special low-boiling point chemical sealed in a glass vial which has had the air evacuated, allowing the liquid to boil from the heat of the bulb, then condense once the bubbles have reached the top of the liquid. This process is explicitly described in the patent filed June 9, 1945, by A. Abramson. "The liquid is of low boiling point and I may employ fluids such as, for example, wood alcohol, ether, or methylene chloride. If it is desired to enhance the ornamental effect, the liquid, tube, or both may be colored or a thin film of pellucid coloring matter coated on the inner or outer surfaces of the tube. Only a portion of the tube is filled in liquid, the balance of the tube being evacuated so as to provide a partial vacuum in which vapor (bubbles) generated in the lower end of the tube may condense and return to the body of the liquid."

The liquid, methylene chloride, is a flammable, poisonous fluid with a low boiling point. This liquid has an extremely strong chemical odor and dries instantaneously if released, permanently staining anything it has touched. Collectors should be very careful if a tube breaks. The white granules, either separated or in large clumps, found in the bottom of the tube are the "bubble generators," and are usually, but not limited to, sugar, borax, and table salt. Another item found in many bubble light tubes is a glass pellet seated near the bottom of the tube. This pellet "catches" the tiny bubbles, "gathering" them up before they are forced between the pellet and glass tube up into the liquid column. This produces the large bubbles that rise up in the liquid. Those bubble lights without the glass pellets in the vials produce very tiny bubbles.

The bubble light idea began with Carl Otis. He filed a patent on November 27, 1935, for Bubbling Display Signs. These signs were designed to spell out a word or to identify a symbol. He later took out a patent in 1939 for bubble lights as collectors know them today.

It would seem most unusual that a product granted a patent in 1939 would not be put onto the market until 1945, since the granted date was two years before the United States entered the war. In situations where products were being put into production while waiting on a patent to be granted, it is simply marked "Patent Applied For." Then that information is substituted for the actual patent number once it has been obtained.

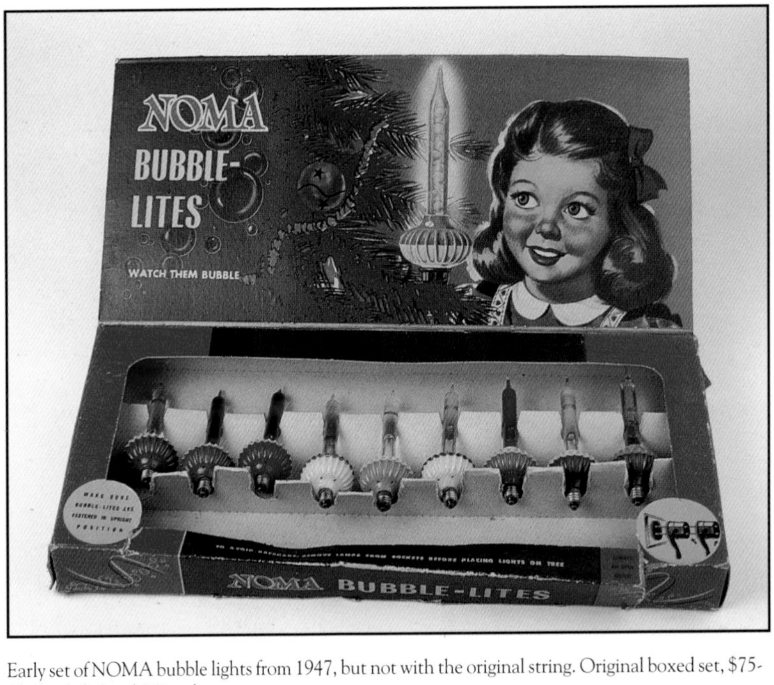

Early set of NOMA bubble lights from 1947, but not with the original string. Original boxed set, $75-80. Single lights, $5-7 each.

Original set of NOMA replacement bulbs from the late 1940s. Original boxed set, $110-130.

Four different boxed sets of bubble lights from the late 1940s. Original boxed set. $85-115 each.

Original boxed set of "Glolite" bubble lights. Boxed set, $95-105.

NOMA Electric of New York was the only company of the ten that Otis approached that was willing to take a gamble on this new idea, and gave Otis a royalty of three cents per lamp sold. Other companies were quick to pick up on the idea and soon marketed their own versions of the bubbler. The most notable of these companies was Raylite Electric of New York. John Petry, an assignor to Raylite, filed his patent on May 6, 1946, and was granted a patent on December 3, 1946. His patent claimed he had improved devices, liquids, and improved construction of the bubbling light. At first they were called Paramount "Kristal Snow Animated Candle Lights." They were "oil" filled, the liquid being made of two types: (1) an organic oil such as grape seed, castor, or cod liver oils, and (2) methylene chloride, chloroform, or ether. When mixed, they produced a slower flow of bubbles, much smaller in size, and in greater quantities, without the glass pellet in the tube. The name "Bubble Lite" was not used, specifically to avoid patent infringement on the Bubble Lite Trade Mark.

NOMA filed suit against the competition, but was offered a settlement out of court, giving Otis a similar royalty offer to the one he was getting from NOMA. However, Otis refused the offer, the case went on to court, and was lost. Otis lost all royalties and no doubt was upset more than once after that, because the bubble light soon came to be the hottest item on the market, lasting for a period of at least two decades. Thus, other companies opened the market for a huge burst of bubble lights. The year 1949 was important in NOMA history. NOMA reissued their famous "biscuit" style lights in the slightly modernized box (a little girl staring in wonderment at the bubbling light had changed her dress from a 1940s style blue outfit to a much more fashionable and attractive solid green dress). That year, one of their bubble light sets was brought into controversy after a Christmas tree fire, that involved a fatality, was directly connected to the bubble lights. After this, a fire-retardant chemical was used in their plastic and that fact was indicated from then on by means of identification on the box itself. However, this chemical causes premature breakdown of the plastic. Collectors will recognize this fact when they discover shrunken and severely distorted plastic bottoms, often with a whitish coating that many novice collectors attribute to spray snow or heat damage. Fortunately NOMA was cleared of their involvement in the Christmas fire fatality, and they ceased the use of this fire retardant chemical in their plastic bases.

The liquid in the bubble light tubes comes tinted in several colors, with purple being the most rare. Purple was only sold the first three years NOMA produced bubble lights. The earliest bulbs have glass slugs. After the Christmas of 1948, they were no longer used. In addition, NOMA changed the style of their bubble lights in 1948. They chose the saucer shape, but the design was very susceptible to heat damage, and was discontinued once all the stock was depleted in 1949. Beginning also in 1948, NOMA marketed a multiple wired bubble light outfit.

May & Scofield, a manufacturing company in Howell, Michigan, was responsible for the alligator-type clips which helped keep the bubble lights upright. In 1936, they had developed a clip to hold electric lights in place on Christmas trees. In 1945, recovering from war-time economic struggles, they began working with Noma Lites Corporation and produced over 100 million of these clips for NOMA, as many as May & Scofield could produce.

In all, approximately thirty plus different styles and brands of bubble lights were manufactured. The word "Lite" was used by NOMA: Glo-Lite (a "generic" brand of NOMA), Reliance, and Renown. "Light" was issued by Paramount: Sterling (a "generic" brand of Paramount), Holly, and Grant. In 1947, 25,000,000 Bubble Lites were made and sold. Due to their success, the retail price dropped from an original $4.95 to $2.40 a set. In 1948, 40,000,000 Bubble Lites were sold, according to S. L. Marshall, assistant to the executive vice president of Noma.

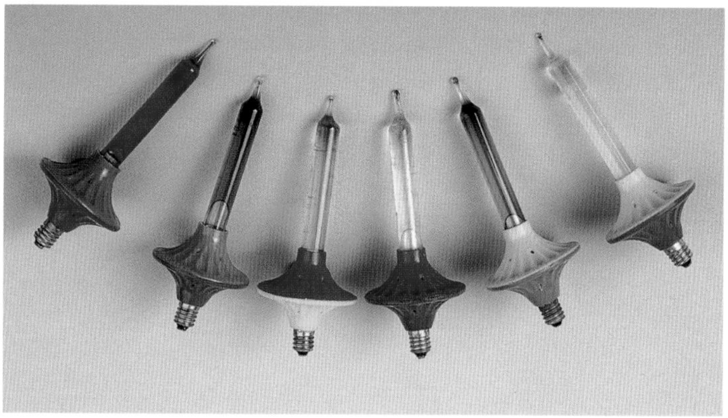

Assortment of NOMA saucer bubble lights from 1947-1948. $7-9 each.

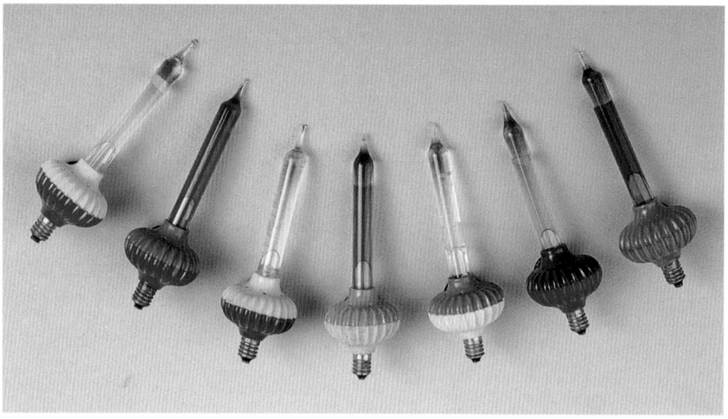

Assortment of NOMA biscuit bubble lights from 1946-1962. $5-7 each.

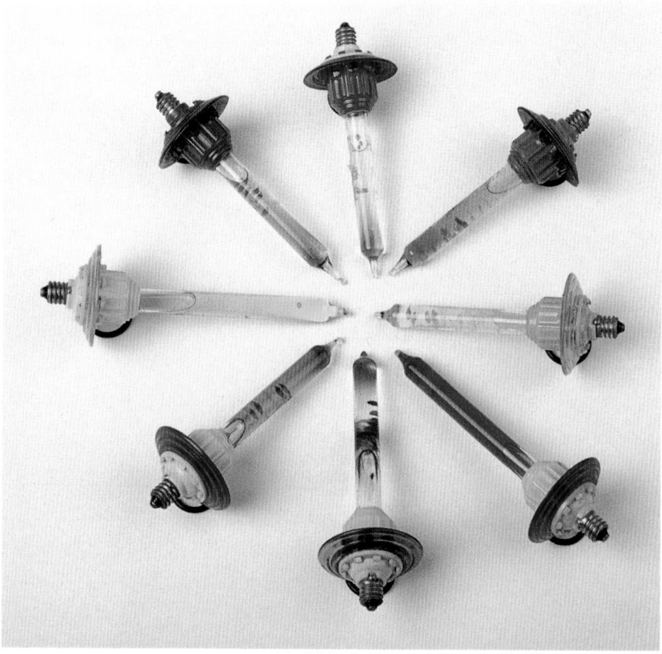

Assortment of Paramount oil bubble lights from 1947-1948. $75-90 each.

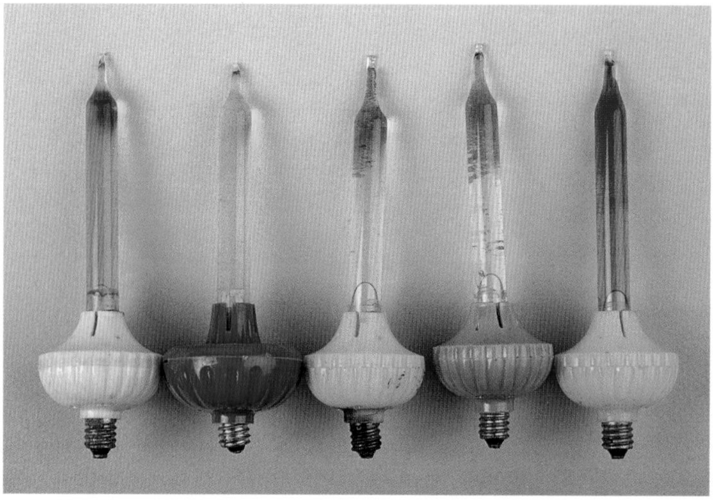

Assortment of Royal Biscuit bubble lights from 1947-1956. $8-10 each.

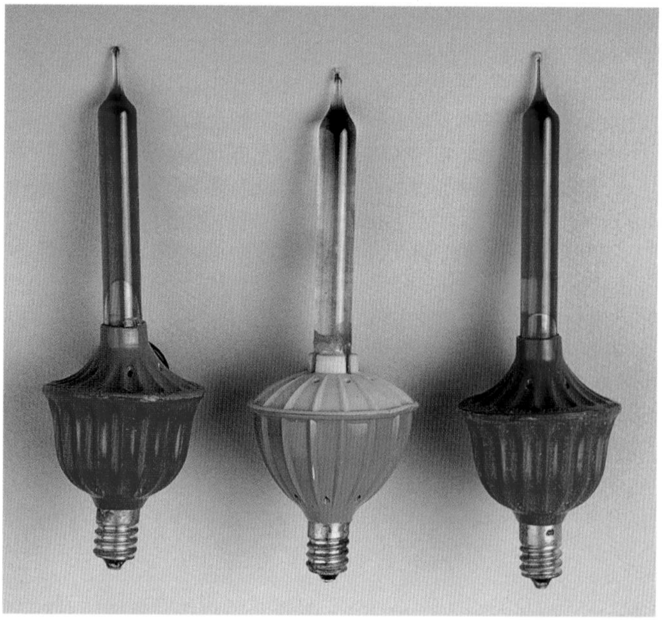

Assortment of Royal Crown bubble lights from 1948-1955. $35-45 each.

"Shooting Star" bubbling lights, produced in 1947 to 1948 by Peerless, are some of the most sought after today by collectors. The tubes contained two different liquids. The bubbles rose rapidly through a thin liquid, then fell slowly through the thicker liquid at the bottom. Many feel the effect is similar to that of fireworks. These rare lights can be identified by the two distinct liquids in the tube, similar in appearance to water and oil.

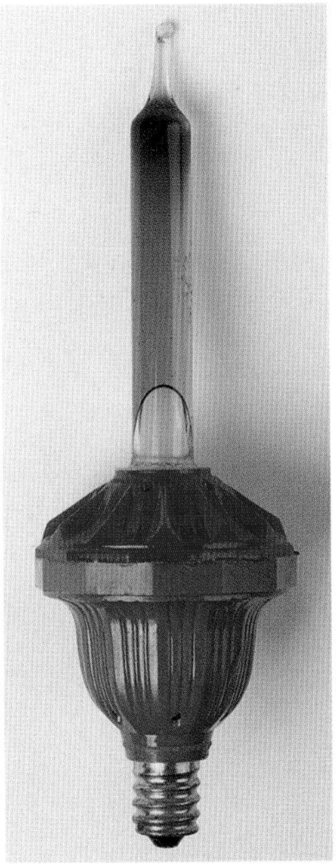

Peerless bubble light from 1949-1955. $15-20 each.

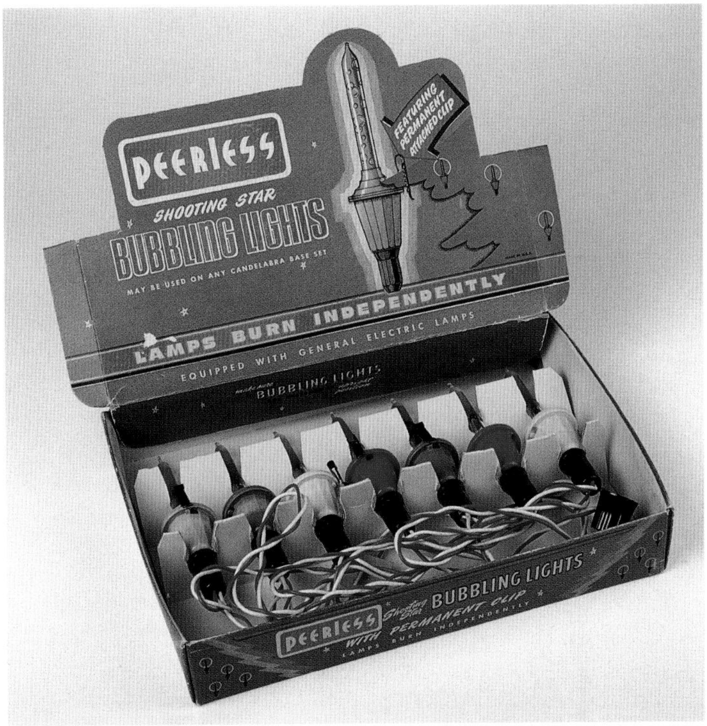

Box of original 1947 Peerless Shooting Star bubble lights in the original box. $350-400 for set. $75 for each bulb.

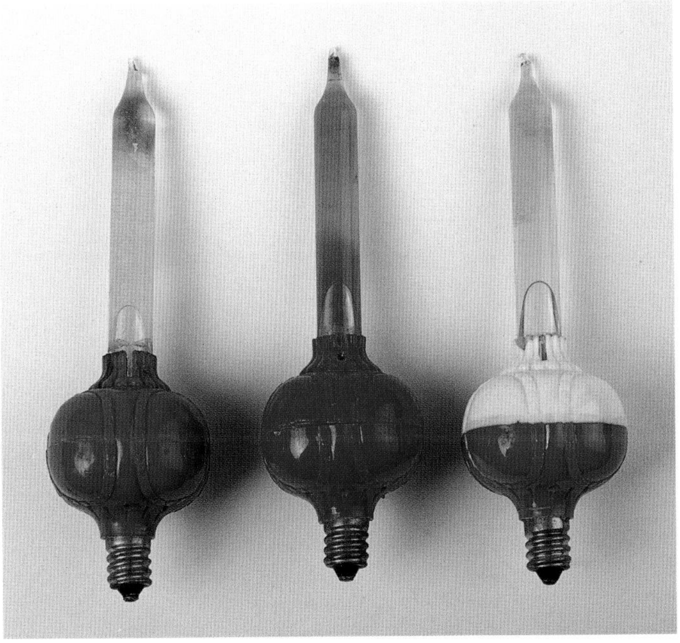

NOMA Tulips (1948-1960) on either side of a Paramount Tulip (1951-1972) in the middle. $15-20 each.

By 1946, a few Christmas lighting sets were appearing in the stores. These new sets followed the form of those sets created before the war, but all were improved in one important detail-the replacement of plastic or synthetic materials closely bonded to the wire in place of previously used rubber and fabric insulation. Thus, this insulation could not readily pull away from the end of the wire where it was attached to the socket, and so leave the conductor exposed for possible contact with tinsel, bare metal, or fingers. One further improvement was a deeper socket to allow the upper edge of the metal base shell to go fully within the socket.

Series-wired sets continued to be sold, but nine bulbs, or even ten, were an improvement over the previous eight-lamp sets. Recommended by Consumers' Research Bulletin in December 1946, were "Noma," "Gem," and "Good-lite." By the mid-1940s, Noma Electric Corporation was the best-known maker of Christmas tree lights. Headed by Henri Sadacca, Noma raised the amount of its assets from $2,639,000 at the end of 1943 to more than $21,000,000 by the end of 1946. Sadacca became vice president in 1927 when Noma was a seasonal business. Young Sadacca had begun the manufacturing of Christmas tree lights in 1911. Competition was keen over the years and forced the firms in this business to form the National Outfit Manufacturing Association (NOMA). Initially it was a trade association, but failing as a stabilizer, Noma finally bought out the other companies and went into production itself. In fact business was so fantastic that Noma was able to deliver only 20% of its orders for lights and ornaments in 1946. In this particular year, Noma produced close to ten million strings of lights. Bulbs were also imported from Japan and China, but were considered of poor quality and they had a short life for the price of 20 to 25 cents each.

Box of NOMA Snap-On bubble lights from 1949-1950. $20-30 each.

Fluorescent lamp sets were introduced in 1945; unlit, they appear to be plain white balls with a black-skirted base. But when lit, they come alive in soft glowing colors of yellow, green, blue, coral red, and orchid (purple); the colors being marked on the base. They are 120 volt, candelabra based sets. However, the bulb is of the size and shape known as "G-16," which means it is globular and two-inches in diameter. Sylvania, Royal, and Miller companies sold them in sets of seven bulbs; replacement bulbs were sold in boxes of ten. Another brand label was the "Polly Xmas Tree Set" in a long rectangular-shaped box. A set of seven "Royal Fluorescent" bulbs, boxed, sold for $6.85. Colors included blue, coral, green, and yellow.

These fluorescent lamp sets were designed for multiple (parallel) operation and could be used also in any cords with the multiple-burning type of incandescent lamps. Each lamp was a complete operating circuit, somewhat similar to the larger fluorescent lamp circuits employed for general lighting. The lamp consisted of a round bulb coated inside with a phosphor or fluorescing material, activated by an electric discharge within the bulb. The ballast was a resistor built into the base of the lamp. According to a 1945 *Sylvania Lighting News*, published by Sylvania Electric Products, Inc. Salem, Massachusetts, "The cathode design lends itself particularly well to other shapes—the limiting factor being the bulb opening through which the cathode structure must be passed in the process of manufacture. Lamps in the shapes of candles, Santa Claus, Christmas trees, crosses, and a host of others are entirely possible." These lamps did not contain mercury as intermediate fluorescent did, and the electrical discharge is of the glow type rather than an arc. They have no filament but work on the same principle as the long tube fluorescent bulbs in kitchen and office fixtures. The white coating is just plain white paint as in some ordinary household lamps.

The color exhibited is due to the color of the gaseous element inside the bulb. Each gas element known to science glows with a specific color when ionized. Argon created the blue and green bulbs; neon created the coral, yellow, and orchid bulbs. The inside of the bulb is coated with colored phosphors. The type of gas used inside was matched as closely as possible to the color of the phosphors in the white coating. (The green is bright because green phosphor is the brightest member if the chemical family and red phosphor is the dimmest. A standard 4-foot fluorescent tube in green is three to five times brighter than a red one of the same size.) The ions created by the glowing gas bombard the phosphor coating, causing it to fluoresce or glow. This is the definition of a fluorescent source. The hue can be varied somewhat by changing the pressure and/or varying the current e electrodes, and gases can be alloyed in various proportions to provide color combinations not available with single gases.

The prices of these fluorescent sets when new were very expensive compared to a regular set of tungsten lamps, even the individual lamps were around fifty cents to one dollar compared to ten cents or two for fifteen cents for milk glass tungsten bulbs. A string of eight lamps sold for about five dollars, considerably more expensive than incandescent lamps. But *Consumer Research Bulletin*, which ran studies on the bulbs, reminded consumers that they were more energy efficient, longer lasting (in excess of 300 hours), and added more soft light to the tree (2-inches in diameter). Sylvania rated their life expectancy at one thousand hours or more which, under average conditions of use, meant several holiday seasons. Good Housekeeping recommended fluorescent lights be tucked into branches on a mantle, or in a basket of greens on a console table. These soft, pastel-colored bulbs burned quite coolly, resulting in an added safety factor.

Set of early fluorescent lights. $120-130 for the boxed set. $8-12 for each individual bulb.

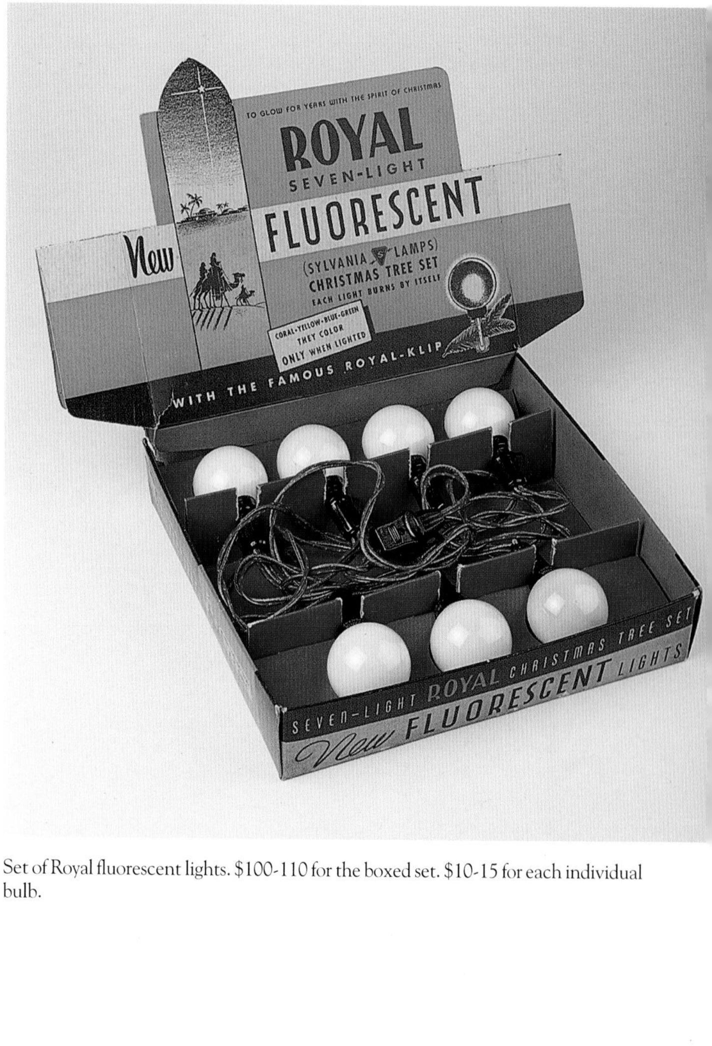

Set of Royal fluorescent lights. $100-110 for the boxed set. $10-15 for each individual bulb.

Plastic, used in the manufacturing of tree decorations, found its way into bubble lights, and most interestingly enough, into figural type lamps. NOMA produced a set of seven fancy figures which snapped over the light for the Christmas of 1949. The set consisted of a rabbit, snowman, canary, angel, Santa Claus, pup, and cat. Made of a Hercules flame-resistant acetate, they were designed for proper ventilation and were advertised as fairly cool to the touch after several hours of illumination. The famous NOMA altar, quite a large item, used to be made of plaster of Paris with glass candles. In 1949, it was made of Tenite I cellulose acetate, giving this decoration ten times the durability of its plaster and glass predecessor and; even though it was more expensive to produce, their customers purchased huge numbers of these altars.

Representative examples of NOMA flame-resistant acetate bulbs. $20-25 per individual bulb.

There were still shortages of lights in 1947 due to the shortage of copper and the continued armament control of supplies of this metal. Sets tested and recommended by *Consumers' Research Bulletin* in 1947 included "Miller," "Noma," "Amico," "Clemco," "Gem," "Glolite," "Good Montgomery Ward," "Park," "Paramount," "Reliance," "St. Nick," "Sterling," and "Tirnco." Not recommended was "Royal," due to poor insulation and shallow socket shells. Clip-on candleholders of ivory plastic with individual 3-foot cords that let you locate each light where desired were sold for $11.00 in 1948. Multiple-wired sets of candelabra bulbs with custom-fit sockets on a 12-foot cord also allowed flexibility when arranging lights on the tree. Noma halos were produced for tree lights or electric candles. Halos were hard, round plastic covers that fit over the socket and tightly around the bulb. The cut edge that circled the halo created an arc of light around each electric bulb when lit. Reflectors, although declining in popularity, continued to be sold; mirror prisms on red, silver, blue, and gold cardboard stars, on the other hand, were the rage of the year. Assorted star designs manufactured from Kristolite, using metal stronger than tinfoil and measuring about 2-1/2" in diameter, were sold in sets of 8 for 24 cents in 1942.

Mantles and mirrors being popular in the 1940s; therefore, it was dictated that designers seek methods for decorating and lighting these items in homes. In December 1941, *Woman's Home Companion* promoted the use of cardboard trees with holes cut out and covered with multicolored tissue paper, arranged with greens and glass spheres, on a mantle. Lit from behind, these trees quickly created a cheery appearing mantle. Another suggestion was to put electric candelabra on either end, with fresh boughs and glass spheres, enhanced by a Japanese string of foil bells spelling out "Merry Christmas." Mirrors came to life also. Angels cut out of construction paper and hand-colored with lights, positioned on a base, and subsequently scotch-taped to the surface were proposed. The mirror, then encircled by glittering tinsel garlands, would sparkle in the darkened glow of the evening. Chenille wreaths, with foil leaves and one or two heavy cardboard foil-covered candles and topped with a 110-volt mazda lamp, all selling for 49 cents and 78 cents respectively, were extremely popular. Also placed in windows were Electric Halo candles in groupings of three, seven, and eight. Ivory or red heavy fiber candles were mounted on ivory colored wood bases. Holly spray decorations completed the arrangement. Prices ranged from $1.19 to $4.49.

Placed on tables, most often close to windows, were life-like "Glolite" trees with Visca branches and a detachable metal cone placed over a plaster ivory-colored base into which a light bulb was inserted. The color came from tips of glass rods, shaped like tiny bulbs, which reflected the light from the bulb contained within. A 10-inch tree with 13 lights sold for $1.19 while a 15-inch tree with 17 lights sold for $5.69.

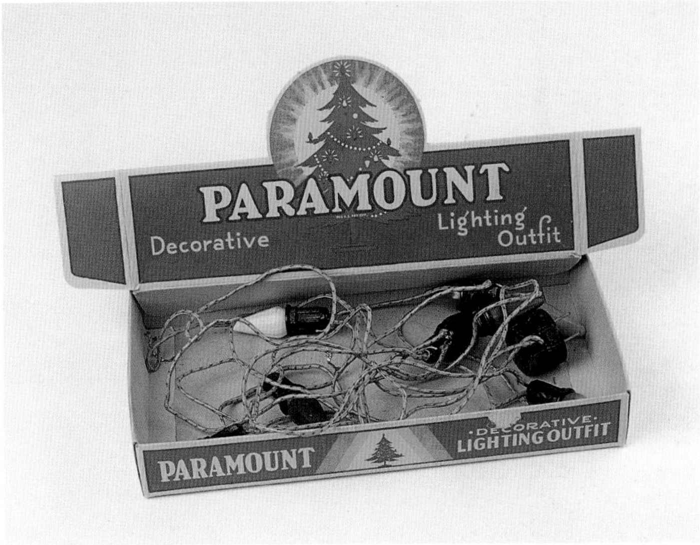

Boxed set of Paramount miniature lamps from the late 1940s. $30-35 for the boxed set.

Late 1940s set of miniature lamps illustrating pink colored bulb (at far left). $15-20 for boxed set. $.50-1.00 for each lamp.

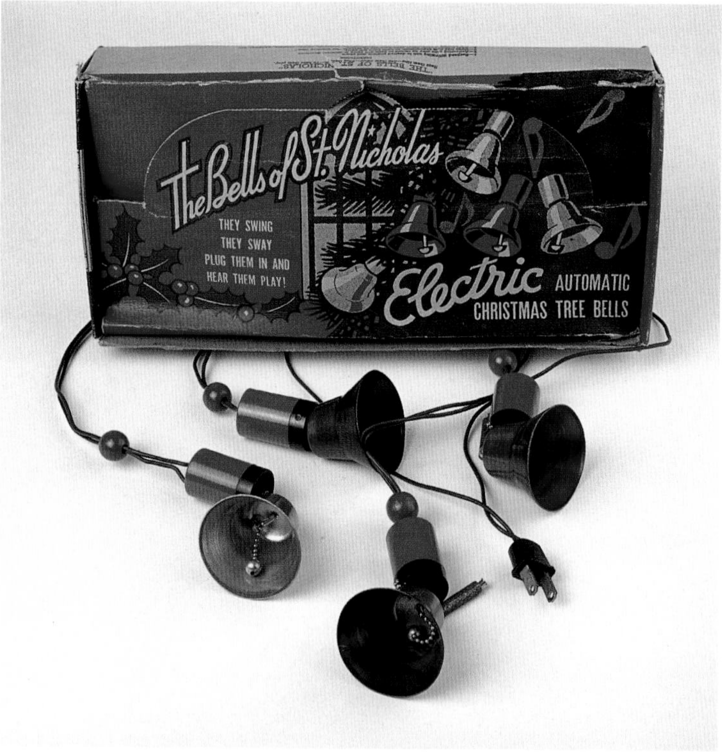

"Bells of St. Nicholas" electric set which rang the bells on the tree through an electrical current. From the late 1940s. $95-110 for boxed set.

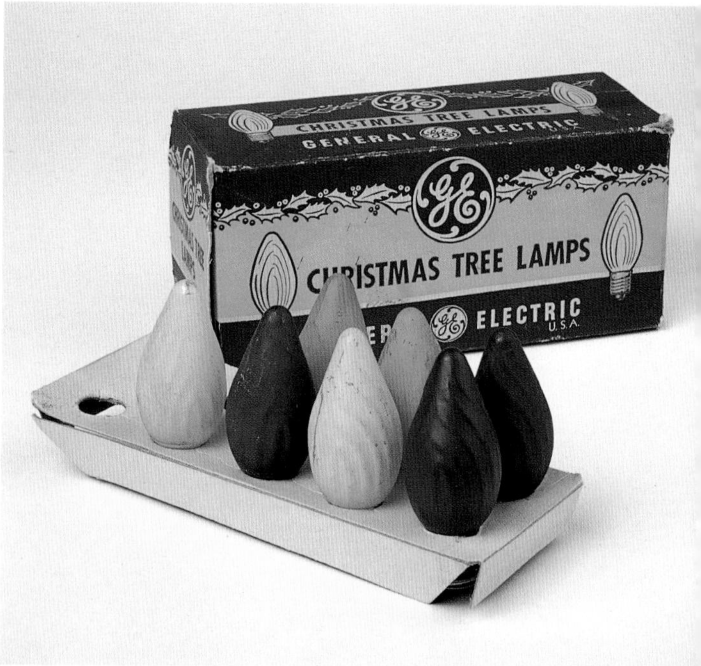

Replacement standard base lamps in original box. $20-25 for boxed set.

Display box of replacement miniature lamps. $30-35 for boxed set.

Replacement candelabra base lamps in original box $15-20 for boxed set.

Bubble Lights continued to be extremely popular in 1949, with a 7-bubble light indoor tree set selling for $4.29. Wired in a parallel string, each bulb burned independently. This meant that when one light burned out, the others stayed lighted. Assorted colored transparent glass candles 4-½-inches long with plastic bases that were screwed into bakelite sockets with metal clip-ons to hold the candles securely in an upright position on the tree. Such sets came in a 13-½-foot plastic covered wire cord. In addition to this set, Montgomery Ward advertised a 9-light set in a 12-½-foot cord for $3.29. However, this set was in a series. This meant that each bubble light was dependent upon the other lights. When one light went out, the entire set went out.

Plastic rosette lights made in Japan appeared with white inserts surrounded by clear colored points in red, green, blue, and yellow. They were intended for use with the regular cone-shaped bulbs to add a little variety to the tree. Sold by Montgomery Ward in 1949, a set of 10 sold for $1.59.

Miniature base plastic Star lights from Japan. Late 1940s into the early 1950s. $4-6 each.

Plastic rosette lights from Japan. Late 1940s into mid-1950s. $3-5 each.

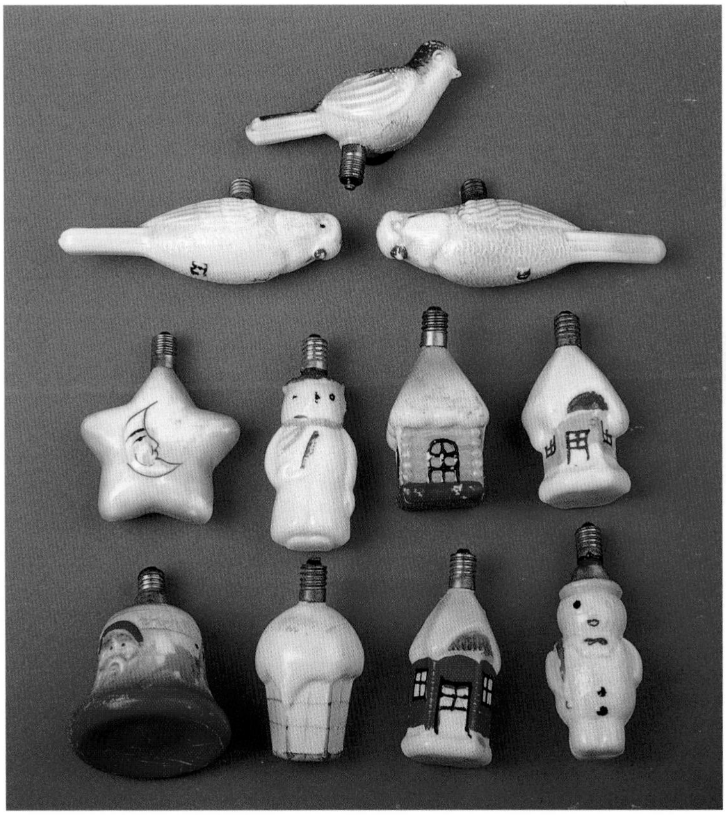

Miniature base milk glass Japanese blown lights. Made from the years immediately following war on into the early 1950s. $10-30 each.

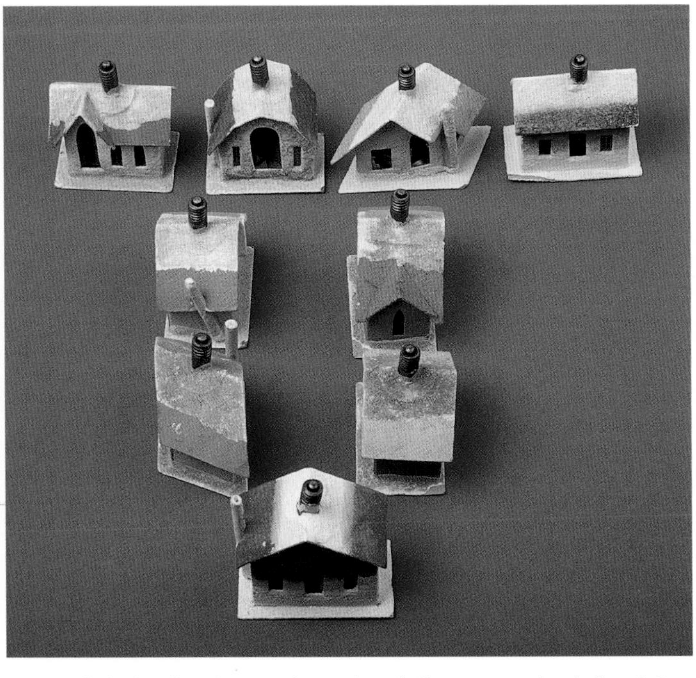

Snow-flocked cardboard Japanese houses electrified by a miniature base bulb each. Late 1940s. $8-10 each.

NOMA lights created from cellulose acetate in the late 1940s. $15-20 each.

An unusual outfit boxed set was marketed in 1948 for the first time. Sold by Sears Roebuck in their mail order catalog, it was called "Sleigh-O-Lites." The lights were stored in a creative cardboard sled which slid out of the box. The sleigh could double as an "unusual decoration for the tree" or a "beautiful and decorate centerpiece for your festive table, either with lamps turned on or filled with fruits and nuts . . . candies or gifts" according to the suggestions on the bottom of the sleigh. It was a typical candelabra base string with seven colored GE lamps. The string was of high quality, as the Snapit Company was primarily involved in the manufacturing of electrical devices. According to sources in the decorative lighting field, this was their one and only holiday item produced for the Christmas lighting business. Another similar interesting set was a set of "Usalite" bubble lights; but, this light set was inserted into a cardboard circus wagon which then fit into the cardboard sales box.

"Sleigh-O-Lights" in original box. $95-110 for boxed set.

Late 1940s Paramount electric wall hanging made from thin cellulose acetate. $50-60.

Plaster and wood table decoration lit by a candelabra based bulb. Swiss-manufactured wind-up music box is in back. Assembled in the U.S.A. Late 1940s. $65-75.

Musical centerpiece from the late 1940s with a music box in the back and a bubble light in lamp post in front of the carolers. $100-110.

Santa light-up from the late 1940s that was manufactured into the mid-1950s. $80-90 with box.

Outdoor Electric Lighting

As a result of the war, many different trends in electric lighting for our trees took root during this decade. Frugality was the key in the early 1940s, as Americans found little commercial lighting available due to the shortage of metal and other materials needed to produce lights. In addition to this, energy conservation was encouraged in an effort to prompt Americans to consider the war effort as far more important than Christmas lighting.

As previously mentioned, the Office of Civil Defense (OCD) discouraged the use of elaborate or potentially dangerous types of outdoor Christmas lighting. This Office highly discouraged the use of any extra outdoor lighting at all in coastal areas. However, it was stated that this was not done for fear of enemy attack, but rather to conserve precious materials and electric power and to reduce the risk of fire. If used on streets, lights had to be able to be turned out quickly. From the position of a war economy, James M. Landis, director, OCD, urged that no new equipment or wiring involving critical materials necessary to the war effort be purchased for Christmas decorations. He reassured the citizenry, however, by stating, "We do not intend that individuals or stores not decorate their window modestly as in previous years, so long as the lighting conforms to any dim-out regulations in their particular areas. It would, of course, be inappropriate for merchants' associations or individual businesses to buy new lighting. It would be better to use money to produce for the war effort."

Outdoor lighting was not eliminated in the early 1940s, but it sharply diminished as Americans turned out their lights, be it for energy conservation or as a symbolic gesture, indicating that this was a time when it seemed out of place to be outwardly festive. Outdoor displays using signs and other symbolic cutouts were suggested as alternatives to using huge numbers of electric lamps on trees and houses.

Outdoor dioramas, cut from composition board and arranged in three planes, with lighting being placed between the planes for optimum effect, were used. Cut out of plywood and subsequently painted, Santa and his reindeer parked on the roof made one of the most common outdoor scenes employed by Americans in the 1940s.

In 1941, *Woman's Home Companion* suggested a huge wreath of pine branches and cones tied with a red oilcloth bow to be placed around a large center window. At night two white floods in nearby shrubbery would bring this simple but dramatic display to life. Christmas floodlighting outdoors had been employed often before 1938. Boston recorded floodlighting its public buildings in color at the beginning of this decade. Therefore, an entire new trend of floodlighting the front door and entryways of both private and public buildings became extremely popular. Blues, reds, greens, and ambers were suggested to obtain various effects.

By the Christmas of 1943, Californians were once again able to celebrate Christmas with extensive outdoor lighting. Californians had been famous for lighting displays since 1769, when a friar at the first "Mission" in San Diego lighted a candle on a primitive altar in preparation for midnight mass.

After the war, plastic was incorporated in the use of exterior light bulbs, enclosing the bulbs in translucent plastic molded into the shape of candles, stars, balls, figures, and endless additional designs. However, during the Christmas season of 1948, some questions were raised about their safety. A number of complaints were received by fire officials to the effect that the ornaments smoked and melted. The plastic material generally used in illuminating ornaments at that time was either styrene or a standard formulation of cellulose acetate. Noma became very concerned. Even though it was definitely proven that no fire hazard was involved, steps were taken to remove the possibility of future trouble. In the early part of 1949, a committee was formed under the auspices of the Society of Plastics Industry, Inc. (S.P.I.), founded in 1937, to make further study of the entire illuminated ornament situation and they made several recommendations.

These recommendations had to do with such factors as close production control of the small 15-volt lamps used for illumination (to prevent overheating); modification of the shape and contour of ornaments; adding vent holes and slots in order to increase ventilation; using adhesives or cements compounded of more heat-resistant materials; making use of a special formula of self-extinguishing cellulose acetate developed and produced by Hercules Powder Co., Wilmington, Delaware; and using "thermosetting" materials such as urea and melamine wherever possible.

By the end of the decade, Noma produced between 7 to 10 million strings of colored lights each year to be hung on some of the more than 25 million trees sold. Americans used about 100 million light bulbs each year. Thus this decade, the decade of dramatic changes in both the electric lighting and decorating fashions of our trees, came to an end. Americans eagerly approached the 1950s, anticipating a new wave of popular, creative, and unusual materials and ornaments with which to decorate their homes. The war was over and we looked forward to a new age of prosperity.

Many different possibilities in molded plastic for exterior display were offered in the decade drawing to a close. Three-bell clusters with a candelabra ½" lamp inside each 5" red plastic bell came with streamers, and later, ribbon, to complete the very popular window and/or door decoration. Appearing in countless windows immediately after the war were the shining metal crosses. The lamp inside the 10" x 7" cross illuminated fourteen red plastic buttons on the white-enameled metal cross with blue painted corners that accented its three-dimensional effect.

Glowlite cross with the original box. $25-30.

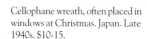

Cellophane wreath, often placed in windows at Christmas. Japan. Late 1940s. $10-15.

Chapter II. The 1950s—
The Industrial Age Molds Our Christmas Traditions

Historical Perspectives—Radical Changes Take Place

At the start of this decade, we once again were not at peace. The United Sates was involved in the hostilities between North Korea and South Korea. Harry Truman, in his annual Christmas message to the Nation, said, "At this Christmas time we should renew our faith in God. We celebrate the hour in which God came to man. It is fitting that we should turn to Him." He reminded the nation that "thousands of our boys are on the cold and dreary battlefields of Korea," and called for prayers for a peace based on righteousness. Once again, in 1951, at our National Christmas Tree Lighting ceremony, the crowd gathered to hear the President's plea for peace in times still plagued by the conflict in Korea. President Eisenhower set aglow the Oriental spruce tree, which had been used since 1941. This was the last year a living tree was used. Beginning in 1954, a cut tree from one of the states was presented each year to the President for use as the National Christmas Tree. Not historically significant at the time, 1951 marked the year Robert May left Montgomery Ward and Co. to spend his time promoting Rudolph the Red Nosed Reindeer, his creation in the previous decade. However, that was short-lived as he returned to Montgomery Ward in 1958. Our 1954 tree came from Michigan and was decorated with over 3,000 lights. That year the ceremony was enlarged an renamed the "Christmas Pageant of Peace." Along the "Pathway of Peace" a life-size nativity scene and eight reindeer from Alaska were added, together with a number of smaller lighted trees bearing names of the states and foreign countries which presented them.

One interesting note occurred at the end of the decade. In 1959, President Eisenhower lit a seventy-one foot tall, eighty-five year old white spruce from Maine. But this was the first year on record that a green dye mixture (1,200 gallons) was sprayed over the surrounding ground to give it a fresh look. It may also seem surprising that Nikita Khrushchev helped President Eisenhower celebrate Christmas by sending a quantity of Russian toys and dolls as Christmas presents for the President's grandchildren as well as Christmas tree ornaments and lights to use for decorating the President's tree.

U.S. shopping displays grew in tremendous spurts during the 1950s. Macy's spent $75,000 each Christmas creating a spectacular window. One of the most well known Macy's displays of the 1950s was a recreation of a 1850s White Christmas. Most stores like Macy's did their own work, but Chicago's Silvestri Art Manufacturing Company and Manhattan's Staples Smith, Inc. did work to smaller stores who did not have the creative talent or time to create displays to attract the attention of shoppers.

In 1951, Americans were beginning to experience the shortages of materials brought about by rearmament. The government shut down the vast flow of many consumer products from U.S. factories. The manufacture of metal-using products was curtailed drastically with shortages to come in toys and other goods requiring metal.

Store displays continued to be very lavish. Wood & Lothrop's in Washington combined Christmas with a storybook theme in their 1952 window. Lord & Taylor of New York City had Santa Claus garbed in red gumdrops and reindeer of brown sugar in a very modernistic setting. J. L. Hudson Co., in Detroit, took a more traditional approach and used a life-sized nativity as the focal point of their window display. The Rockefeller Center tree lighting ceremony was televised on *The Kate Smith Show*. The tree received even more national publicity when the *Lucky Strike Hit Parade* broadcast its Christmas show from the Rockefeller Center.

In this decade, the "Christmas Bonus" became a controversial issue. A firm reduced its Christmas bonus in 1951 and the union appealed to the National Labor Relations Board. The board ruled the bonus was not a gift at all, but a part of company compensation. The company was not free to reduce it or to discontinue it. In the executive branch, gifts of money and merchandise approached a national scandal, bordering on bribery. Therefore, the Internal Revenue Service placed a limit on gifts of $25 in value.

In the early 1950s, Mr. and Mrs. Santa Claus discovered Moose Landing, Alaska, and it was renamed the North Pole. Con Miller appeared on the scene in 1952, dressed up as Santa each year, and built "Santa Claus House." In this gift shop, countless Christmas ornaments and decorations appeared. Of great value are those cards and envelopes stamped with this early North Pole label.

In 1952, Macy's reported giving away over 120,000 lollipops, selling over six million greeting cards, and selling over 1.5 million toys. Twelve Santa Clauses, working in shifts, talked to over 10,000 children a day. Macy's spent over $75,000 dollars on their window display, illustrating a white Christmas of 1850.

Economically, Christmas 1955 was one of the best ever, with holiday sales up by eight percent over the previous year. American spent more than six billion dollars on Christmas.

In the 1950s, Christmas Crackers continued to be popular with many English families who had immigrated to the United States. However, crackers were a bit more difficult to locate; World War II had taken its toll on factories that had produced these crackers. After World War II, Caleys, a major producer of crackers, (also bombed during the war) merged with Smiths. *College Crackers* was started in 1950 in Camden Town on Royal College Street. Their traditional crackers were typical of the 1950s decorative themes.

"White Christmas," the Christmas song of the 1950s actually had its beginnings in the previous decade. While filming *Holiday Inn*, Bing Crosby received the sheet music for a new song a few weeks before filming this new movie. The song, of course, was "White Christmas," destined to become a Christmas classic.

In 1956, *Life Magazine* profiled John Matison, who had batted around the world as a seaman and various other uncertain jobs for most of his sixty-four years, until he came to the point of no return—no job and no home. But, in New York, he found a home and a job with the Volunteers of America—that practical, understanding organization that existed to help the not so prosperous. For four glorious weeks ever year, from ten to six every day, Matison was Santa Claus, making children happy in homes and schools, but he came to offices as well. When he came to offices, he asked for donations to make youngsters happy with presents and to buy dinner for them and their families.

Christmas in the 1950s with bubble lights, candy canes, and metal icicles on the tree. $40-50.

Christmas 1959 with a traditional tree illustrating wrapped packages, brush trees, and European glass beads produced before World War II. $25-30.

Christmas 1954 with an artificial tree, so popular in the early part of this decade. $40-45.

Christmas 1953 with a tiny tree, chemistry set, and a Fort Apache toy set. $40-50.

Two girls looking up the chimney for Santa with stocking hung, ready to be filled. Early 1950s. $20-25.

Christmas 1959. The television set becomes part of the setting as kids excitedly open presents. $25-30.

Christmas 1958. Small flocked tree decorated with American ornaments in a single, solid color. $15-20.

L. J. Calkins and son posing for Christmas 1955 in Ft. Forth, Texas. $40-50.

Little boy posing with his newly received "Lone Ranger Outfit." $40-50.

Heavily flocked tree in the 1950s. Note the TV and the clear glass American ornaments on the tree. $30-35.

Christmas 1954 with a pedal tractor and baby buggy that must have delighted this boy and girl. Very simply decorated tree. $30-35.

This photo of a 1956 Christmas illustrates a beautifully decorated period tree with a Paramount plastic tree top, tinsel roping, and lead tinsel. $20-25.

That is a new Sears bike and a teddy bear proudly displayed during the Brenner's Christmas in 1959: Left to right, back: Dan, Bob, Marilyn. Front, left to right: Virginia and Carol. $Priceless.

Van Pelt Store Christmas Party, 1950. Note the bubble lights and wonderful Santa suit. $25-30.

Early 1950s Christmas. Very lavishly decorated tree with candelabra-base lights. $30-35.

Christmas in the country. A wonderful example of a rural, electrically decorated tree with a large plastic star at the top. $10-15.

Dick Wilder with his Christmas tree in La Crosse, Wisconsin, in 1952. Note the use of popcorn chains. $15-20.

Christmas 1956 in La Crosse, Wisconsin. Note the wrapped presents under the tree and the plastic "Glow in the Dark" icicles. $15-20.

A postcard from 1952 showing Taunton, Massachusetts, decked out with a lavishly decorated town square. $25-30.

Christmas 1955. This picture was not taken until February in Merrill's house, however, where he kept his tree up until Easter, lit with miniature-base candle lights. $20-25.

Generation photo from Christmas 1952.$20-25

Gas station and garage in Peoria, Illinois, decorated for Christmas in the mid-1950s. $40-45.

Cards, Wrapping Paper, and Paper

Whereas the traditional card continued its popularity, companies such as Designers & Illustrators, Fravessi-Lamont, and Irene Dash all manufactured cards that were sophisticated and untraditional in a sleek manner. Religious themed-cards reproducing the work of 15th, 16th, and 17th century Italian painters in smaller sizes were also quite popular. Those who wished to send larger sized cards, in good color on high-quality paper, favored "Gallery Artists" including Grandma Moses, Winston Churchill, and Norman Rockwell.

Some of the cards of this decade poked fun at trying to live in a world filled with nuclear armaments. The Korean Conflict was reflected in cards with a proliferation of doves and the word "Peace" appearing on many of our cards.

Whitman's in Racine, Wisconsin, produced many of the inexpensive Christmas cards. Myron O. Lawson headed the greeting card division until his retirement in 1956. Lawson was considered to be one of the top greeting card executives in the country and he had built the Whitman line to a volume of 120,000,000 cards per year.

Lawson's experience in design, color, and plate making in Western's Photo Engraving Department helped him immensely to put Whitman in one of the top positions as a greeting card manufacturer. By 1956, Lawson had become one of the top greeting card executives in the country, and he had built the Whitman line to a volume of over 120 million cards a year. All of their cards were designed by freelance artists who submitted sketches to the Greeting Card Division for approval. Verses for their cards were selected in the same manner. Once designed, cards were printed by the offset lithographic process on huge printing presses which reproduced full-color illustrations in one step while moving through the presses.

Lawson's experience in design, color, and plate making in Western's Photo Engraving Department helped him immensely to put Whitman in one of the top positions as a greeting card manufacturer. By 1956, Lawson had become one of the top greeting card executives in the country, and he had built the Whitman line to a volume of over 120 million cards a year. Whitman commenced producing valentines in the early 1950s. Again, these cards were designed and given verse by freelance artists who submitted their material to the Greeting Card Division for approval. Whitman's line was specifically intended for the low-end market. Most of the cards were sold by the box in "Five and Dime" stores such as Kresge's and Woolworth's

Carl Gildemeister was the foreman in charge of greeting card production during the years after World War II. He remembers Myron Lawson going out once a year on buying trips and coming back with orders for millions of cards. The orders kept his department busy all year long. "In the summer," Carl recounted, "I'd have to hire a couple of hundred high school and college kids to do finish work by hand on our Christmas cards."

While most of Whitman's cards were marketed in syndicated "five and dime" stores, Whitman also produced colorfully boxed Christmas cards in assortments of 25 or 50 cards and envelopes. A few Christmas cards were created individually for corporate sponsors. One such card, produced for the General Drafting Company, won an award for its graphic design in 1954, and another created for the Outboard Marine Corporation, won a similar award in 1957. A number of religious cards were drafted for the Catechetical Guild—a Minnesota firm which published books for Catholic churches and schools and which was eventually purchased by Western and became one of its many subsidiaries. In 1957, ten paintings by Sister Monica—who was then head of the Art Department at Dominican College in Racine—were produced on Christmas cards to be sold by the guild.

One popular, but expensive, card was the card with a real etching reproduced on it. Such cards were stamped from copper plates on which the artist had spread a coating of "etching ground." On this surface, he scratched his drawing. Following that, the plate was immersed in an acid which ate into the copper only where the lines of the drawing were. The sketched plate was then steel faced to stand up under continuous printing. If color was applied, it was done by hand. Thus these cards were quite expensive.

But the most common method used was offset printing in four colors: black, yellow, blue, and red. Frequently, other colors were added to produce special effects. First, the original sketch by the artist was photographed "down" to the proper size required for the card through a fine screen, and filters were used to separate the different colors. The subsequent negatives were retouched by a lithographic artist and then printed on a thin sheet of aluminum or zinc, which was then treated with chemicals. Once inked up, it was ready for the proofer. Each separate color had to go through the process.

After the proofer received these sheets of metal, he proofed the yellow first, following with each subsequent color used. The designs selected for the form, together with verses and titles, were photo-composed on a sheet of glass as large as the sheet of paper to be used. After every detail was lined up, the sheets of glass, one of each color, were placed in vacuum frames and everything was transferred to zinc or aluminum by a photographic process. Once the sheets were deep etched, the plates were ready for the printing process.

After the yellow "plate" was transferred and prepared, it was clamped around a cylinder on a large fast-running press. These offset presses consisted of three cylinder rollers. One contained the "plate," the second contained the rubber blanket, and the third contained the impression cylinder, which contained the grippers for carrying the sheets of paper. When form rollers charged with ink rolled over the plate, the printing process commenced. After passing through the press, these sheets were deposited in large piles on trucks so they could easily be rolled from one end of the press to the other for each color. After all the colors were completed and perfectly dry, the sheets were sent to the cutting department. Large cutters then cut them into single cards, ready for the finishers. Once separated, the cards were stacked for inspection. Next came the folding, for which complicated folding machines were created. If there were any attachments such as ribbon, sachets, satin, or other additions, the cards went to a separate processing department. Once inspected for the last time, the cards were ready to be boxed and sent to wholesalers.

Inflation eventually killed the Whitman line. Gildemeister recounted the fact that a Hallmark card printed in four colors could be sold for a quarter in a fancy gift shop, but Whitman cards of the same quality had to be priced at a nickel or a dime at variety stores where they were most often found. The profit margin dwindled and Whitman greeting card production was discontinued in the early 1960s.

Assortment of more unusual greeting cards from the early 1950s. $2-3 each.

Assortment of more common greeting cards from the mid-1950s. $2-3 each.

Assortment of more common cards and boxes. $4-6 for set.

Assortment of mechanical and novelty greeting cards from the mid to late 1950s in the original boxes. $15-20 complete set. $2-3 each.

1950s advertising greeting cards with metal money clips, book markers, and other advertising give-a-ways. $6-7 each.

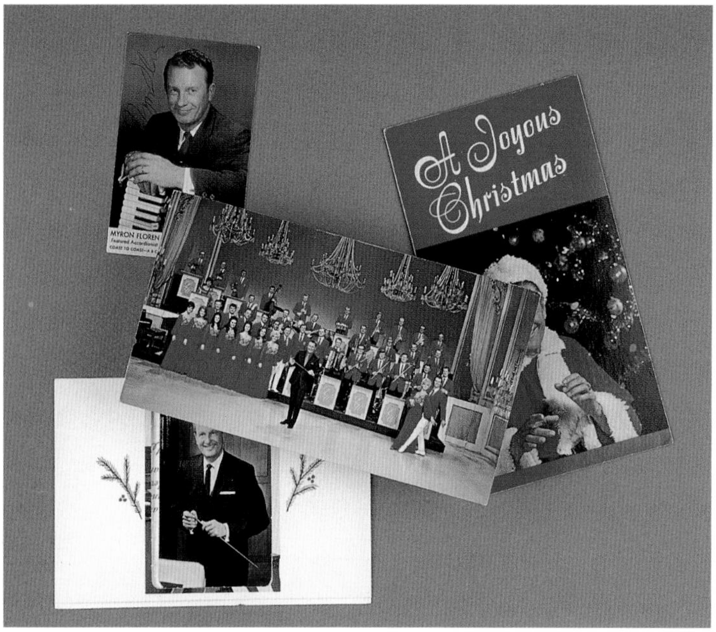

Array of Lawrence Welk 1950s Christmas cards. $5-7 each.

Original wrapping paper with gift cards. $15-20 for complete set.

Stickers and seals for wrapping presents. $2-3 for original set.

Assorted gift wrap and seals from the late 1950s. $3-4 per sheet.

Rarer wrapping paper in rich designs. $3-4 per sheet.

Gift boxes from department stores of the early to mid-1950s. $15-20 per box.

Gift boxes from department stores. Used in place of wrapping presents individually. $10-15 per box.

Advertising calendars from West Germany. Air-brushed and completed with a calendar booklet at the bottom, they made inexpensive premiums for customers at Christmas. $45-55 complete with calendar.

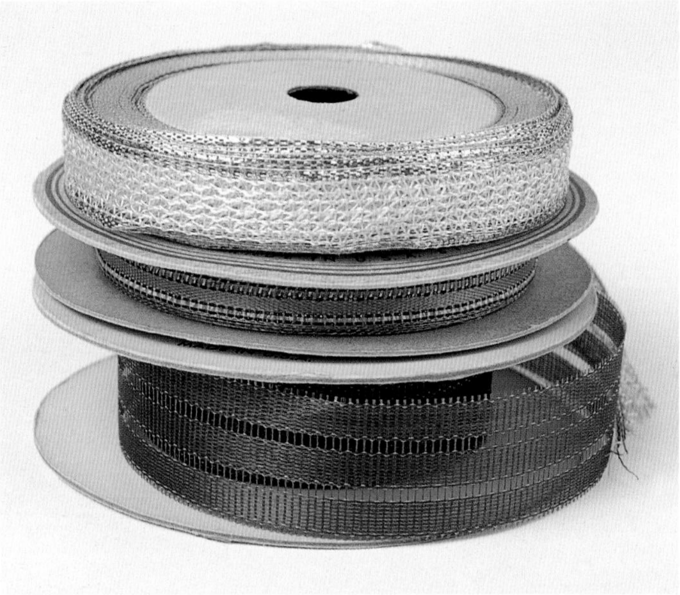

Ribbon in elaborate patterns. $2-3 per roll.

"Kiss L Toe" store display selling mistletoe at Christmas. $160-170.

Assortment of Augsburg Christmas Annuals from this decade. Richly embellished with illustrations and history, these make interesting historical reading. $5-10 each.

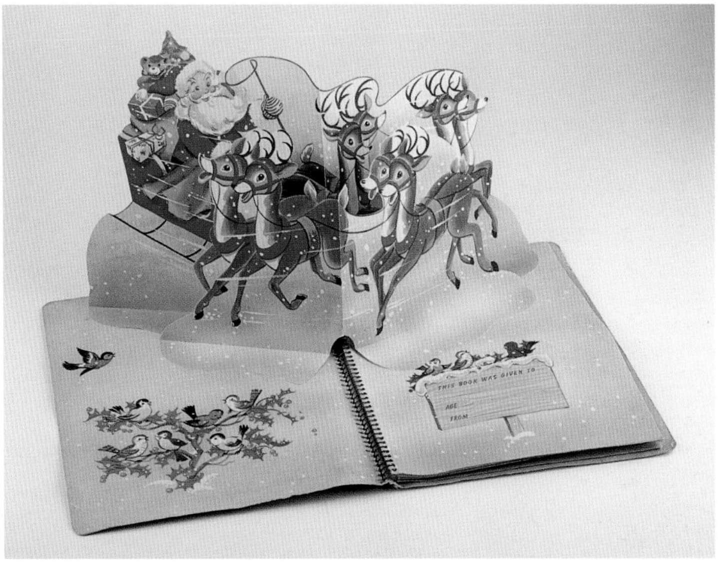

Santa Visits Mother Goose pop-up story book from 1956. Opened to just one of the richly decorated pop-ups in the book. $75-85.

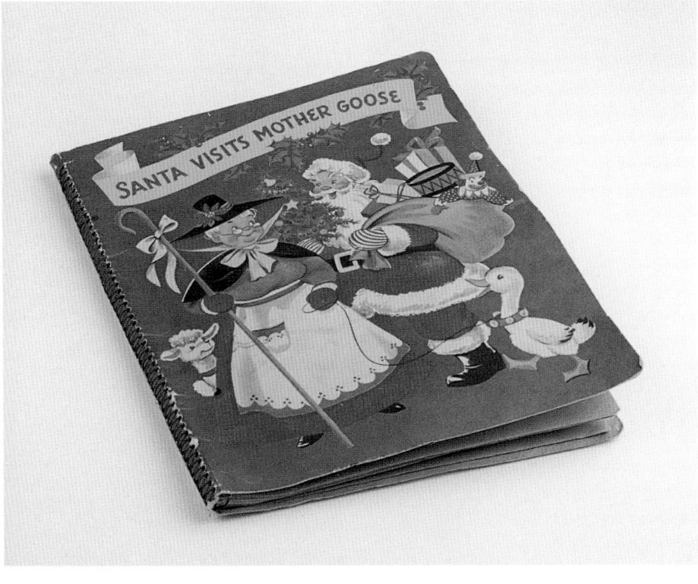

Santa Visits Mother Goose pop-up story book from 1956. Unopened. $75-85.

Trio of large children's story books from this decade. Whitman Publishing of Racine, Wisconsin. $25-30 each.

Trio of large children's story books, all of which have been flocked for added attraction to little children at Christmas. $40-50 each.

Mechanical, pop-up, and heavily decorated children's books. $60-70 each.

Children's comic books. $25-30 each.

Children's coloring books. $25-30 each.

Jigsaw puzzles from the mid-1950s. Printed in Ohio on thick cardboard stock. $35-40 each.

Large 36" display Santa used most often in schools and stores. $85-95.

Smaller sized 14" Santa figures. USA. $25-35 each.

Rudolph tin board. Once part of a game. $20-25 incomplete, as is.

Rudolph fiber beverage tray. $45-55.

Rudolph cake mold on left, $25-30 and Jello mold on right, $15-20.

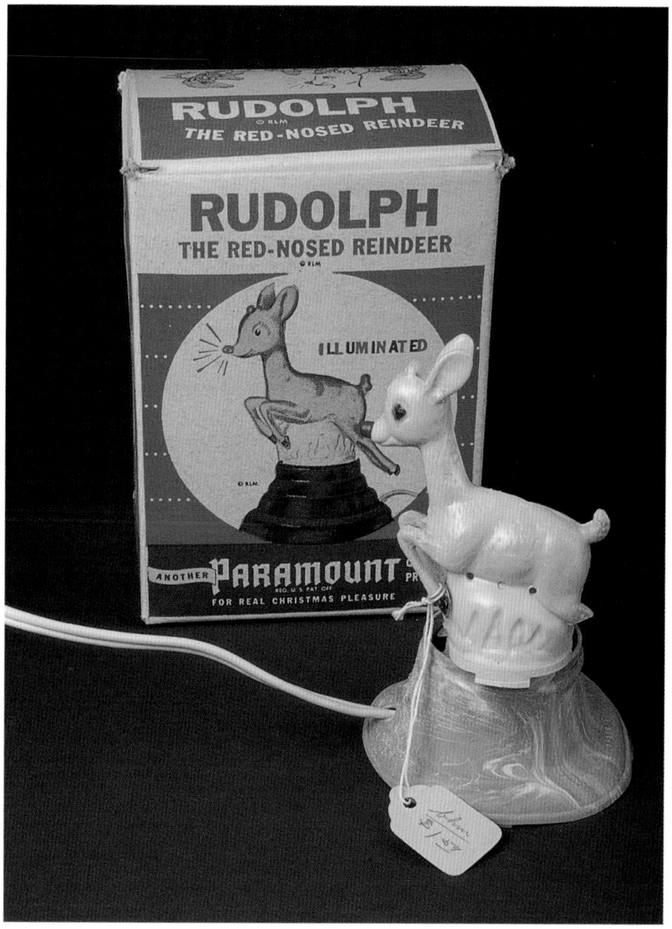

Rudolph night light for childrens' bedrooms. $75-85.

Large heavily flocked Santa figure and tree. Whitman Publishing Co. of Racine, Wisconsin. $35-40 for set.

Our Trees

Live trees once again continued to be popular, as Americans sought to decorate trees like those before the war. America's live tree of choice was the spruce with its short, sharp needles, and downward-hanging cones. Second was the fir, which has softer needles, usually curved, and cones that stand straight up. Pine trees and red cedar trees were also favorites, but never reached their peak of popularity in this decade.

Thirty-one million live trees were sold in 1954. Balsam came from the Maritime Provinces of Canada and from Maine; black spruce came from Wisconsin and Minnesota; Douglas fir came from British Columbia, Washington, Oregon, Idaho, and Montana; and Scotch and other long-needled pines came from orchard farms in several Eastern and Midwestern states and from near Toronto. Scotch pines gained favor with Americans in the late 1950s; red spruce remained the favorite of the Pennsylvanian Dutch, who would have no other tree other than the traditional short-needled variety.

Thus, giants in the Christmas field like Fred Musser of Indiana, Pennsylvania, continued to enjoy the financial benefits of providing live trees for Americans. In the mid-1950s, Musser had over 8,500 acres of trees, cutting approximately 200,000 trees a year. Red pine was his top seller in both the Christmas tree market and the nursery.

Paul Kirk of Tacoma, Washington, was called the "Christmas Tree King" by *Better Homes and Gardens* in 1954. He distributed 4 to 5 million trees a year. It all started in 1918 when an El Paso, Texas, florist could not obtain any trees for sale. He mentioned this to a friend, who suggested the florist contact W. R. Kirk (Paul's father), his brother-in-law. Paul Kirk had a little company up in Washington State that cut poles and posts and did a little logging. The loggers cut only the skinny seedlings, stacked almost 5,000 small firs in a railroad car and sent them to El Paso. The next year the florist wanted two railroad cars full of trees and the business was born. Over 20,000 acres was devoted to the growing of trees in the mid-50s. In December 1957, *Sunset* listed Mr. and Mrs. Howard Nielsen of Santa Cruz, California, and Mr. and Mrs. Drew Michaels of Salem, Oregon, as being pioneers in western Christmas tree farming.

Another giant was Roy Halvorson of Duluth, Minnesota, who started peddling Christmas trees from door to door when he was twelve years old. He discovered early that falling needles meant no sales. North of Duluth there were forests of scraggly spruce trees; the tops, thought Halvorson, would make miniature Christmas trees for use on dinner tables and in small apartments, if he could find a way to preserve them. So Halvorson started experimenting with a chemical which would keep trees fresh for about a week. Gradually Halvorson improved his chemicals so they would color the needles green, silver, or white and keep trees alive-looking for one to three months. He perfected a secret formula using water and plant foods which, when sealed in a metallic tree base, acted as an artificial sap. These flocked trees were among the first to be promoted in the United States.

Fire-resistant tips included a solution containing a gallon of warm water, a cup of boric acid powder, and 1-1/2 cups borax as a mixture for the Christmas tree stand. Some even suggested spraying the boughs with this same solution with a vacuum-cleaner sprayer or spray gun. By the mid-1950s there was keen competition in the live Christmas tree market to the point where a surplus of some 35,000 trees occurred in St. Louis for the Christmas of 1955.

The 1950s especially found America going through a new period of experimentation, while still attempting to get "back-to-nature." This was reflected in their decorations. One of the interesting innovations was the use of aerosol-dispensed "snow" in 1951. "Make It Snow" was produced under the guidance of Noma Electric Corporation. Boyle-Midway, one of the biggest companies in the household chemical field, was having its product, put up by Bridgeport filler Connecticut Chemical Research Corp. Other companies turning out "aerosnow" were Fluid Chemical (Newark, New Jersey), Continental Filling (Danville, Illinois), Frank Paper Products (Detroit, Michigan), Water Repellents, Inc. (Indianapolis), and Minute Spray (Chicago). The cans came out in 6-oz. and 12-oz. sizes, priced competitively at 98 cents (by 1954, the price had dropped to 84 cents) and $1.95 respectively. Three million dollar in sales of aerosnow was the recorded for Christmas 1951. Sales continued to grow as Americans sought to bring a little outdoor atmosphere to their green trees. It was highly recommended that the decorator spray the tree, let it dry, and then added the ornaments. However, many added snow as an afterthought when the tree was completely decorated. Thus, many glass ornaments, lights, and other decorations still bear the visible evidence of "snow happy" Americans in the 1950s.

If you didn't want to purchase snow, you made your own. A box of ordinary household detergent or powdered soap and a mixer turned out the fluffiest snowfall this side of the North Pole. Recipes were simple. "Just pour a cupful of packaged soap or detergent into a mixing bowl, add a little water, and beat to the consistency of a super-stiff meringue," was the suggestion of *Design* magazine in November 1957. If you wanted a soft color, you needed to add a few drops of food coloring to the mixture just before beating. Then it was suggested that decorators dip a wooden spoon into the mixture and lightly pat it along the boughs. For special effects, glitter was sprinkled onto the branches while they were moist. Once dried overnight, the tree was ready for decorating. But, once again, many Americans added this snow at the end, after decorating, and much of this soap landed on both the lights and glass ornaments.

Feather trees left over from before the Second World War were once again sold, especially in small 18-inch sizes convenient for mailing to soldiers and sailors in Korea. Made of real goose feathers in Germany and set in a white wooden base, they came with 24 miniature glass ornaments from Japan. Other feather trees were sold, often with the "Made in Germany" label sanded off so as not to offend anyone who still was sensitive toward this country after the war.

Visca (straw-like rayon) trees continued to be popular in smaller sizes for those who had only a small space for a tree. Most Visca trees were placed on coffee tables or in corners on end tables. Sizes ranged from 36 to 84-inches and were placed in plaster-type bases. The branches folded flat against the trunk for easy storage. Green and white colors were available. Since flocked trees were somewhat in vogue, Visca trees flocked in pink and blue were produced. While consumers resisted the larger size floor to ceiling type trees (often considered "unsightly" or "homely"), many people in apartments purchased the smaller trees. Most of the interest was shown in Visca trees which came already wired with glass rods (electric light bulb inside) or wired with sockets for bubble lights.

In 1951, Sal Puleo began hand-making artificial trees in the back room of a florist shop in Elizabeth, New Jersey. As a result of these trees' immediate popularity, operations were soon moved to three one-car garages. Flocked trees in pastel colors were the items originally produced by the Puleos. Macy's and Bamberger's department stores were two of their customers in their first year. The business expanded to such an extent that they became incorporated as Puleo's Novelty Co. in 1956 and moved into a 7,000 square foot facility, and expanded once again to a 50,000 square foot facility. Expanding their product line as well as their facility, they began producing soft needle trees and the first natural and most realistic looking Scotch Pine trees. Their largest customer for these was Sears Roebuck and Company.

By 1959, American manufacturers began producing a more realistic outdoor-looking Visca tree, the "Forester." It was six feet tall, five feet across at the base, and contained over 300 thick, fluffy branches. Actually, consisting of fifteen graduated-size trees, these branches fit quickly into a pre-drilled trunk for very fast assembly. Selling for about $26.95 from Aldens, Sears, and Spiegel, it was a vast improvement when displayed along with the traditional Visca tree, whose branches folded against the trunk for storage. One other interesting development was the production of a dark green vinyl tree in a seven-foot size containing about 120 branches.

Eight-foot Visca tree in a round wooden pot. Late 1950s. $45-55.

Six-foot Visca tree in a square base. Early 1950s. $35-45.

Spun glass "Angel Hair" used to put on tree branches as well as under the trees on cotton batting sheets. $5-10 for box.

Artificial snow used to sprinkle on branches of tree after they had been flocked with soap flakes. $5-7 for canister.

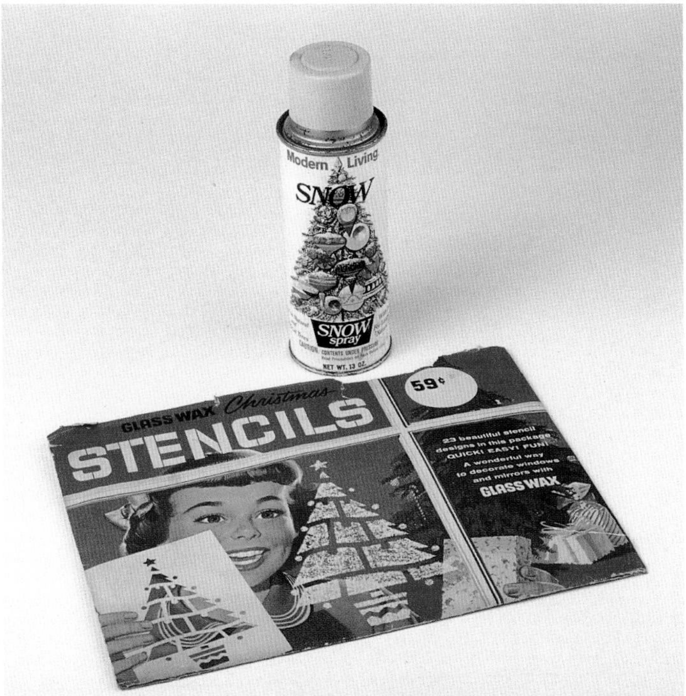

Spray aerosol snow can and stencils from the late 1950s. Snow was used this way on windows and mirrors as well as sprayed onto trees for a winter effect. $3-5 for a can of snow. $2-3 for a complete set of stencils.

Assortment of tree hook boxes illustrating styles used during this decade. $1-3 for boxed set.

But by the middle of the decade, the tree was to change forever, or at least that is what many Americans thought, as the "aluminum" tree was created as the ultimate in artificial trees. Aluminum trees traced their origins to silver aluminum foil ornaments which were used after World War II. *Better Homes and Gardens* in 1956 illustrated and gave directions for a variety of foil decorations made from aluminum pie plates and foil. The glitter and fascination for these ornaments on a tree caused some decorators to wonder what a whole tree created of aluminum would be like. An advertisement in a Garrison Wagner catalog in 1950 listed base metal "evergleam" trees in turned aluminum bases in all silver, ice blue/silver, green/silver, fuchsia/silver, or chartreuse/silver. Trees were one to four feet in height and sold for $6.50 to $25.00 respectively. Other aluminum foil decorations included puffed foil on a heavy wire form six-feet in height, aluminum foil shaped belts, and aluminum roping. Making an appearance as early as 1950, aluminum trees were quite the revolutionary idea. These early experimental trees were more intended for display in department stores and various businesses.

Thus Reynold's aluminum was used for a stainless-aluminum tree made by Aluminum Specialty Company of Manitowoc, Wisconsin. The tree came in a compact carton, with each branch in its own separate sleeve. Available in sizes ranging from two to eight feet and colors, in addition to natural silver, including pink, green, and gold. Larger trees came in two sections which fit into a stand. For assembly, individual branches were taken from cardboard sleeves and fitted in pre-drilled holes in the trunk. A seven-foot tree containing about 200 branches sold for around $60. Although the use of low-voltage lights was possible, floodlights were recommended because of the danger of a short-circuit in the metal tree caused defective wiring.

Although quite the rage, aluminum trees were shunned by many who thought it sacrilegious to have a tree so contrary to what once was tradition. In fact, Irene Dunne, one of our more famous actresses of the period stated, "We in the movie industry take a very dim view of silvered or gilded Christmas trees. Our family trees are almost always natural green. As a matter of fact, I have seen only natural greens for sale so far this year [1954]. Possibly we resist silvering our trees because it suggests to us makeup, and therefore work, and we feel strongly about not taking our work home for Christmas." Nevertheless, aluminum trees were sold by the thousands by the end of the decade. A seven-foot version with 100 branches sold for $16.99 and was available from Montgomery Ward in 1959.

In 1959, a trade catalog from Star Band Company, Inc. of Portsmouth, Virginia, advertised aluminum trees. Their trees were advertised as having "branches fully assembled with unbreakable aluminum rods, ready to insert into a tree trunk drilled with holes scientifically spaced to form a symmetrical arrangement of branches, secured in a light weight Genafoam tree together with trunk and tree base." They suggested to their dealers that they display the tree against a black background, using a floodlight to bring maximum luster. Star Band further suggested that an unusual effect could be obtained by winding miniature imported lights around tree trunk before assembling branches, trimming the tree with solid color ornaments in assorted sizes, and then using a small fan to give the branches motion.

Beginning to be illustrated in the 1950s were flocked trees like those from decades past. In a time when much experimentation was being done, some decorators seemed to be clinging to tradition by decorating these flocked trees with "fruits" made of ribbon-wrapped plastic-foam balls and old light bulbs. Those available by mail order and most gift shops were of the small apartment and table size variety. A three-foot tree with down-swept branches made of white plastic and planted in a wooden stand sold for about $10 in most stores.

For those who used real trees and didn't want the expense of a commercially flocked tree, which was beginning to be somewhat in vogue, there was "Sensational Sno-Flok." The Sno-Flok spray gun fit with all attachment-type vacuum cleaners. It was advertised as "Won't fall off-lasts 30 days or more-fire retardant-prevents needle dropping." Trees could be made "Snowy White," "Frosty Pink," or "Silver Blue." The outfit, which sold for $4.49 and was made in conjunction with General Mills, contained a special spray gun, plastic jar, one pound bag of Sno-Flok crystals, color tablets, and, of course, instructions.

"Silver Spruce" plastic trees, manufactured by Warren, were sold in six-foot heights, in shades of pink, white, or green. Visca trees wound around rustproof wire branches in green and white continued to be sold, but virtually disappeared from the market in the late 1950s.

White pine tree strayed with aluminum paint to give it that 1950s look without purchasing an artificial tree in Racine, Wisconsin. Left to right: Paul Klinkhammer, Susan Klinkhammer, and Kathleen Gehrig.

Four-foot aluminum tree with original box. $95-105.

Early revolving color-wheel floodlight. $80-90.

How We Decorated Our Homes

During the 1950s, it was possible to decorate modestly with home-fashioned ornaments, traditionally with old world-type Christmas decorations, the American-way with modern American-made glass ornaments, or quite stylishly with plastic ornaments. Bells, snowmen, and canes of foamed plastic were manufactured from kits available for 75 cents in 1954. They were created at home by using molding material which was hardened in an oven and decorated with aluminum foil and mica chips.

During the shortage of materials, much scrap was used for Christmas decorations. Many novel ideas were further promoted by a group of individuals who felt Americans should continue to "recycle materials." Pressed paper cones that held thread for the power machines were painted with bright colored tempera, dried, and then decorated with painted designs and subsequently shellacked. The paper from egg crates was cut in various shapes, especially crosses, which were then hung in windows at school and at home. They even found their way onto the decorated tree.

The larger circles from apple crates were shaped into angel and doll faces. Angel wings, choirboy collars, Santa Claus beards, crepe paper hair, and other things were glued to these faces.

A large number of household decorations were wholesaled during the 1950s to specialty shops and florists by Garrison-Wagner Company of St. Louis, Missouri. Three-dimensional decorations, lithographed in full color on non-flammable rigid Vinylite sheets, made their appearance for the Christmas of 1950. Produced by Stanley Wessel & Co., New York, these appeared in a series of four Santa Claus jolly faces. Each Santa face was wreathed in a smile and the same Santa was found in a Christmas wreath on a die-cut star background as well. An angel on a star background and a reindeer ornament and door decoration were also produced. Each piece was molded in deeply drawn, three-dimensional form and became even more striking when backed by an electric light on a Christmas tree, or over a mantel, or on a door. Non-warping, scratch resistant, and light in weight, they easily attached to a tree or wall.

Helen Cole, Inc. of New York suggested some very beautiful decorating schemes for the Christmas of 1952, including one for a protected, inside door. Luminous bows, tinsel, tarlatan, pleated paper fans, and cornucopias full of winking stars on gilded wires was one suggestion. Cardboard cut into the shape of a Santa Claus mask, musical instrument, or Christmas stocking, then painted and trimmed in a creative way was another period suggestion. Instead of candles in windows (far too dangerous), it was suggested that electric lights be placed in outside window boxes in gold, red, or white colors. One other very popular house decoration of the mid- to late-1950s was a Christmas mobile. Made from coat hangers or wire, it was hung with either purchased glass ornaments or home crafted ones cut in shapes of birds or other familiar Christmas symbols. Influenced by our newfound affection for Scandinavian furnishings, it seemed only natural to copy their love of Christmas mobiles in our country.

As previously mentioned, many designers promoted the idea of using luminous bows, tinsel, tartalan, pleated paper fans, and cornucopias full of winking stars on gilded wires, all combined together in a very novel door arrangement. Aluminum foil was incorporated into many of these decorations. Foil trees, bells, and even wreaths sparkled in windows and on doors. Directions were provided for creating these ornaments at home or they could be purchased commercially.

Traditional European-style ornaments were promoted by illustrating novel ways to use them to their full effect. One idea was to take silver candlesticks, wrap them in silver tinsel, hang tiny glass balls from the bobeche (the glass collar on the candle socket), and insert an elaborate, German-blown tree top into the candle hole. Clip-on birds were used in topiary arrangements for tables and corners of living rooms. Even fresh fruit was combined with glass fruit (primarily apples, pears, and oranges) in bowls for a most intriguing centerpiece. Glass beaded garlands were intertwined into chandeliers above dining room tables to match the old-fashioned table arrangement. Plastic prisms, almost as elegant as the cut-crystal ones, appeared on the market and were combined with glass ornaments and other plastic figurines.

White Visca trees in one to three foot sizes were placed on end tables and decorated with felt and sequin fruits finished with green fabric leaves. Placed on a circle of bright red or green felt, this made a stunning arrangement.

Candles were still used in windows, but many turned to the new electrified types for convenience and safety. Thousands of orange-flamed lamps inserted into plastic candles appeared in windows across America.

In an effort to create an American Christmas, some interesting sleek centerpieces and decorating schemes were advanced. Golden orbits created by mobiles cut from gilt paper were incorporated with simple glass spheres and suspended from chandeliers over tables. Satellites of Styrofoam balls encircled with foil were hung in garlands and strings from ceilings. Pendulum-shaped gold cornucopias finished the scheme. Snowy white stars, snow comets and star rockets, all cut from paper and cardboard, embellished with honeycomb tissue, were suspended above fireplaces and in corners of living rooms for an almost futuristic, modernistic approach to Christmas decorating.

One of the most prolific decorations of this decade was the papier-mâché Santa head, which was ideal for business decoration. This head averaged about 16" x 12". Also very popular was the artificial snow in shades of white and pink available in aerosol, pine-scented cans. These cans of artificial snow were coupled with stencils to create a wide variety of designs on the tree, windows, or mirrors.

Commencing in the late 1940s, plaster was also a popular medium for creating Christmas figures. Snowmen, angels, and trios of carolers were often combined with wire trees, star-shaped frames, and ovals. Standing Santa figures and Santa's complete with sleigh and reindeer were also molded from plaster. These figures were quite heavy and sometimes lightened with the use of vermiculite with the plaster. These figures were all American-made. Produced in the U.S. Zone of Germany, however, were miniature plaster angels about 2-¾-inches high. Delicately molded with gold foil wings, they came with cords for hanging on trees if desired.

In the early 1950s, papier-mâché was still quite popular. Santas, angels, and snowmen were manufactured in that egg carton-type of material. While most home decorations did not exceed 12-inches in height, many larger items, such as 38-inch tall angels and choirboys, were created for store displays. While papier-mâché items fell somewhat out of favor, primarily due to the expense of manufacturing such items; American ingenuity came to the rescue with Styrofoam items in abundance. Also on the market in 1959 was Genafoam, a new tough, resilient, water-proof plastic which could be molded into intricate shapes for use inside and outside on the ground, on wires to trees, on the roof, and wherever else home owners wanted a touch of Christmas. Genofoam was sold in various sizes of blocks, balls, stars, wreaths, and bells. Genofoam was easy to cut with a bread knife, coping saw, or even a razor blade. Its uses were varied in centerpieces, as Christmas ornaments, and other Christmas displays.

Also prevalent were illuminated figurines for mantles, tables, or for use as a child's night light. A Hi-Ho Santa riding a reindeer, a shining angel, and a lighted musical church (which played "Silent Night"), a Frosty-the-Snowman, and an animated musical sleigh with light were the favorites.

Who could resist the musical Santa dolls of this decade? Made with a happy face of washable, all-vinyl, the body was made of crush-resistant rayon plush in a colorful red and white. Cuddly and soft, these dolls were stuffed with "feather foam." The most desirable had a removable music box in a zip pouch which played various Christmas tunes. In assorted sizes, they were advertised in retail catalogs, wholesale catalogs, and in various store displays. Also they were given as premiums by many gas stations. With a complete tank of gas, they became a popular give-away during the months of November and December.

A similar model included a plush dressed Santa on a cardboard base, which played "Jingle Bells" as Santa turned.

In the late 1950s, ceramic products from Japan became the craze of the day as thousands of Americans purchased angel bells, sleighs, Santa figures, and even snowmen in countless sizes and forms. Their popularity lay in the inexpensiveness of such products as well as the colorful detail and paint.

Lefton China provided countless such ceramic Christmas decorations as well as utilitarian dishes for holiday entertaining. Plates, cups, saucers, creamers, sugar bowls, and platters abounded in dark green and white, all with the distinguishing green holly leaves and red holly berries. Candy-striped edges finished one of the earlier lines. Candle holders, candy dishes, and relish trays finished out the line of products which enticed many a gift buyer in this decade and in the one to come.

During the1950s, Holt-Howard started designing Santa Claus coffee mugs and pitchers. The Holt-Howard Company was started in 1949 by John and Robert Howard, and their friend Grant Holt. They were students at Amherst College, in Amherst, Massachusetts, and started the company with a nine thousand dollar loan from their families. During their early years, they primarily made Christmas items, but since they realized they could not survive alone on holiday items, they branched out into kitchen items as well.

Interestingly enough, these mugs were so popular that they started creating coffee mugs for everyday use. As a result, Holt-Howard is generally credited with pioneering the coffee mug as we know it today. Their designs were always magical, spending a great deal of time capturing that perfect facial expression on Santa's face. Holt-Howard marketed many serviceable, holiday collectibles, including an amazing array of cookie jars, planters, candy dishes, ashtrays, serving trays, salt and pepper shakers, and an infinite variety of candleholders. Holt-Howard ink-stamped, signed, and copyright-dated most all of its early 1950s Christmas items. A few pieces were not signed and some only had a tin foil sticker. "Holt-Howard," "HH," and occasionally "Japan" was part of the signing since all of the items were made abroad. In the late 1950s, the red and gold foil label was most often used, replaced by a silver and gold label during the early 1960s.

Ceramic Letter Vases and Candleholders. Made in Japan. Napco Ceramics. Distributed by National Potteries of Cleveland, Ohio, in 1956. $60-70 for a boxed set.

Set of four Santa face mugs. Late 1950s. Japan. $35 for set. $4-5 for each individual mug.

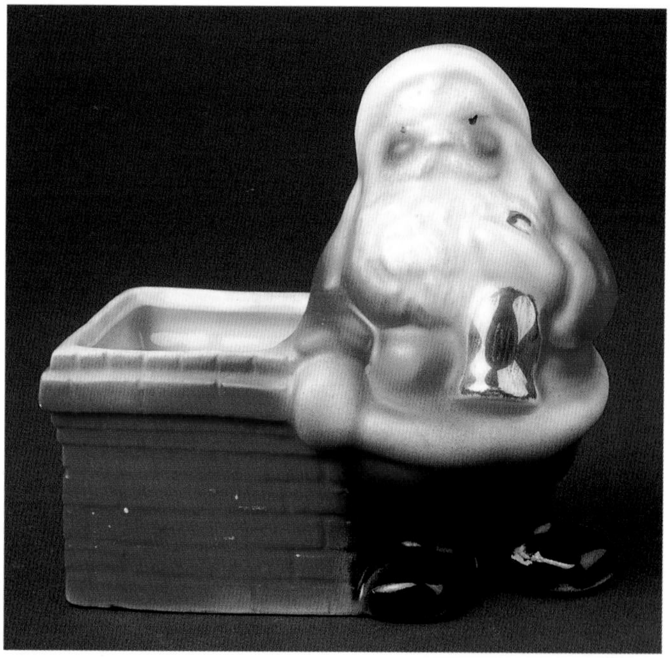
Santa planter. Marked "Japan" in black ink. Late 1950s. $15-20.

Left: Santa planter. Marked with "A988 Relpo." Made in Japan and distributed by Relpo Ceramics of Chicago, Illinois. $35-40. Right: Santa planter. Paper label "INARCO Japan" and numbered with black ink "E-762." Mid-1950s. $35-40.

Table decoration. Napco Ceramic. Black ink mark "4JX4090." Early to late 1950s. $85-95.

Santa planter on green skis. Marked in black ink, "Japan." $25-30.

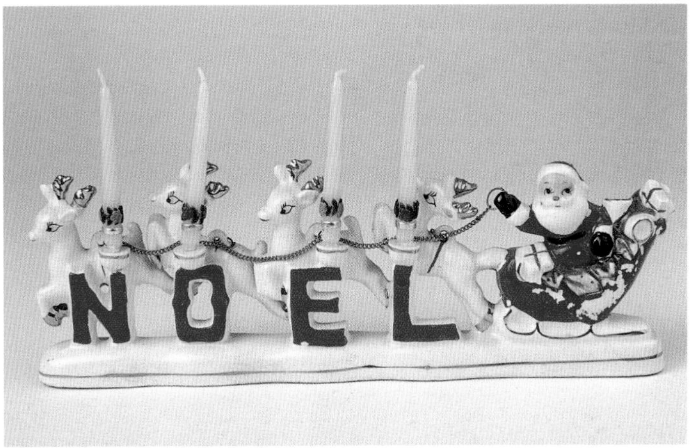

Table decoration. Marked in red ink, "Japan." Mid to late 1950s. $55-65.

Salt and pepper shakers. Marked in black ink "Geo Z. Lefton." $20-25 for set.

Assortment of heavily flocked pieces from various manufacturers. All typical of mid to late 1950s. $10-40 each.

Salt and pepper shakers. Marked with paper label, "Napco." $12-18.

"INARCO" Japanese-manufactured. Left to right: Elf with present, 15-18. Angel with present, $20-25. Angel with squeeze box, $12-15.

Salt and pepper shakers. "Napco." 1959. $10-15.

Santa candleholders for dining room tables or mantles. Mid to late 1950s. Marked "Japan" in black ink on bottom. $60-70.

Santa candleholders. Marked with paper label, "Napco." $30-35 for pair.

How We Decorated Our Trees

Helen Winslow in *Horn Book* of December 1952 writes of her "Christmas Cookie Tree." Cookies continued to be as popular as tree decorations as they were before World War II, but new history was made as the cookie shapes changed. Her patterns included Ping, Raggedy Ann and Andy, Dr. Dolittle, Pinocchio, and others. Even Little Black Sambo, the Little Engine that Could, Mary Poppins, Heidi, Thumper, and Alice in Wonderland all appeared on her Christmas tree as cookies. Thus, another decade of history in Christmas ornaments was to be recorded with popular personalities of the day appearing as decorations.

One of the more revolutionary suggestions was to decorate with ornaments that reacted to black lights and to produce black-light tree bulbs to make them glow. Many home decorators used luminous fluorescent treated fabrics, fluorescent paint, and a kit for black-light Christmas ornaments made by Magic Corporation, and black light fixtures manufactured by "Stroblite."

Color was a strong factor in creating a new look for the tree. Helen Cole of *Good Housekeeping* suggested that a gold tree be created by gilding laurel leaves on a wire frame. Pink and red paper carnations were to be its only trim. Another novel idea was to spray a pine tree dark blue, trim it with tiny clip-on glass birds from West Germany, add pompons of pink, and finish with silver tinsel. Another novel idea of hers was to create a mobile-type tree out of coat hangers and hang only German figural glass ornaments from its wire branches.

Another popular trend of the 1950s was to create star rays, snow comets, and star rockets cut out of paper and cardboard. All of these designs blended well with the simple-cut furniture and decorating schemes of newer homes built in this decade. Celestial spirals, golden orbits cut from foil, star towers constructed from wire, satellites, and stylistic stars were further suggestions for some radically unique decorations unlike those of decades past. All of these were often combined with simple five to seven-inch glass ornaments of one color blown by American companies.

Ethnic trees were promoted as a means to give identity to certain nationalities which needed a sense of roots when it came to the family time of Christmas. Decorations from Lithuania were perhaps the most unusual in that straw from the fields was strung with needle and thread to form intricate geometric designs, bell towers, birdcages, and a host of religious symbols. The "straw" bird cages are ideal for housing fragile eggshell birds so loved by the people of Poland who used empty eggshells as the basis for all kinds of ornaments, including animals and birds. Scandinavians expressed an intense personal patriotism by trimming their trees with paper chains made in the national colors and by draping long garlands of miniature flags on the tree.

French descendants used large white snowballs of cotton or foam plastic, silver paper cornucopias with hard candies, and an abundance of tinsel as their only tree decorations. The German tree was decorated with candles, Christmas cookies, apples, oranges, and popcorn balls. Many British families decorated their trees exclusively with Christmas cards on colored cord or hung individually from ribbons. Even the Japanese were not to be left out. Americanized to the point of having a tree, they still decorated with an Oriental motif with tangerines, kimono-clad dolls, fragile glass-blown ornaments, and little rice wafers known as "sembei" containing fortune-telling slips.

European Influences on Our Glass Ornaments

Glass ornaments became available once again after World War II, but their popularity was not immediately established for several reasons. Countless Americans refused to purchase items manufactured by a former enemy, while numerous others just simply wanted a charge. They were starting new with new families in newer style homes and these European creations simply did not fit the climate of the time. However, by the end of the 1950s, we were once again paying some serious attention to glass figurals imported from Europe. These glass treasures were severed inside and wrapped with crinkly wire as faithful copies of those made before the war

Germany Continues to Create Ornaments

While many Americans scoffed at the idea of using European glass ornaments in the period after World War II, Germany continued to produce ornaments somewhat like those created by their predecessors. However, their popularity was slow to catch in the United States in a time in which we were creating our own American identity, not wishing to be reminded of our European pasts. Thuringian glassblowers who crossed over the border to make their home in the West created these glass ornaments. Some of the most well known craftsmen included Walter Haehnlein, Paul Heinz, Arno Sauer, Max Langhammer, Adolph Koehler, Heinz Muller-Pulver, Erwin Eichhorn,Senior, last but not least, Waiter Schuenzel.

In 1957, sixteen East German glass blowers founded the first cooperative of Christmas decorations, the PGH (Produktionsgenossenschaft Handwerk) "Heinrich Rau" in Steinheid. In 1959, the VEB (Volkseigener Betrieb), the state owned company was formed in Lauscha. The sales department of Thuringian Christmas Tree Decorations was the leading promoter of the Christmas decoration industries. Involved in the formation of VEB were Gerd Ross, Greiner & Co, Hermann Lins, Carl Boehm-Casper, and Carl Meusel. There was a concentrated effort to produce ornaments as had been done before the war. However, these first years were difficult since there was little demand for their ornaments. Some of this was due to the lack of American interest in East German-produced ornaments and some of that lack of interest was due to the poor quality of these first ornaments. With a brownish tint to their paints, a lack of quality detail in the painting, and poor molded detailing to begin with from over-used molds, the East German ornaments often created little interest in the market.

After the Second World War, the glass blowers' cooperative of the Meiningen highlands that had existed since 1907 unchanged continued its business. A new department for producing "Feenhaar" *("fairy hair")* was equipped in the building 75 Bahnhofstrasse *(Station Road)* in Ernstthal that had been built in 1921 and had been the headquarters of the cooperative's management and the production place for cartons to supply members since 1924.

On November 21st, 1959 in the House of Culture of the VEB Glaswerk *(glass works)*, Ernstthal, the PGH Christbaumschmuck *(Christmas tree decorations)* was founded. This way the formation of socialist production conditions in the tree decorations production line was completed. To this cooperative belonged glass blowers from Lauscha, Ernstthal, and Spechtsbrunn that had been members of the glass blowers' cooperative and their employees.

As a first measure taken toward using modern production methods and in stepping up the productivity of the work, the company inserted converted ampoule automatic machines to produce the "little pieces" (spears) and, therefore, the production of "fairy hair" was shut down because another factory was manufacturing this product and it seemed to be duplication of sorts to the East German government. At the same time, preparations were being made to start using flask blowing machines and to establish a central processing department. A one-story building was put up at the factory area as a storehouse for tubes and a garage. The production program of the cooperative included a normal range of Christmas decoration articles. Some glass blowers traditionally produced special articles like miniature decorations, garland pearls, cans, vases, trumpets, and horns. These articles had to be taken out of the line when the employees who had produced them reached retirement age.

Spun glass continued to be a viable part of the ornament industry in Eastern Germany. One of the businesses primarily involved in this manufacturing had existed at 11 Kirchstraße *(Church Street)*, Steinach, for many years and was known as Greiner & Co. Besides being a distributor for Christmas decorations, they also started to produce leather dolls. Around the turn of the twentieth century, 45 persons were employed in the company.

In 1920, the production had changed to the mechanical production of Feenhaar *('fairy hair')*. At that time, the use of glass sticks of different compounds guaranteed the curling of the spun glass after taking it off the spinning wheel. In 1935, the production of technical glass fiber for insulation started. The old production rooms weren't big enough for the extended production. A new house was built in the street Oberer Rottenbach and the spinning moved there in 1938. The processing of the spun glass, like today, was completed in this old company.

For the resumption of the production of fairy hair after 1945, the different glass sticks weren't available any more. New paths had to be trod in fairy hair production. From that time onward, the spun glass was put in the rakes that had been designed in the company and the curls that were formed this way were stabilized by heating in an instantaneous oven so that use as fairy hair was possible. The company became the only producer of this export article. Besides fair hair, they also produced fiber mats for insulation.

In 1959, the state's participation started with the VEB Thüringer Christbaumschmuckverlag *(Thuringian Christmas decorations sales department)* Lauscha. Stabilized in its work as distributors, the company's production achieved a growth rate of 50%. In 1962, the production of the so-called 'Elflafa'-garlands made of an artificial silk yarn started on an imported machine. In 1972, after the import of a pressing machine, their product line was extended by the production of tinsel made of silver plated copper wire. The constantly increasing demand for this product that was used as Christmas tree decoration could only be met by building another pressing machine.

In April 1972 this company, producing fairy hair, glass fiber mats, and garlands was connected to the VEB Thüringer Glasschmuck *(Thuringian glass decorations)* Lauscha as the production department in Steinach. The employees that were working as distributors in the company together with them at the same time joined the Bernhard Matthäi KG company. Together, this conglomerate made up the Steinach warehouse department of the sales and foreign trade department.

While East German ornaments were not so widely recognized, West German ornaments quickly attracted the interest of the American importers. As more East German glassblowers moved to the West, Fritz Rempel considered the possibilities of a large factory for ornament production. The Oberfrankische Glas und Spielzeug" (toy goods) at ist Neustadt near Coburg was a cooperative business providing glass, paints, and molds to cottage workers. In 1948, Fritz Rempel, a teacher, founded Oberfrankische Glas und Spielzeug. His idea was born from the fact that in this year glass blowers were bringing their ornaments in baskets in the still open Soviet border to Neustad to barter for food and money. Oberfrankische Glas commenced the distribution of glasswares on a seasonal basis and delivered them to customers. Their business flourished with Woolworth's, Montgomery Ward, Sears Roebuck, and Kresge's. Rempel's first show room was actually the living room in his modest home. In 1962, it was evident that the Russians would keep the border with West Germany completely closed. Rempel persuaded glass blowers to escape over the border at night so that that they could come to work for him. The company continued to grow over the years.

Another company who went this way was the Ernst Paul Eckardt Company. Eckardt crossed from Oberlind (near Sonneberg), East Germany, to ist Neustadt near Coburg, West Germany. Ernst Paul Eckardt was a brother of Max Eckardt (Shiny Brite), New York.

Krebs & Sohn, identified by their 'B' with the Bear trademark, offered many different glass ornaments. Their standard packages contained one dozen balls each in sizes 3, 4, 5, and 6 cm and one half dozen packages containing 7, 8, and 9 cm balls. Silvered ball-shapes were available in solid colors of silver, pink, green, blue, gold, and red. Decorations included white painted and glittered stars, stripes, snow tops, and dots. Multitudes of indents and pear-shaped ornaments were sold. Tree tops wrapped with tinsel and finished with miniature glass bells were among the most elaborate made after Word War II.

Figurals included bells, birds, mushrooms, grape clusters, pinecones, bugles, horns, and Santas with hangers and on clips. Even tiny goldfish, lamps, peacocks, ducks, teapots, owls, violins, dogs, cars, and pipes were made, many of them recognizable from molds used before the war. Boats, balloons, and other indents were wrapped with silver crinkly wire, but the wire was thicker and not as fine. Glass beading in pear-shaped and round-blown forms as well as tinsel stars, chandeliers, and pendants were also sold.

Cotton ornaments included bells and icicles. Lead tinsel, gold and silver lamenta, and angel hair in various sized packages were very popular imports into the United States.

Contrary to popular myths, the Germans also employed ribbon machines like those which created the envelopes for electric light bulbs. The walls of these ornaments (unlike those made in America) were extremely thin, which then did create some problems in final decorations because the paint had to be applied with very light pressure. After being coated inside with silver nitrate, the outside lacquer was added, and these glass ornaments were placed on a conveyor belt which ran under a series of lights for drying. Then they were decorated by the silkscreen or stencil method in which the design was first "printed" on a silk or nylon screen by means of light-sensitive emulsion. The screen was stretched across a wooden frame fastened to a semi-automatic machine. As the glass Christmas ball rotated, the screen moved at the same speed as the surface of the ball. There was a rubber squeegee within the screen frame that forced the paint through the open areas of the silk (which were not covered by the printed design), and the design was impressed on the glass. Naturally, the screen could only contact the area near the circumference of the ball as it rotated, and that is why all machine-decorated spherical ornaments have designs only around the center. To decorate near the top or bottom, the striping method was used in which a brush replaced the silk screening. Other methods included veiling (wavy lines) and spraying.

Elaborate tree tops being blown in an East German glass blower's home during the 1950s. While there was factory production, Germans preferred to work at home in Lauscha.

Glass pine cones being blown at the lamp in an East German glass blower's home in the mid-1950s.

Ornaments being packed by co-operative employees for shipment to Russia and other satellite countries since exports to the United States were too high due to very high tariffs being placed on East German goods.

Woman in her Lauscha home applying glitter to hand-blown and painted ornaments. Note the spikes on which the ornaments were placed to dry.

Machinery used in East Germany to create glass rods for German glass blowers. Once the rods were produced, glass blowers would then heat these rods at the lamp and create ornaments.

East German government posed picture publicizing the production of glass ornaments in Lauscha during the 1950s. Note that the entire process of blowing, painting, decorating, and packing are being displayed in this one photograph.

Advertisement displaying the array of glass objects made in Lauscha for the United States and Europe. Even though there were high tariffs, some goods were shipped to the United States and other goods were smuggled across the border and then stamped as "West Germany" even though these objects were manufactured in East Germany.

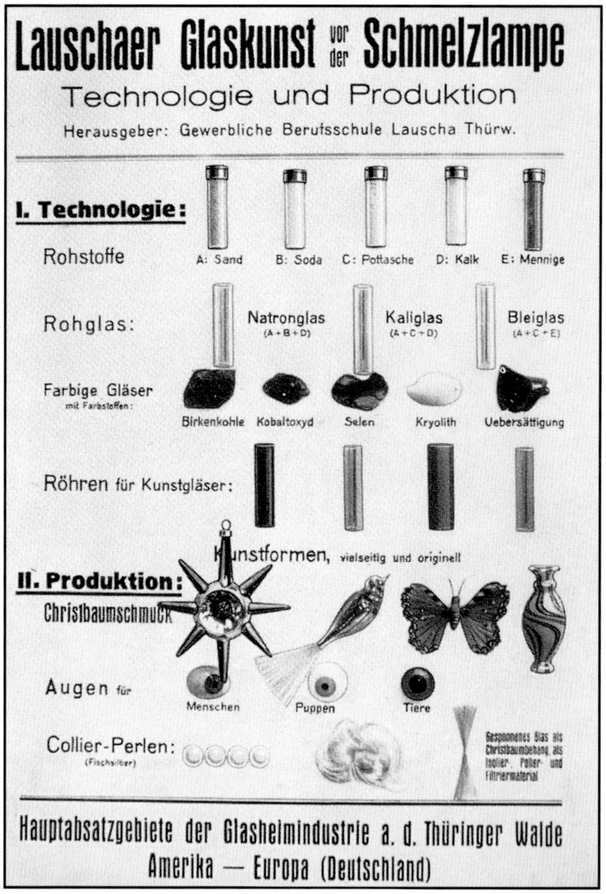

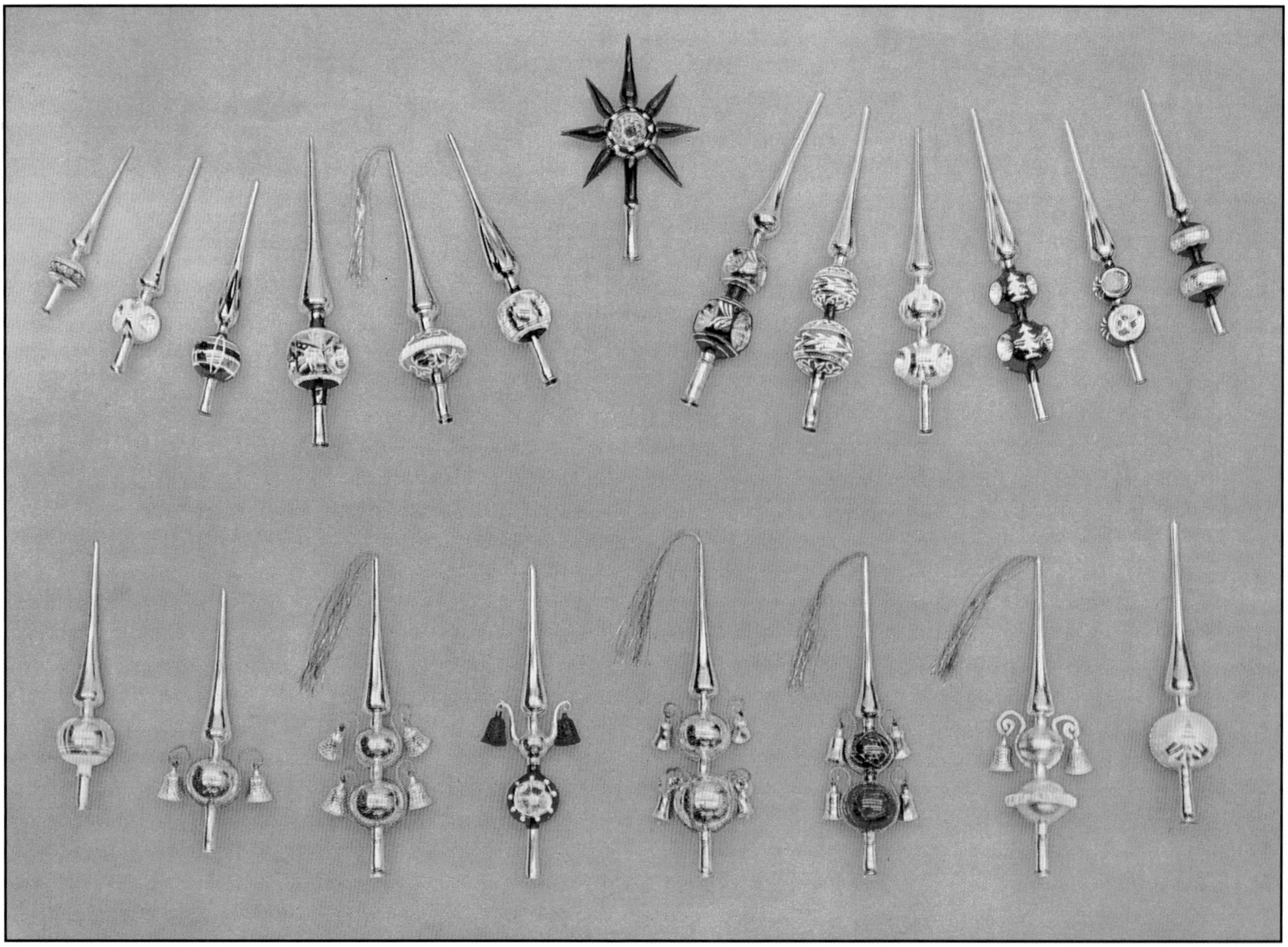

Lauscha-produced glass tree tops from a 1954 catalog from Lauscha.

Assortment of 1954 produced figural ornaments including pipes, sailboats, wire-wrapped birdcages, and balloons.

Elaborate wire-wrapped ornaments from 1956. Note the brown-tinted yellows, greens, blues, and reds.

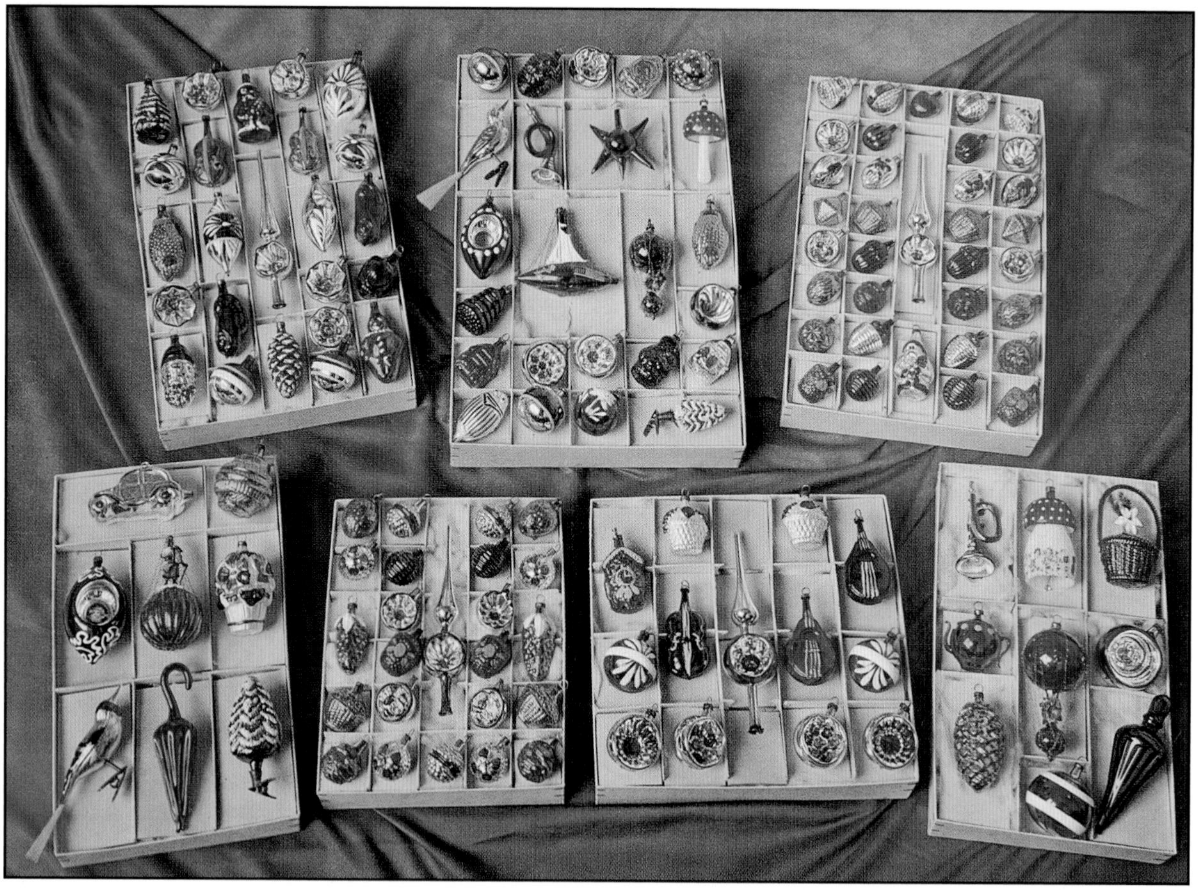

Boxed assortments from 1956. This is the decade when Americans more than ever wished to purchase a complete box or even several to get an "instant" collection of ornaments for their tree.

Early 1950s production items, all of which were blown in the same molds just before World War II. Painting tints and details are quite good.

Early 1950s production items, illustrating the employment of mold blowing plus the creative free blowing done to complete these ornaments.

Items from this decade illustrating the abundant use of silver and the absence of great detail.

Assortment of birds on clips illustrating the styles and sizes available during this decade.

Great examples of fruit ornaments continued once again in the 1950s, using the same molds as before the war and even with most of the same coloration. However, the greens still contained that brownish tint so characteristic of this decade.

Assortment of early 1950s ornaments from West Germany. More common shapes. $7-20 each.

Rare West German figural ornaments from the early 1950s. Bear, $65-70; angel, $55-65; birds, $25-40; thin man, $65-70; and kitten in shoe, $55-65.

More unusual shaped West German ornaments from mid-1950s. Clowns, $40-50 each; Santa figures, $25-30 each; angels, $40-45 each; frog, $50-55; and bird, $15-20.

In order to refuel an interest in European-blown ornaments, the symbolism behind many of the various glass figural ornaments was publicized. Apples were symbols of the real fruit once used on trees, and then fed to farm animals, those lowly witnesses when Christ was born. Lanterns symbolized lights used in former days to help light the trail to church for early dawn's Christmas mass. Silver cones come from the ancient legend where each day a good but poor old woman gathered pinecones to be used for fuel in her home. Even though her husband was bedridden, she did not complain and was known throughout her community for her good deeds. One morning, while in the woods, an elf came along and put some cones in her basket, and asked her not to peek until she got home. When she returned home and dumped out the contents on her kitchen table, she was astonished to find they had turned to solid silver.

The yellow canaries pinched with clip-on fasteners were reminiscent of the canaries that found refuge in a fir tree during a fierce blizzard on Christmas eve. The canaries sang all night, praising the power of Christ who guided them to the protection of that old Christmas tree. The bell came into prominence during the Medieval Ages when bells were employed to call people to worship. Angels, of course, heralded the birth of Christ in the skies to the shepherds. Such legends, and more, were widely distributed in an effort to revitalize America's interest in old-fashioned European ornaments.

In 1953, the United States imported $367,000 worth of glass Christmas tree ornaments from Poland; East Germany supplied $127,000. West Germany, outside the Russian orbit, was our largest individual overseas supplier, with imports valued at $508,000. Most considered the ornaments from Europe to be of better quality than their American counterparts, although the American companies were quick to dispute that point. Japan was another large supplier, but primarily of the small, inexpensive ornaments. Italy also commenced importation of ornaments after World War II. Imports of glass Christmas tree ornaments from all foreign sources totaled $1,355,239 in 1953.

Three-inch Polish ornaments in various shapes, all richly painted and detailed. $4-6 each.

Two-inch Polish ornaments in various shapes. $3-4 each.

Four-inch Polish ornaments with exquisite hand-painted detail. $5-6 each.

Making an appearance in the 1950s were ornaments from the U.S. Zone of Germany. In the first years, the shapes were very simple, being pinecones, grape clusters, bells, and indents. By the mid-1950s, Marshall Field & Company advertised a set of West German ornaments including a wire-wrapped bird on nest and a Santa Claus. Also available were sets which included a snowman, boat, urn, clock, candelabrum, bird, bell, church, and frosted musical instruments. All the ornaments were elaborately painted and trimmed, somewhat unusual for this period of history when many Germans were relearning the art of blowing, painting, and decorating glass ornaments.

While wire-wrapped ornaments appeared for sale, the wire used was quite different than that used before World War II. Immediately After the war, when East Germany was under Russian control, much of the wonderful Bouillon wire (Gold 9k) and silver (800) went into dumps. Most glass blowers did know how to market their products and simply threw away all the "makings" and attempted to make their livelihood in other ways. In West Germany, they commenced making the wire once again when they discovered more markets for wire-wrapped ornaments. It came in numerous hues: silver, gold, bronze, brass, and even red, green, and blue.

Assortment of mid to late 1950s wire-wrapped ornaments from West Germany. $40-60 each.

Wire-wrapped balloons from the early 1950s. West Germany. $55-65 each.

Pinecone people were so very popular throughout this decade. From Germany, West Germany, and Italy. $7-10 each.

Boxed sets of ornaments appeared in multitudes after World War II. Many of them were inexpensive and somewhat crude in their appearance. One of the most popular sets of twelve sold for about $1.00 and included two cottages, two mandolins, two peacocks, an angel, an elf head, carousel, cuckoo clock, Santa, and mushroom. The colors were that distinguishing brown-shaded red, green, blue, and yellow. Much silvering was evident as the ornaments were merely painted with a minimum detail. Some of the more elaborate pieces were wire-wrapped and finished with tinsel and paper flowers.

Krebs & Sohn, Chrisbaumschmuck GmbH of Rosenheim, Germany, produced many of these ornaments. One of their catalogs from 1955 illustrates pages of spheres, trimmed in a variety of ways. Delicate tree tops reminiscent of those made before World War II also appeared. Some ornaments included elaborate star shapes, bells with clappers hanging from extended arms, and elaborate indent shapes. However, all illustrated tops do have that dull color scheme with an abundance of silvering appearing in areas not painted. Songbirds, storks, pipes, bugles, horns, mushrooms (some on clips), Santa figures, pinecones, lamps, and teapots abound. Some of the baskets, balloons, and bird nests were wire-wrapped. Less than ten percent of the ornaments listed in their thick catalog of over forty pages included figural ornaments. The rest were spheres, pear shapes, and bells, all painted and sold in boxed sets.

Several German factories played a prominent role in the production of glass ornaments in this decade. Krebs and Sohn was one of those very large factories who produced thousands upon thousands of glass ornaments for the American market. After World War II, the Krebs family settled in Rosenheim, Bavaria, in what was then West Germany, at the foot of the Alps. Through those difficult post-war years, the family managed to build up a production of traditional ornaments which is now recognized as one of the largest of its kind in Europe. The Krebs family developed exclusive colors and designs, for which they have become famous.

In 1947, their original business was founded by grandmother Erika Krebs, who was trained in the ornament business as a child in German Bohemia and Czechoslovakia. After World War II, Erika and her son Helmut moved from Czechoslovakia into West Germany. They found themselves in a home which had hundreds of worthless German banknotes in a back storage room. They traded this worthless paper money for cardboard and together Erika and her son created miniature houses, churches, and other village buildings like those manufactured in "olden days." These ornaments made from cardboard were heavily flocked, airbrushed, painted with details, and often glittered in various colors. With a tiny wire spring-clip pushed into the top of the building, these ornaments were somewhat popular when made by Helmut and Erika.

They once joked that they started their business with billions of German marks! The Krebs soon realized that while these buildings appealed to Europeans, they did not appeal to any large extent to Americans who were much more interested in glass ornaments. Thus Helmut and Erika employed an old-world trained glass blower to work in their home. It was here that the actual production of glass spheres and figurals commenced.

Over the years, their business continued to thrive and grow due to the very lavishly decorated and perfectly blown ornaments. It was not long before Helmut married Wilma in 1950, bringing with him into this business a very dedicated and skill artist who worked beside her husband for years, eventually even with her three sons, Michael, Wolfgang, and Eberhardt.

Many other glass ornaments were produced near Coburg, in eyesight of the Castle Coburg, by the Wegner family. Their family was originally from Sonneberg. Erich Wegner was originally a partner in a wholesale company that sold glassware and laboratory glass parts such as thermometers and hourglasses. In 1949 Horst and his family left Communist East Germany and settled in Coburg, where Erich established his glass ornament factory. Wegner earned the distinctive honor of providing over 2,000 huge ornaments in 1958 for the Christmas tree on the lawn of the White House.

Inge-Glas had its beginnings as well just after the close of World War II. In 1951, Heinz Muller-Blech decided to escape communist East Germany and settle on the western side. He arrived in Neustadt, just twenty miles from his home, but a world away from what he left. Heinz met and married Inge and built a home on a quiet lake. They began by producing ornaments in their basement and selling to local wholesalers. They named their firm "Inge-Glas." At this time, glass ornaments like those he produced were still not very popular and Heinz was forced to work as a policeman to survive. Gradually, business increased and he was able to devote his full time energy to his glass blowing enterprise.

While Inge-Glas prospered, the glass blowers in Lauscha were under the weight of communism. The traditional cottage industry of mouth-blown glass ornaments turned to modern machines to create round ball-shaped ornaments. The painting quality declined due to the lack of incentive and the industry continued to decline.

Czechoslovakia Regains Strength in the American Market

Since 1952 Christmas decorations have been exported by the Czechoslovakian JABLONEX Foreign Trade Corporation. As a result, their ornaments started to adorn trees in the United States, France, the Soviet Union, Great Britain, Italy, Sweden, Holland, Canada, and other countries throughout the world.

The production of modern Christmas decorations in Czechoslovakia underwent dramatic changes after 1930, due to the Research Institute of Glass-making at Hradec Kralove. The economic depression of the 1930s caused the decline of market demand for the decorative blown hollow beads produced by Smrzovka, near the town of Jablonec, since 1862. For that reason, these manufacturers searched for other possibilities in applying their acquired glass blowing skills. A glass blowing cooperative was founded at Zdobin, near Dvur Kralove, and then production was extended into other parts of the country. And commencing in 1934, their decorations were exported abroad.

Single beads, bead-rows, bugles, drawn beads, bangles, rocailles (seed beads), and other such shapes went from the manufacturer (glass factory), to the supplier (company which facilitated the home cottage industry in Czechoslovakia), to the cottage worker (homes in which these ornaments were shaped). Knobloch & Berger was one of the principal producers of these shaped glass ornaments after World War II. This company, and most others, were centered in the Gablonz area, not too far from Prague.

Up to 1951, exports took place via the Glassexport (Skloeport) company; after 1951, the company was divided: Glassexport concentrated on flat, hollow, pressed, and art glass; Jablonex focused on bijouterie (a collection of trinkets, ornaments, or jewels). The graduates of the technical school produced designs in the sample departments; the objective was to produce professional examples for the home cottage workers to emulate. The sketch was carried out as a design and presented at various trade and toy fairs. Up to three thousand different samples were viewed by buyers from all over the world. Only one collection a year was produced that featured Christmas ornaments. Jablonex organized sample exhibitions of their work in foreign countries. Christmas tree ornaments made up ten percent of their entire bead production, with the rest going for the jewelry and fashion industry.

Their ornaments reflected some very vibrant folk customs. On the eve of December 5, St. Nicholas legendarily descends from a gold cord with an angel and devil to reward or admonish children. At Christmas Eve supper, a chair is left vacant for an eventual poor traveler. After supper, someone secretly lights the candles and sparklers and puts the gifts under the tree so that the children think that Santa Claus arrived. Then he rings the bell and everyone goes to the tree. One of the most intriguing customs involves heating a piece of lead on an old spoon under a candle until it changes into a liquid. Then it is poured into a can with cold water. Lead creates different shapes and people find similarity to something—things, people, activities, and animals—from which they forecast the future of a person for the next year. In all homes, people display small paper, wooden, or ceramic "Bethlehems"—models on a smaller scale of the stable/manger scene in Bethlehem with figurines of the Christ child, Joseph, Mary, and the animals. After Midnight Mass, children often sleep on straw by the manger, reminiscent of Christ's birth. On January 6, Epiphany priests write C+M+B over the doors of homes, placing a cross between the letters which stand for the initials of the Magi and a Latin phrase meaning, "May Christ bless this home."

Late 1940s into mid-1950s, Czechoslovakian blown ornaments. Simple shapes. $6-10 each.

Late 1940s into mid-1950s, Czechoslovakian blown ornaments. Unusual shapes including a windmill, baby buggy, spinning wheel, balance scales, and sprinkling can. $35-50 each.

Late 1940s into mid-1950s, Czechoslovakian blown ornaments. Rare shapes including: airplane, helicopter, boat, cannon, and zeppelin. $70-80 each.

Mid-1950s Czechoslovakian blown ornaments. Simple shapes. $15-20 each.

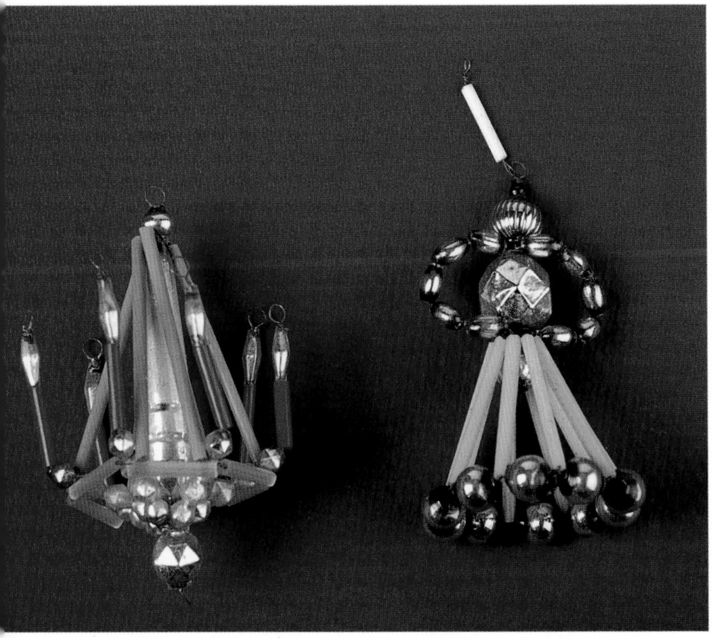

Mid-1950s Czechoslovakian blown ornaments. Chandelier and angel. $25-30 each.

Examples of Japanese counterparts. Early to mid-1950s. $8-12 each.

Italy Commences a Rich History of Glass Ornament Production

In the late 1940s, after World War II, German Christmas traditions began to manifest themselves in northern Italy, in the northern regions of Lombardy, and Lake Como. At the end of the war, the German manufacturer Karl Becker left Germany to settle in sunny Como, near the Swiss border. There he started FLORIDA, a company which produced and marketed artificial trees and garlands. Becker encouraged the Italian glassblowers who made decorative and utilitarian glass objects to adapt their skills to supply Becker with ornaments to sell. This was not a great leap since both countries did share the concepts of art glass. In the 1920s and 1930s, German glass blowers had experimented with many free-blown forms such as birds, swans, anchors, and numerous other animals. The Italians had the rich tradition of fanciful Venetian glassware. Thus the Italians were able to cross this bridge and begin producing free-blown ornaments, without the use of any molds. It should be noted that the Italian glass ornament companies did produce some mold-blown ornaments as many of these earlier molds were discovered in back storage areas of Italian glass factories. However, the almost complete turn to free-blown ornaments occurred because Italians just could not compete with German mold ornaments, and quickly realized that the market for free-blown shapes was a unique corner of the market for which they could be famous.

Although Italy had been exporting different items for sale at Christmas since 1947, it was not until 1952 that Italy began exporting glass figural ornaments to the United States. In 1955, Italy exported just over $22,000 worth of ornaments.

All these ornaments were hand blown in the old manner, being shaped by paddles as the glass bubble is slowly blown. A glass tube which varies in size according to the size of the ornament being produced, was quickly heated and pulled by the artisan to create first the body then the head of this ornament. Then arms and legs were created from tiny tubes of glass attached at the appropriate spots after being heated.

The glass is extremely thin and fragile due to the extended legs, arms, and other such features. Stork's beaks and feet, as well as the arms and legs of other figures, are carefully drawn out into the thinnest of appendages. Thus, caution must be practiced in their use and storage. In addition, many of the first ornaments in the 1950s were trimmed with inexpensive materials such as feathers, cotton pipe cleaners, maribou, and plush.

Among the most rare of Italian figurals to first be imported into the United States was a set of Peter Pan related figurals including Peter Pan, Captain Hook, and an alligator with a clock painted on his belly. In 1955, a set of Italian figurals reached this country which included a ballerina with a skirt, an ice skater with cotton trim around the neck and skirt, a skier complete with thin wooden skis, and a doll complete with cotton hair. The set sold for $2.98 and started an unbelievable variety of different figurals sold through the years. Some other early documented production items included a ski jumper on thin cardboard skis, a skater wearing cotton "furs" and thin blown ice skates, and a helicopter with metal propellers.

Italian figurals. Left to right, top: Soldier, $85-95; Sorcerer, $100-120; and Indian, $100-110. Left to right, bottom row: Turbaned Indian Man, $90-100; American Indian, $110-120; Ballerina, $90-100.

Italian indents from the mid-1950s which included plastic inserts. $5-10 each.

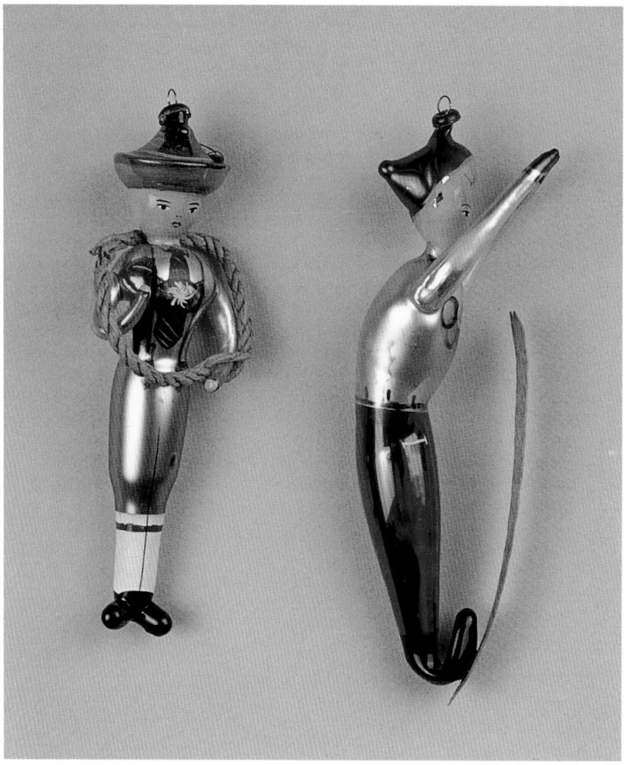

Two pieces from an original four-piece 1955 Sears set commemorating the Winter Olympics. $135-140 each.

Early 1950s Italian ornament exported by FLORIDA with original box. $140-150.

Wicked stepsisters with fairy godmother. $100-110 each.

Late 1960s cotton-decorated winter figures. $95-105 each.

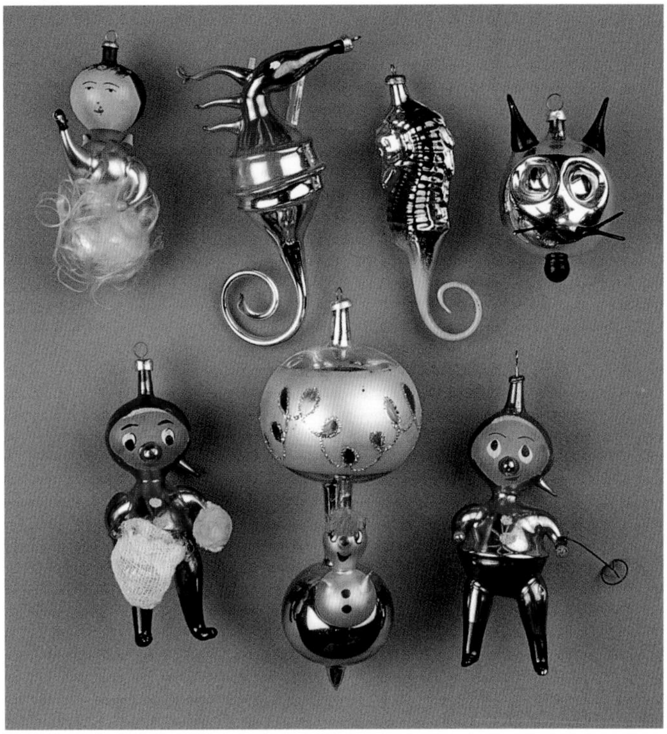

Italian figurals. Left to right, top: Angel, $45-55; seahorse, $125-140; seahorse, $100-110; and cat head, $100-110. Left to right, bottom: Elf with snowball, $90-100; clown below mushroom, $120-130; and elf with skis, $85-95.

Rare Italian figural ornaments. Left to right, top: Musketeer, $140-155; Captain Kid, $165-175; football player, $110-125; and Mexican, $130-140. Left to right, bottom: Samurai man, $180-190; French soldier, $150-160; and cowboy, $145-160.

Russia Plays a Small Role in Ornament Production

After World War II, Russia, through experiences with Germany and other European countries, began in earnest to once again produce Christmas ornaments as they had done previous to the Second World War. However, their ornaments did not accurately reflect Russian culture as artisans created icicles, squirrels, nuts, houses, and other simple shapes. An order from the Central committee in 1955 decreed that more ornaments should be made to emphasize the power of the working classes. It was in this period that a profusion of fairy tale characters from around the world were blown in different shapes from glass. Most of the glass figural ornaments now found on the market for sale in the United States were made starting in the 1950s.

American Influences on Our Glass Ornaments

Americans continued to produce the largest number of ornaments for the market during this decade. New glass ornaments, primarily spherical in shape, were silvered inside and then silk screened with Santa and his reindeer, holly sprays, the Star of Bethlehem, a Parade of Toys, Patterned Stars, village snow scenes, or train scenes. These ornaments were new-styled ornaments.

Many of these 1950s ornaments were manufactured by Santa Heim, started in 1938 by W. J. Thompson, a veteran Woolworth buyer, and Harry H. Heim, who came to tree decorations by way of ladies' dress designing and window trimming. A 150 year old duck mill and a village of 100 houses were bought in rural Maryland, gaily-painted red and white, and named Santa Heim. Workers turned out 2,000 to 2,500 ornaments a day. Different shapes including pinecones partially encrusted with white snow, elaborately indented "reflectors," and violins. A Santa in bas-relief and others were exact replicas of traditional German ornaments. One of their more popular items was a swan indented with a shiny reflector on both sides, which was hung on the tree from an annealed glass hook at the top. Dipped in a red lacquer, and finished with a few white swags of white enamel, the bird was immensely popular in several different sizes. While ornaments in six and seven inch sizes were produced for large commercial trees, Heim also produced a "Tiny Tim" line of miniatures—some tinsel-trimmed for Lilliputian-sized table trees. However, they were more expensive than the miniature Japanese manufactured ornaments and therefore could not compete in price.

One of the first American importers of tree ornaments was B. Schackman and Company, a New York City wholesaler and retailer. Immediately after the war, they once again commenced importation, and quickly filled their warehouses. They catered to the upper brackets, carrying items not carried by the chain stores which did the bulk of ornament retailing. Breakage of glass ornaments at that time was estimated to be ten percent; therefore, with 39 million trees being decorated in 1950, there was ample room for importation growth.

In the late 1950s, extravagant wire-wrapped figurals disappeared, since Americans favored simpler ornaments for their trees. While red, silver, blue, green, and gold continued as favorite colors, Americans were quickly attracted to pastels such as violet, pink, and chartreuse. Figurals tended to be as simple as pinecones, grape clusters, and fruit baskets. The rest of these sets were finished with melon-shaped ornaments, bells, and reflectors. There were indents and balls with silk-screen motifs such as Santa with reindeer, a parade of toys, and a village scene.

American-made glass ornaments produced in sets were sold in profusion. Industry statistics stated that ten percent of the glass ornaments used on American trees broke every year, so with 39,000,000 trees in the United States, steady sales were assured regardless of any additions to family inventories.

These American-made ornaments were formed in iron molds, most of which were supplied by the American Brake Shoe Co., Engineered Casting Division, Rochester, New York. The castings were not a high-production job, but the requirements of surface finishing and accuracy at the parting line of the mold cavity were high. Low production might mean three or four molds, while there may be as many as 150 of one popular design.

By the 1950s, glass ornaments were made by Corning Glass Works at the rate of 1,000 a minute which amounted to over 1,440,000 per twenty-four hour day per machine. Designs were planned two years in advance. The first step was to make a full-size wood pattern of the ornament. After sample castings were made and designs approved, patterns were returned to Corning for refinement and pattern alterations for more economical production. This usually consisted of making the pattern such that it could be mounted and, if necessary, making a plaster corebox for producing the cavity core. If only a few molds were needed, the corebox was eliminated and the cavity made directly in the pattern. The next step included the addition of synthetic molding materials to create the fine detail in the cavity. The molds were then sent to Corning Glass where they were fitted onto their ribbon machine.

While Corning Glass supplied most of our domestically produced ornaments in the 1950s, there were others who played a minor role. American Teens Co., a Chicago firm engaged in glass blowing, was established in 1957 by a group of teenagers. Many hurdles, including the procurement of raw materials, continual breakdown of flame stations, and their ignorance of glassblowing techniques, did not prevent them from selling thousands of ornaments. Indents and spheres were the two principal types of glass ornaments produced. Their advisor, Chris Altier, a Viennese glassblower, helped this group of teens to form the first glassblowing firm in Junior Achievement History. Unfortunately, no ornaments from this company have been recorded.

Frank J. Maietta, design director for Max Eckardt, changed many of the older traditional forms. This was due to practicality since the designs were applied to the glass surface by hand and by machine. A design that was to be reproduced by machine had to repeat itself so that it could be applied to the surface of a glass ball in a continuous, automatic operation. A design applied by hand had no limitations, except the time of the individual artist. When an ornament was decorated by hand, several artists worked on the same ornament, because each man had his specialty. Stripes, dots, and stars, which appeared on hand-painted balls were each applied by an artist, one at a time, in what was known as a labor pool.

In many cases, after the original design had been accepted and given back to the labor pool to copy it, quite often it came back looking just a little different—the personality and technique of each artist was added, so that although the finished design resembled the original to some extent, actually no two hand-decorated ornaments were ever the same. In many cases, the original hand-painted design was altered slightly to make less expensive to produce in quantity. At their fingertips were paints, jewels, crinkly wire, glitter, and paper.

Shiny Brite ornaments. Assorted clear shapes. Continued to be made into the mid-1950s and then disappeared. $2-3 each.

Typical boxed assortment of Corning manufactured ornaments. $5-6 for boxed set.

Varying colors and sizes of U.S. spheres so popular for use with aluminum trees, the fad of the latter portion of this decade. $.50-1.00 each.

Assorted solid-color U.S. spheres so popular for use on aluminum trees. $.50-1.00 each.

Indents were so very prevalent in the mid-1950s. U.S. $2-3 each.

Fancy U.S. shapes from the mid to late 1950s. $.50-1.50 each.

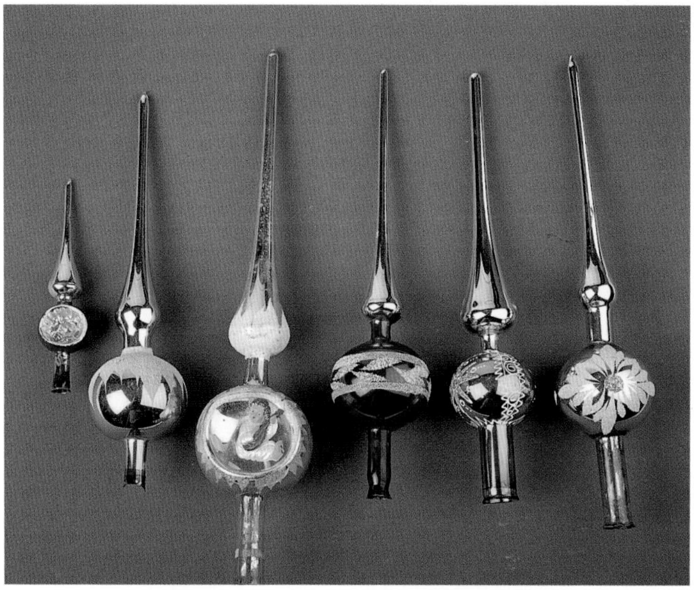

Simpler shaped 4 to 14-inch blown West German tree tops. $4-8 each.

A Closer Look at Other Tree Decorations of This Decade

Tree Tops

Plastic became the rage in the 1950s when it came to tree toppers. Most of them were constructed with a wire frame at the bottom to fit on the tree. Most had an opening in the back into which an electric bulb could be placed. Topper shapes included angels, Santa Claus, and stars. The Glo-Lite plastic Santa-Glo tree top manufactured in Chicago, Illinois, was advertised for use as a tree top or a stand-up for the mantle or a fireplace. It has a felt-covered plastic front with a metal back. Constructed of translucent, unbreakable plastic, and artistically decorated in "Christmas red," this 8-½-inch figure came package in a very colorful display box. For most Americans, it was their first and most memorable tree top.

NOMA created a plastic star, illuminated from the center, the light passing out through five triangular prisms, clipped to a pentagonal centerpiece. Before the war, the angular points were made of glass. After the war, they were made of high heat-resistant polystyrene. Thus, there was far less breakage in the plant, far fewer returns, and an actual savings of 1 ½ cents a star.

In the late 1950s, NOMA created the Star of Bethlehem. It was sold right after the first Soviet and American satellites were launched. It contained a bright red center with numerous plastic white spikes protruding from the globe. Also extremely popular were foil stars into which an electric light was inserted. A thin tinsel wire somewhat reminiscent of tops before World War II surrounded many of these foil stars. The NOMA Christmas Angel made of plastic with a golden star-capped wand in her hand also appeared at the top of so many trees during this decade.

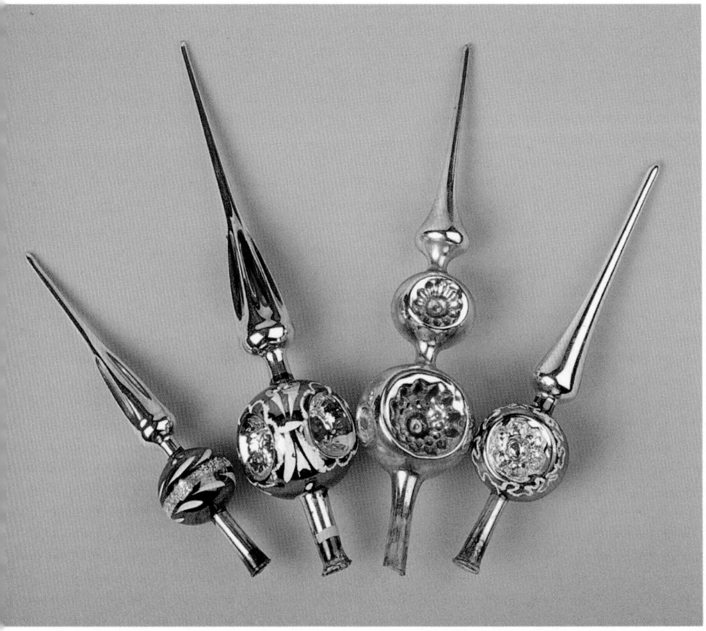

More elaborate 12 to 14-inch blown West German tree tops. $8-10 each.

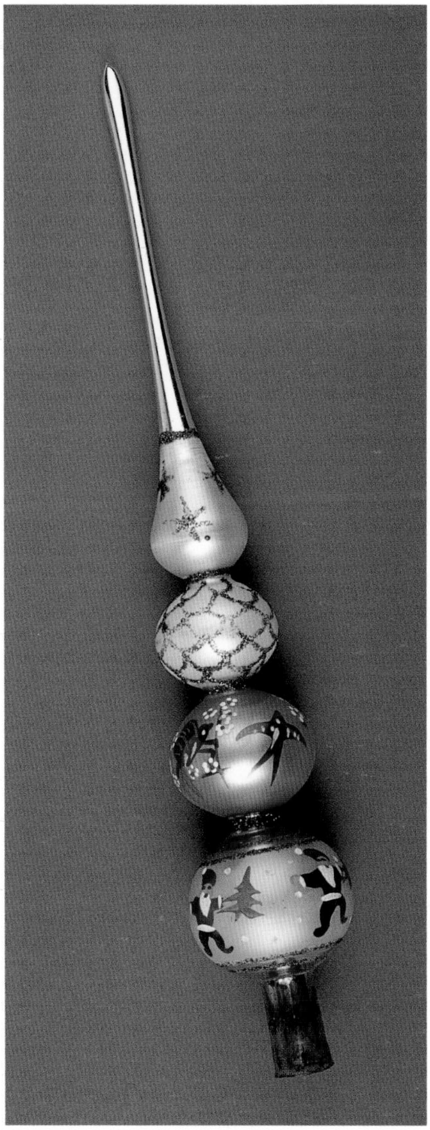

Polish tree top. 16-inch. Mid-1950s. $45-55.

Unusual tree top with white plastic angel. Early 1950s. $40-50 complete with box.

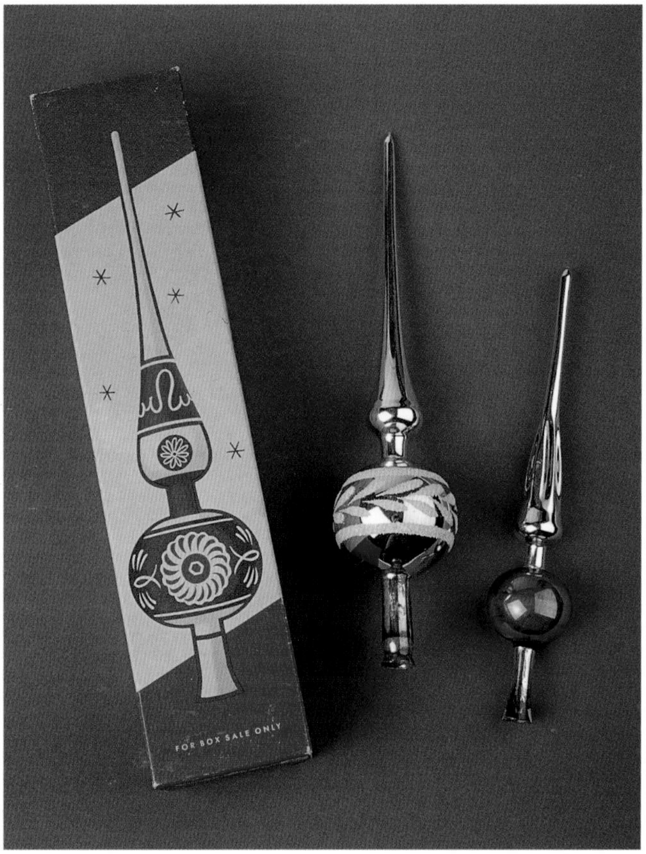

American blown tree tops. $3-4 each.

Late 1940s into 1950s, Paramount tree top. Electric. $8-15.

Late 1950s aluminum coated plastic tree top. Electric. $45-50.

National Tinsel Company's 1950s version of a previously produced tree top. $35-40.

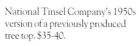

Early 1950s cellulose acetate tree top. U.S. $25-30.

Glass Beading

Not available any longer from Germany, thin, glass-blown beaded chains which were draped on the branches of trees were replaced by simple beaded chains. Produced in Japan in lengths of about nine feet, glass beaded garlands were sold by the thousands in the 1950s. Distinguished by their heavy glass molding, they most often appeared in one color. However, alternating colors and even some different shaped beads were employed on the more expensive garlands. Six strands usually sold for $1.39. Even though they were more durable than the thin-blown German models, they failed to recapture their spots on the tree. Most of these chains were used for room, mantle, and door decorations rather than being draped on the tree itself.

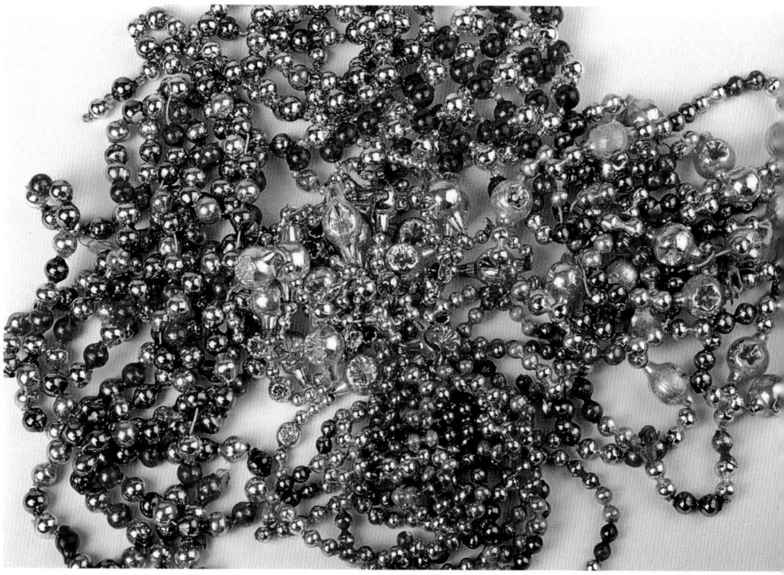

Solid color beading chains. Japan. 3 and 4-foot lengths. $6-8 per chain for simple beading. $15-20 for indents and other unusually molded beaded chains.

Solid color beading in original packages. Japan. $20-25 for original container and chain.

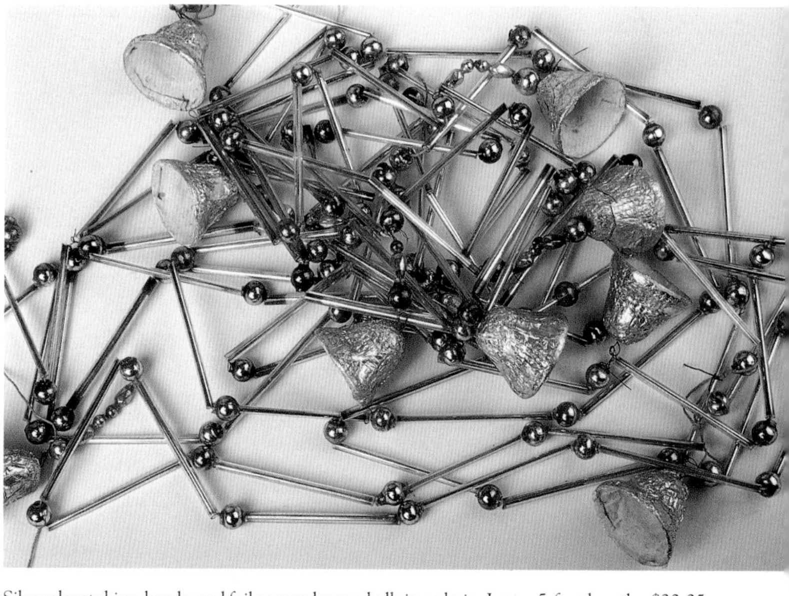

Silver glass tubing, beads, and foil covered paper bells in a chain. Japan. 5-foot lengths. $20-25 per chain.

Candy Containers

While the tradition of presenting school children with a gift box of candy at Christmas programs continued in schools, the sizes of these containers changed quite drastically. In an era were money was more plentiful, children expected more and more. Thus manufacturers increased the size of these candy boxes to fit consumer demands. Candy boxes, triangular in shape, came in half-pound sizes in red and white holiday designs. In addition, Wisconsin Deluxe Company sold one pound sizes with cloth tape handles for $4.50 in 1951.

Also very popular were red net kiddy stockings filled with hard candy. Finished on the top with a bright lithograph of Santa and a red and white candy striped cloth hanger, they first appeared on the tree and were then distributed to children. One large 12-inch stocking was filled with toy plastic automobiles of all descriptions with other toys and candy novelties.

Also becoming more popular were candy house kits. Then youngsters (and parents as well) could fashion a cottage complete with gumdrop trees, licorice doors, and a sugar-wafer roof. Sold by Marshal Field & Company in 1954, their set included sugar wafer candies, licorice and caramel whirls, candy cigarettes, rock candy, gum drops, spearmint leaves, fairy breathlets, and green sugar to attach with powdered sugar paste, all for the price of $2.95!

Plastic containers appeared on the scene as well. Red plastic Santa boots 2-¾" in height were filled with suckers to be used as tree ornaments, present tie-ons, or as table favors for Christmas dinner.

Even a candy-filled hand puppet was a popular choice. With a lifelike Vinylite head, the body was set on a cardboard chimney chock-full of cellophane-wrapped fruit drops.

Imported candy containers. Left to Right: Austrian Santa box, $75-85; Japanese fireplace (mantle lifts off), $60-70; and Japanese foil-covered stocking with celluloid Santa face, $85-90.

Plastic USA candy ornaments filled with tiny toys and candy. $15-20 each.

Glass candy containers from the early to mid-1950s filled with original candy. Left to right: Musical instrument, $25-35; telephone, $40-45; and lantern, $15-20.

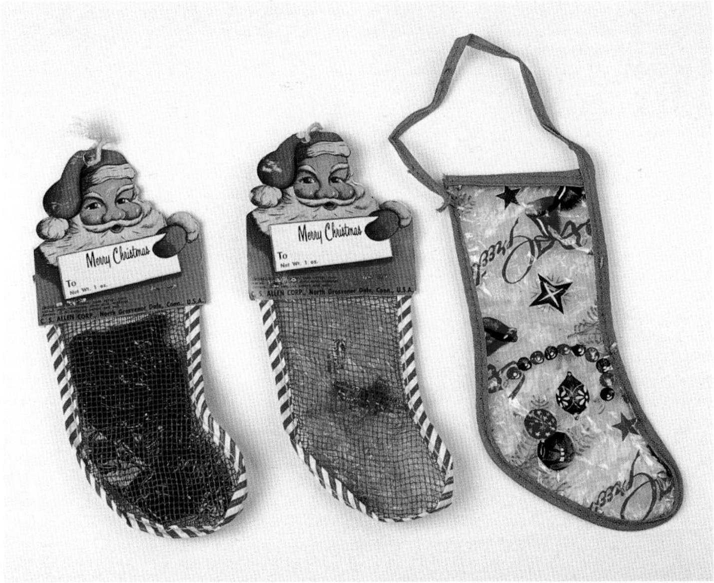

USA manufactured stockings, originally commercially filled with toys and candy. $35-50 each.

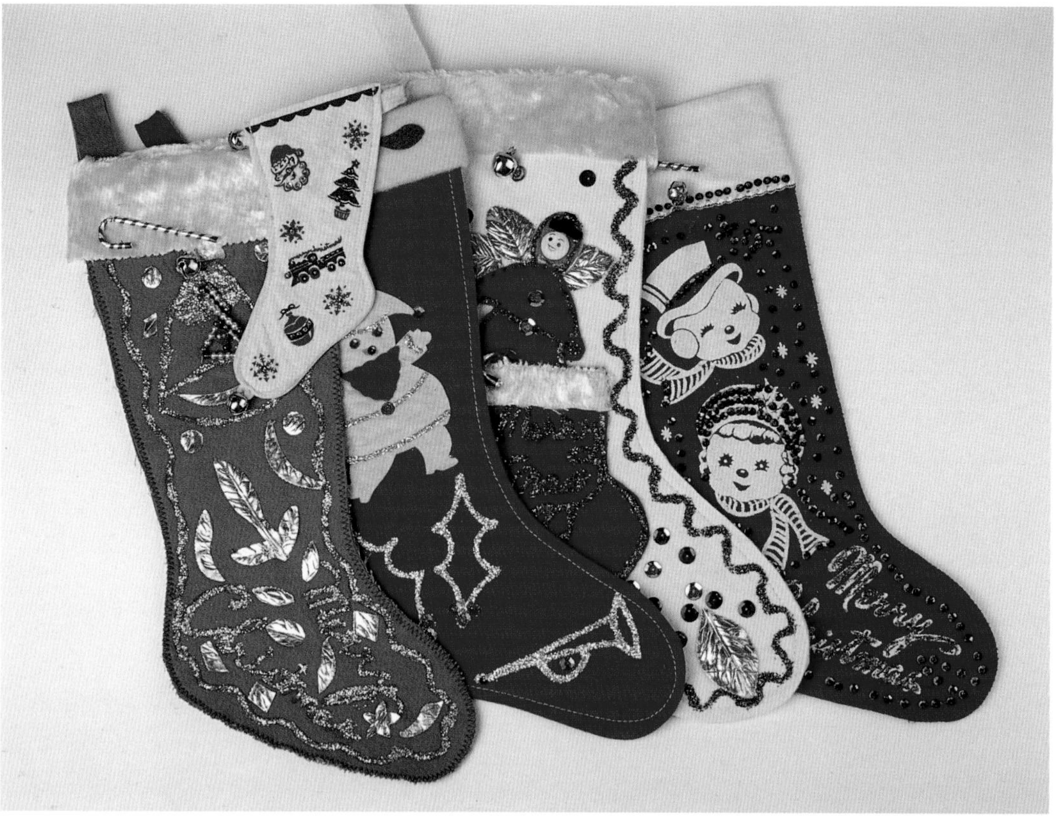

USA manufactured stockings meant for Santa to fill at Christmas. Larger sized. $40-50 each.

Santa box originally filled with chocolates. $75-85.

Candy box place settings eventually found their way to the tree for use as tree ornaments. $10-15 each.

USA candy boxes meant for school and church use. Early 1950s. $15-20 each.

USA candy boxes intended for school use. Late 1950s. $8-15 each.

Metal tree ornaments from England. These ornaments separate in the middle and were originally filled with hard candy. $4-5 each.

Wax Santa heads originally filled with hard candy. $4 each.

Paper and Cardboard Ornaments

Dresden ornaments continued to appear in the 1950s, but aluminum foil was used with lacquer to create the gold color. Before World War II, real silver and bronze (termed Dutch-gold leaf) was glued to the stiffened paper before embossing. Dresdens were constructed by stamping a 1/32-inch sheet of cardboard between two dies. One die was the stamping die, the other the receiving die. The intricate details on the stamping die were raised and the details on the corresponding die were depressed. These "newer" Dresdens are marked "Germany."

However, the rage of this decade were ornaments which combined cardboard and pine cones. Made mostly in Japan, a few were made in East Germany as well as West Germany and other countries. Markings for Japan include "Japan" and "Made in Japan" in blue and red ink. Markings for Germany include "Made in West Germany," "Western Germany," and "Germany USSR Zone." Others located have included markings such as "Austria," "Italy," "Foreign" (Japan), and "Made in Paris, France."

The German variety generally are painted with greater detail and have richer colors incorporated into their design. The Japanese versions are a bit simpler and less detailed. The figures have as a body, a flocked pinecone, and are attached to a flocked cardboard base. Paper, crepe paper, tinsel, celluloid, wood, cotton, chenille, and flannel were used as trim. Figures hold all sorts of items: sacks, skis, walking sticks, brooms, ladders, lanterns, bells, trees, mushrooms, songbooks, and even musical instruments. The whimsical fantasy of these ornaments is unbelievable as one starts to collect the multitudes of different available styles.

Marzipan and circus peanuts used as tree ornaments by a farm family in Wisconsin from late 1940s to 1956. $3-5 each.

Lead Tinsel Icicles and Tinsel Garlands

The National Tinsel Manufacturing Company of Manitowoc, Wisconsin, did a $3,500,000 business in Christmas decorations in 1950. They were among the leading producers of the almost eight million pounds of lead foil produced each year to replace this amount annually discarded with trees.

Double Glo continued to be the dominant force in the sale of lead tinsel icicles in the 1950s. Made of quality tinfoil cut into narrow strips, these heavy icicles hung from the tree in a most elegant fashion.

Another leading producer of lead tinsel was Star Band Company, Inc. of Portsmouth, Virginia, who prided themselves on packing their icicles in especially constructed sturdy boxes with reinforced side walls to prevent crushing. Each box was then wrapped in cellophane. They packaged their tinsel in boxes of 400, 500, 900, and 1,500 strands. Also heralded as an alternative to lead tinsel was Saran icicles produced by the Dow Chemical Corporation. A Dow Chemical Company newsletter in 1956, heralded these two icicles as possessing the ruggedness of saran and the glittering beauty of metal. This newsletter stated, "The new product has inherited from saran its exceptional resistance to tearing and breaking, and the combination of saran and metal provides a soft, shimmering produce which will not mat or tangle. They were advertised as stronger, reusable, lightweight, and resistant to tangling or breakage. They were sold in boxes of 150, 200, 400, and 500 strands.

Circus crackers and vanilla candy hung with butcher string and was used from the late 1940s into 1956. $2-3 each.

Heavy tinsel garlands in 12-foot lengths by ¾-inch widths were the most popular for use in this decade. For those willing to try something new, Double Glo sold aluminum foil garlands in 14-foot lengths. Many Americans quickly purchased this garland for use outdoors since it was not affected by climatic conditions as were the crepe paper decorations.

Also continuing in popularity was the fiber roping imported from Japan. Manufactured of rice wood, it came in 60-yard bolts in red, green, and white. Japan also exported brilliant, high luster red and green cellophane roping in 18-foot bolts.

Another extremely popular garland was the two-color aluminum foil garland in either red and silver or green and silver. About 7/8-inch thick, it came in 10-foot lengths. The more inexpensive garlands appeared in silver only and were marketed in 14-foot lengths. Foil blinker sets with 20-foot garlands of 180 metallic plastic disks of assorted colors were also popular, especially when combined with foil figures, snowflakes, stars, balls, cookie designs, and bells.

Once again being imported from Germany, as well as being made in the United States, were silver tinsel ornaments in pom-pom shapes, stars, and circles. All were very simple silver, some with a tiny bit of red cellophane for color in the center.

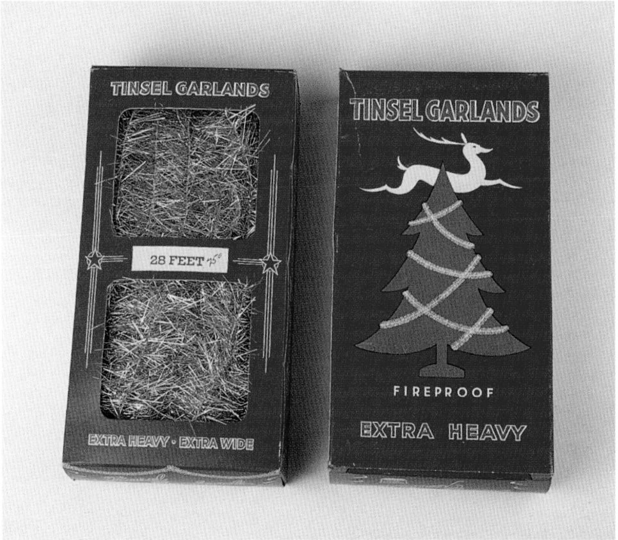

Front and back of National Tinsel garland boxes from the mid-1950s. $12-15 for garland and original box.

Fiber foil garland in 15-foot lengths from Japan. Red and silver, silver, and blue and silver were the most popular colors. $5-7 per individual garland.

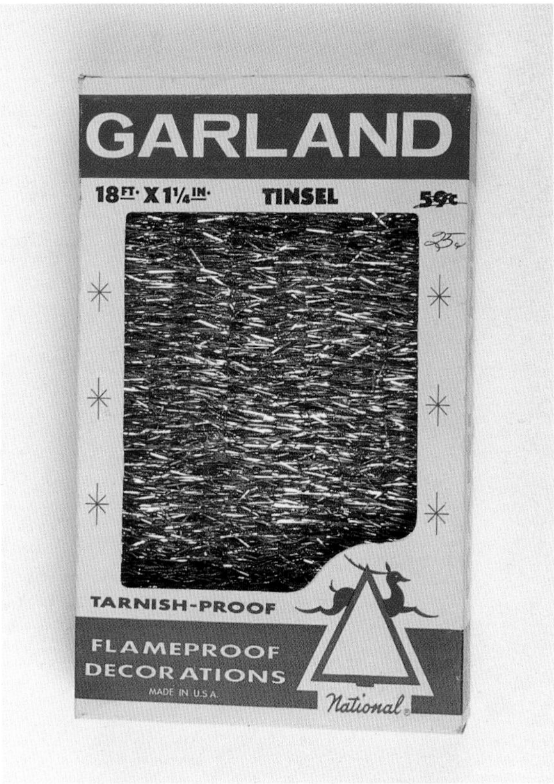

National Tinsel 18-foot garland in cellophane and silver tinsel. $14-18 for garland and original box.

Tinsel and cellophane roping from Japan. Early 1950s. $7-10 for 15-foot lengths.

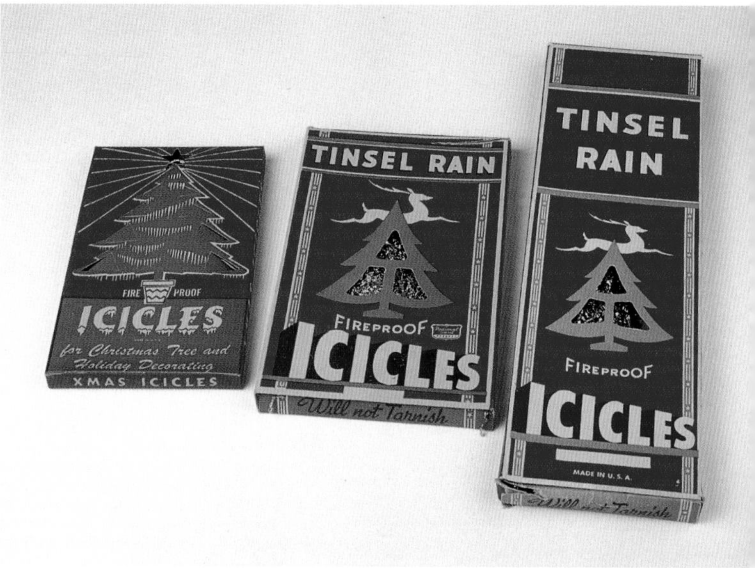

Representative examples of 1950s lead tinsel. U.S. $5-10 for box.

Tinsel ornaments from the U.S. in the original box. $50-55 for the whole set and box. $1-2 each.

Lead tinsel in silver and gold. $8-10 for box.

Wax Ornaments and Decorations

Some wax ornaments with metal hooks continued to be popular choices for tree decorations. Angels, Santa Claus figures, and snowmen appeared along with boots. All of these were hollow and painted with sparse detail. However, figural candles became more and more popular. While most were used as table decorations, many were hung on the branches of trees with string.

Caroler themed candles. Tavern Candle Company. $2-3 each.

Wax boot ornaments originally filled with tiny bits of candy. $3-5 each.

Various range of 1950s tree candles. U.S. $2-4 each.

Rudolph candles. Gurley Candle Company. $4-5 each.

Original set of potted wax plants and candle figures. Tavern Candle Company. $15-20 for complete set and box.

West German wooden Santa centerpiece with candleholders on both sides. Early 1950s. $10-15.

Wooden Ornaments and Decorations

Wooden nutcrackers and small wooden decorations continued to be brought home by servicemen serving in Germany. Around this time, Midwest Importers of Cannon Falls, Minnesota, and Kurt. S. Adler began importing nutcrackers. The first ones came from Erzgebirge, where the new East German government, keen on acquiring "hard currency," formed family-owned businesses into "people's cooperatives," subsidized production, and invariably exported all of what was produced in Germany. The Steinbachs and the Ulbrichts, two of the prominent families in the field, left Erzgebirge at this time.

The Steinbachs moved to Hohenhameln in the foothills of the Harz mountains and opened a new factory. Otto Ulbricht moved his family to Lauingen on the Danube and rebuilt his business there. Both the Ulbricht and the Steinbach families realized that in order to compete with the East German nutcrackers, they would have to produce nutcrackers which were far more elaborate, more creative, and much more tailored to the American market. They were quite successful in meeting this competition and both families made wonderful nutcrackers which became very desirable to Americans.

Occupied Japan wooden centerpiece which expands from 4 to 8-inches when totally unfolded. Mid to late 1950s. $25-30.

Assortment of German wooden ornaments. From 1-2-inches in height. Mid-1950s. $3-5.

Metal and Ceramic Decorations

Tinkling long-handled bells with clappers in a shining metallic lacquer finish of red, green, blue, fuchsia, silver, and gold were sold with loops for hanging from the branches of trees. Also making their appearance were white china bells with clappers—all hand decorated in a variety of colorful Christmas designs. These china bells were sold in sets of twelve with six round and six oblong-shaped bells.

Plastic Decorations

The 1950s really started Americans in the direction of using plastic decorations for the tree. Some of the first plastic ornaments offered for sale included a white angel with halo, choir boy with taper, reindeer, Santa, and Santa's helper. This American-manufactured set was made of hard plastic and was colored with silver. Bradford Novelty provided many of these decorations, while starting once again to explore the possibility of importing glass ornaments from Germany. Other plastic ornaments, in the shapes of snowflakes and icicles, were sold in clear or white which glowed in the dark. Interlocking snowflakes and plastic prisms were sold in crystal clear, blue, pink, green, or red. They were available in translucent, opaque, or metallic finishes. One popular item was a candy-striped cane made from cellulose acetate tubing distributed by Frank Paper Products Corp., Detroit, Michigan. These canes came in a tube and solid rod. The smaller sized canes, of the seven sizes available, were extruded in red and white cellulose acetate, while the larger ones were ribbon-wrapped and hollow.

Other plastic, silver plated ornaments in the shapes of lanterns, balls, and bells were also sold. Figurals for sale included angels, candles, altar boys, elves, reindeer, and Santas. One bargain assortment of 47 plastic ornaments, sold in 1951 by Spiegel, included balls, bells, reindeer, snowmen, Santas, and icicles. They were distributed by numerous companies including Plaxal, Inc., Rabar Plastics, Inc., and Modern Mittex Corp.

While glass still held the lead in sales, its great fragility opened the way for heavy sales of pure-white foamed styrene, metal-plated cellulose acetate, sheet cut and formed on machines in all sorts of shapes, and molded styrene balls, icicles, and other pieces. One set sold by Aldens in 1951 included six precision molded white plastic ornaments and a palate of five colors and brush for creative finishing at home.

High heat resistance, high impact strength, and flame resistance were all reasons thermoplastics made their entry into the Christmas tree ornament industry. In 1950 the retail dollar value of the ornament industry was in excess of $100 million dollars with plastics gaining quickly $40 to $45 million dollars of sales. Thirty million of this was spent on electrically illuminated decorations.

By the end of the decade, Americans found a new craze. They began to decorate Styrofoam balls by pinning on sequins, rhinestones, and bits of broken jewelry, combined with satin ribbon, gold cloth braiding, and miniature pearled string beads. This decorative treatment grew out of Styrofoam ornaments that were snow-white and crisp looking, but lacked the festive glitter of other ornaments. Thus, decorators suggested glitter and sequins at first, and it did not take long for companies to commercially produce these for sale. Many commercially manufactured ornaments were available, including some very stunning examples from Robert Offergeld of Place Noel in New York City.

In 1952, Marshall Rauch was the owner of a small textile company. Inspired by the newly introduced Japanese papier-mâché ornaments, and using processes employed in the Rauch factory, Rauch's employees developed the satin tree ornament. It was then patented. Rauch began selling the ornaments to the same accounts, mostly variety stores, that bought his threads and cords. Rauch's line gradually expanded to include a wide variety of ornament styles and materials as well as other Christmas items.

Schwab & Frank, Detroit, Michigan, produced a line of candy-striped Christmas canes made from cellulose acetate tube and solid tube. Frank Paper Products Corp. of Detroit distributed the canes both for use as tree decorations and to brighten Christmas corsages. The smaller sized canes, of the seven sizes available, are extruded in red and white cellulose acetate, while the larger ones are ribbon wrapped and hollow. The smallest measured 4-¼-inches while the largest was 28-inches. These canes were lightweight, easy to handle, and washable. At the same time, they were advertised as being strong enough to withstand the rough usage that Christmas packages were apt to undergo.

Bells, canes, and snow men of foamed plastic created from plastic modeling material that could be hardened in the oven found their places on the tree. These products enabled Americans to fashion some of these decorations as a family at home. "Saran" wrapped candy wreaths and other decorating ideas employing toothpicks, Styrofoam balls, and other miniature plastic ornaments helped to create a demand for five to six million pounds of plastic by the late 1950s. However, much of that plastic was employed as "phenolics" (special plastics used for molding and insulating) in socket bases of tree lights and vinyls for wire coatings. By 1950, according to a plastics industry specialist, plastic decorations accounted for almost ten percent of market sales. Steady growth though the decade made for a 25 percent share by 1959.

Polystyrene, a true synthetic plastic, was the material of this decade. It was made from ethylene (from petroleum or natural gas) and benzene (a by-product created by converting coal or coke). It was first produced commercially in 1937 when the Dow Chemical Company introduced Styron. Polystyrene was so important because of its negligible moisture absorption, its resistance to fading, and its excellent dimensional stability. By the late 1950s, ornaments and toys molded from polystyrene (hard plastic) quickly replaced those molded from polyethylene (soft plastic).

Clear molded plastic icicles with tops at the top appeared in the early 1950s. Due to their instant popularity, they quickly were manufactured in a white plastic and even in shades of pink and blue for those more adventuresome in their tree decorating schemes. Other plastic decorations with a metallic finishes appeared in sphere-shapes, bells, and stars. More expensive sets, including balls with figures, filigree balls, indent balls, and carolers' lamps, were sold in sets of 12 for $1.77.

An even more elaborate set of 18 sold for $1.89 and included angels with spread wings, reindeer (complete with antlers), Santa, and choirboys holding candles.

Styrofoam ornaments made a noted appearance on countless Christmas trees. One popular set of 41 ornaments sold for $1.49 by Sears Roebuck in 1953. Thirty-one pieces were decorated with multi-colored glitter while 10 larger shapes were up to 5-½" tall in bells, reindeer, snowflakes, stars, etc. Some Americans sought to return to a more natural look for their tree and relied heavily on white Styrofoam snowballs for their decorations.

One of the more revolutionary ideas was a 23-inch white plastic tree complete with 150 all plastic ornaments which included 6 assorted circle designs, 6 stars, 12 angels, 60 bells, 12 fancy ornaments, and 48 bell-shaped ornaments in assorted styles. The complete set sold for $5.49.

Snow domes or globes as sometimes termed by collectors had a Renaissance in the 1950s after World War II. They enjoyed immense popularity prior to the war due in part to an RKO Radio Pictures release, *Kitty Foyle: The Natural History of a Woman,* staring Ginger Rogers, who was also recognized for her performance by winning Best Actress at the Academy Awards. A snow globe with a bisque figure of a young girl sledding down a hill from an elegant castle is the transition between major scenes. When these globes reappeared after the war, they were produced employing both a plastic base and a plastic dome top. Japan and Hong Kong were the principal suppliers during this decade. There are thousands of different holiday designs from which to choose. Santa, cottages, snowmen, tree scenes, and carolers abound.

In the mid-1950s and well into the 1960s, Kurt S. Adler imported the first quality made snow globes from West Germany. These snow globes, also termed snow domes, featured Christmas scenes with Santa and other holiday characters.

Some of the most popular silver-coated plastic ornaments were produced by the Bradford Novelty Co. in the early 1950s. Left to right: Deer, $4-5; church, $5-7; angel, $5-6; choir boy with candle, $7-8.

Assorted deer in plastic. Early to mid-1950s. $4-5 each.

Three deer, coated with gold-colored plastic. $5-6 each.

Assorted musical instruments. All 3" to 4" in length. From the mid to late 1950s. $4-6 each.

Fluorescent plastic tree ornaments which all glow in the dark. Mid-1950s. $10-15 each.

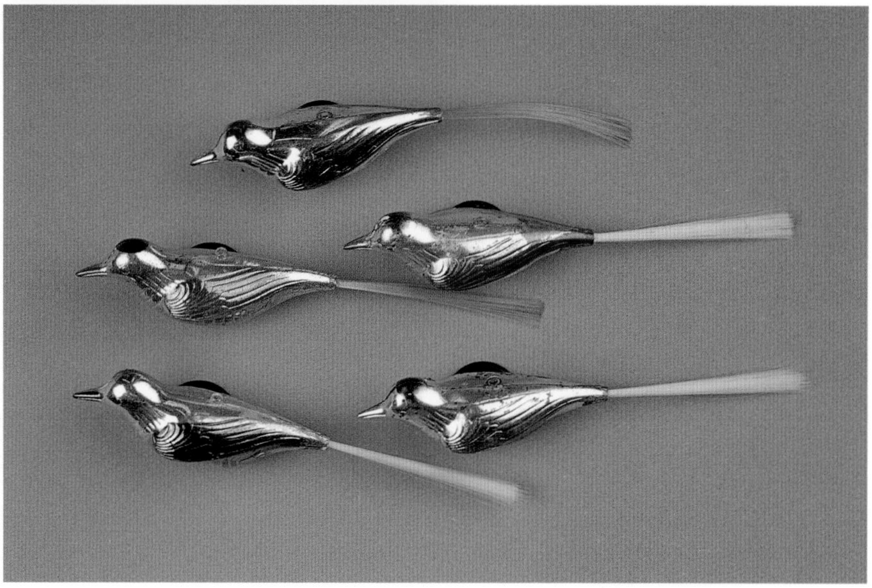

Silver coated plastic song birds with fiber tails. Marketed by Sears Roebuck in early to mid-1950s. $7-10 each.

Elaborate plastic ornaments from the early 1950s from Bradford Novelty. Three to four-inches in height. $8-12 each.

Four representative examples of simple silver coated plastic ornaments from Bradford Novelty. Four-inches in height. $4-6 each.

American made plastic stars with silver coating. $10-15 each.

More elaborate plastic ornaments, including two tops and a chandelier ornament in the middle. Five-inches in height. $10-12 each.

Rudolph the Red-nosed reindeer, marked "Robert L. May." On the left is a rare top for a 45-record player, $75-85; on the right, two reindeer ornaments, $8-12 each.

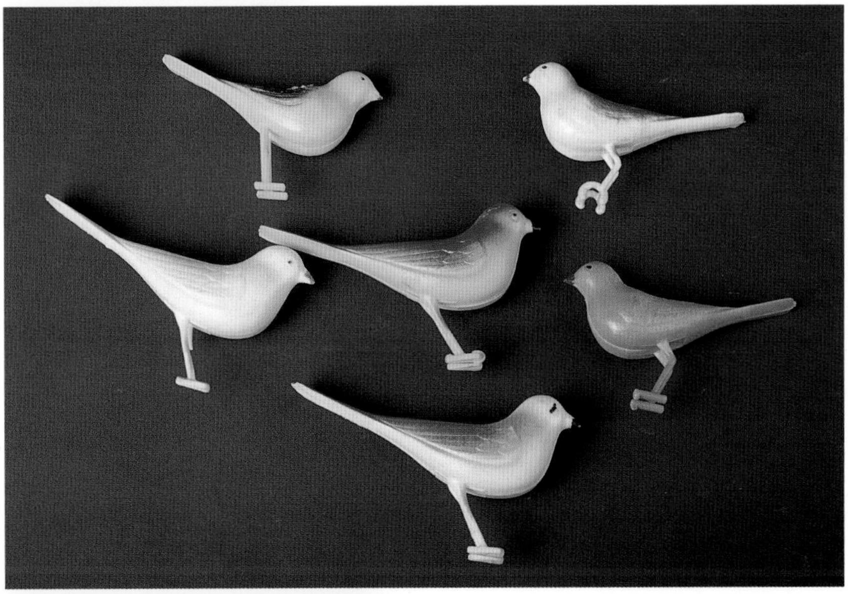

Plastic birds from the late 1940s on into the early 1950s which were snapped onto the tree through their molded feet. $3-4 each.

Two to five-inch Santa ornaments. On left, $25-35. Santa on right, the back of which contains a opening for an electric light when placed on the tree, $40-55.

Assortment of plastic Santa ornaments from this decade. Santa on skis, $12-18; Santa ornament, $6-10; Santa in sleigh, $18-20; and two white trimmed Santa ornaments on the right, $12-18 each.

Set of five Santa Claus figures made of hard plastic. Each one is equipped with a different tool. $40-50 each. $350-400 for the complete set.

Hard plastic set of three wise men in the original box. $50-55 for boxed set.

Hard plastic ornaments in clear, red, pink, green, and blue. All snap together to create a three-dimensional ornament. $4-5 each.

Array of red plastic boots from three to four-inches. All contained candy at one time. $3-10 each depending upon size.

Elf ornaments made from early 1950s to 1956. $7-10 each.

Glow-in-the-dark Icicles. Most common color: white. Rarer colors: pink, blue, and green. $1-2 each. $15 for boxed set.

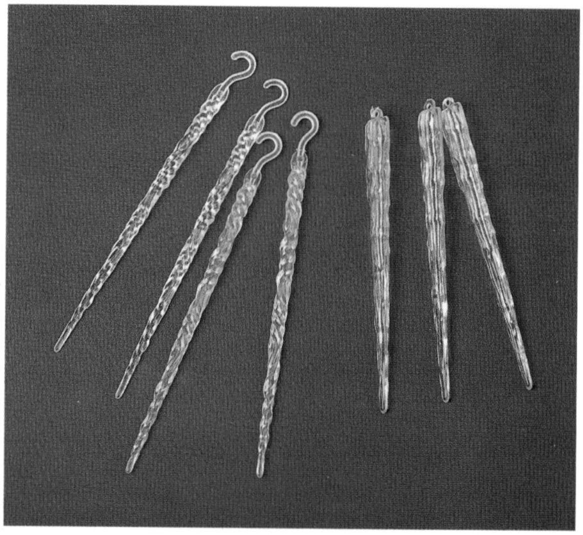

Two varieties of clear plastic icicles. Those on the left are simple, hang on the branch flat-types, $.50-1.00 each. Those three-dimensional type on the right are attached by means of a hook through the opening on top, $1.00 each.

Under Our Trees

Nativity Scenes

Inexpensive nativity sets which lit and played music were manufactured in Japan. Each was lit by a candelabra-sized electric bulb and contained plastic figures combined with a fiberboard stable and a green "grass" mat base. Heartland of Wisconsin and many other companies who produced plastic decorations for our trees produced inexpensive plastic nativity sets. Most of these sets were simply airbrushed or painted with very little detail. But they were extremely affordable and appealed to many mail order companies who could easily ship them to rural areas.

Also sold were large nativity sets manufactured in the U.S. Zone of Germany. With a stable constructed of rustic looking coarse-grained wood, these papier-mâché figures ranged in size from 6-½-inches to the tiny 1-inch baby Jesus.

Marolin in Steinach, which did lie in East Germany, produced many of these sets. They were stamped such to avoid tariffs on communist goods (to be explained in the 1960s chapter). Julius Weigelt joined Richard Mahr in the 1920s, and they produced countless crèche figures. After the Second World War, Steinach fell behind the border in Communist East Germany where private business was firmly discouraged. They gradually ceased the production of these cribs. Precious few of these sets were imported into the United States.

Composition figures were produced before the war by Pfeifer (later named Tipple-Topple), Elastolin, and Lineol. Lineol completely ceased making crèches in the early to mid-1930s as the Third Reich was born. As the war ended, Lineol was appropriated by the East German state and no Communist state could sanction the production of crèches. However, some limited production continued to the mid-1950s when their composition figures started to be replaced by new ones made of plastic.

Large nativity figures from 1954, West Germany, 4" to 14" in height. Complete set including camel, wise men, shepherds, sheep, animals, and holy family. $300-350. Individual figures, $25-70 each.

Sturdy tree stands were necessary as Americans decorated more floor-to-ceiling trees than ever. The basic stand was the red and green metal variety. For those with some extra dollars, a family could purchase a "Snow man" tree stand with a holiday scene lithographed on a red enameled base.

Cardboard crèche scene, American printed and marketed by Catechetical Guild of St. Paul, Minnesota, in the 1950s. $40-45 complete in box.

Large 36" wide cardboard crèche printed in the USA, primarily sold by Sears Roebuck and Montgomery Ward through their mail order catalogs. $50-60.

Italian crèche scene with Swiss music box in back. Carved from wood. Mid-1950s. $60-70.

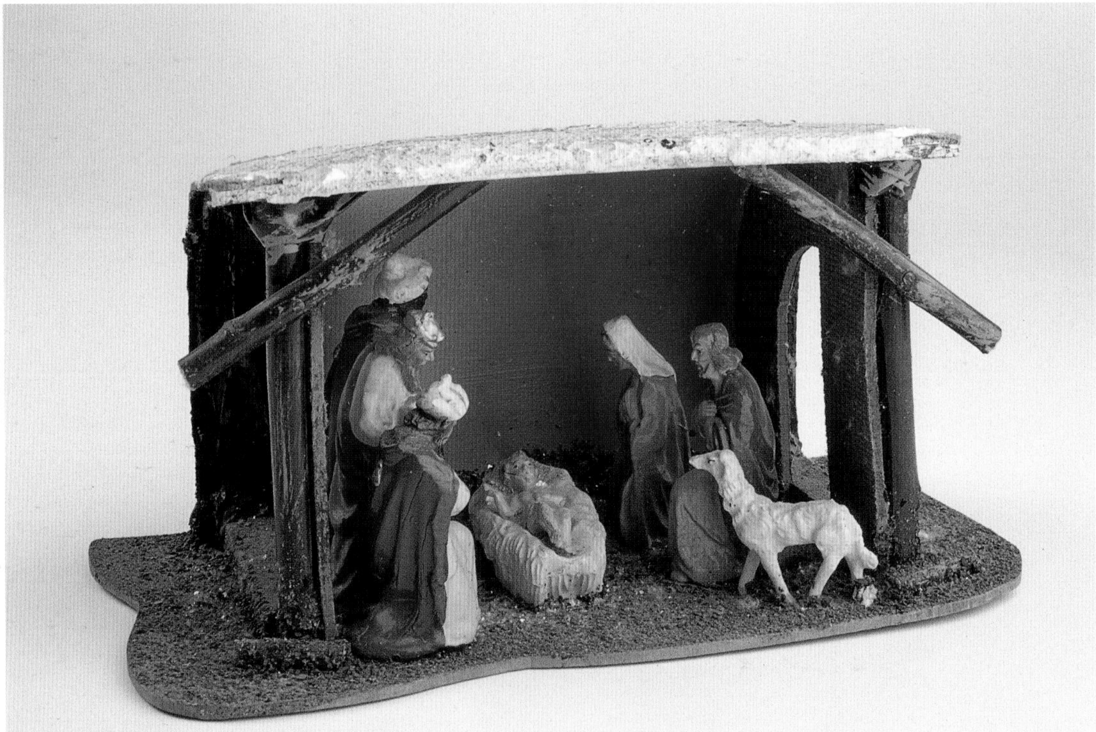

Typical Japanese-manufactured crèche scene of this decade. Figures are glued onto the base. $35-40.

Fences

While simple red and green wooden fences continued to be made, plastic and metal fences also appeared. One set was produced with wooden poles and woven, hoop green wire and came in an 18-inch square. Also popular were little 6-inch sections of white plastic picket fencing which could be assembled in a variety of shapes under the tree.

Village Houses

In the early 1950s, miniature villages continued to be popular under the tree. Churches average about 6-½" high while individual houses averaged about 4". The earlier houses were constructed entirely of cardboard with cellophane windows and doors. However, later versions included cardboard houses mounted on plastic foam bases.

Miniature Christmas houses in a 3-¼" size continued to be placed on mantles, on tables, and under trees in various village scenes. But most houses were much smaller than those used in previous decades. All were, of course, lit with a bulb. The ingenious Christmas scene creator put the light strings under a white-cotton blanket, cut slits for the bulbs and inserted them through the base so that a perfect setting might appear.

Early 1950s Japanese-manufactured houses, all of which have holes in the back for the insertion of electric lights. $20-25 each.

Larger style 1950s Japanese-manufactured houses, all of which have holes in the back for the insertion of electric lights. $25-35 each.

American-manufactured houses for use under the tree, each of which contains a hole in the back for the insertion of an electric light. $20-25 each.

Brush Trees

Brush trees continued to be a popular decoration on table arrangements as well as under the tree. During this decade, sizes up to nineteen inches were made. Some of the Japanese-manufactured trees had chains of multi-colored glass beads draped in a spiral fashion on the trees. The applied snow was not as fine as it was in earlier decades. It was applied in clumps and often had glitter sprinkled on it. In order to fit the Fifties home décor, these trees appeared in some very novel colors, including a bright pink, pale and dark blue, deep red, and even a yellowish-green.

Large 12-inch Japanese-manufactured brush trees, complete with glass beads. Note the flat cylinder base, typical of this decade. $40-50 each.

Rarer Japanese-manufactured red brush trees. Small, $6-105. Large, $25-35. Other colors included pink, blue, purple, and white.

Assortment of Japanese manufactured brush trees from this decade in the typical green color with white flocking. $10-20 each.

Animals and Figures

One of the most popular figure settings of the 1950s was the three plastic wise men in silver-colored metallic finish with gold-colored trappings. Each wise man was molded in great detail and stood 4-¼" tall. This decade more than any other found Americans turning to hard plastic for nativity figures, as well as animals and other human figures for their village scenes under the trees. Many of these were manufactured by companies who supplied model train hobbyists with similar train accessories.

Papier-mâché "egg carton" type Santa figures, snowmen, and boots continued to be made by a variety of manufacturers. While there were companies on the East Coast in New York State, the majority of these pieces were produced in Milwaukee, Wisconsin, by the same producers of the 1940s. However, from Milwaukee, Wisconsin, in the 1950s, the "Pulpco" name was marked on Santa candy containers, boots, and snowmen which that firm produced, helping collectors to more easily date marked items to a general period.

While celluloid ceased to be produced in any large quantities during the later part of this decade in the United States, Japan continued to produce and export many such items to the American market. Items between 1945 and 1952 are "Occupied Japan" pieces and are often marked as such. Celluloid items were especially great give-aways at Christmas by many businesses and even educational institutions due to their relative inexpensiveness. Therefore, these animals and figures continued to be used in great quantities at Christmas for decorating purposes.

Silver-painted celluloid deer from Occupied Japan. Five-inches in height with glass eyes. $25-30 each.

All Japanese-manufactured celluloid items for play and for use "on ponds" (mirrors) under Christmas trees. $8-10 each.

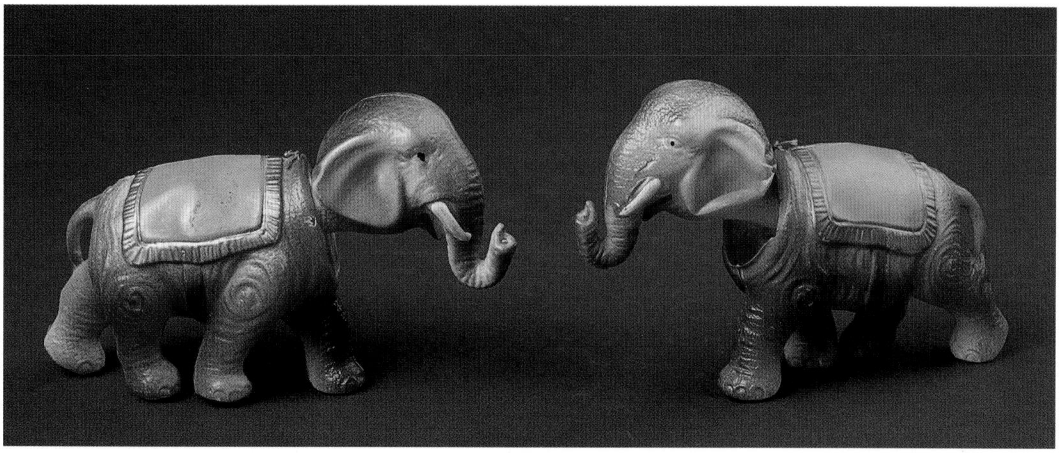

Nodding elephants marked "Occupied Japan." $65-75 each.

Marked "Occupied Japan." Left to right: Bear, $20-25; dog, $15-20; and sheep, $20-25.

Cellulose acetate American-made items by Irwin in the period just before hard plastic was perfected during World War II. Left to right: Standing Santa, $15-20; Santa on metal skis, $40-45; miniature Santa figure, $8-10; large Santa with celluloid sled and reindeer (antler-less). $40-45.

Array of cellulose acetate items. Left to right: Santa rattle, $20-25; Santa roly-poly, $25-30; reindeer with Santa sleigh (red and white), $65-75; Santa on sled with toys, $50-60; reindeer with sleigh (red, green, and white), $85-95; and taller Santa rattle, $60-70.

Cellulose acetate Santa figures produced by Irwin. Smaller, 5", $50-60, and larger, 12", $90-110.

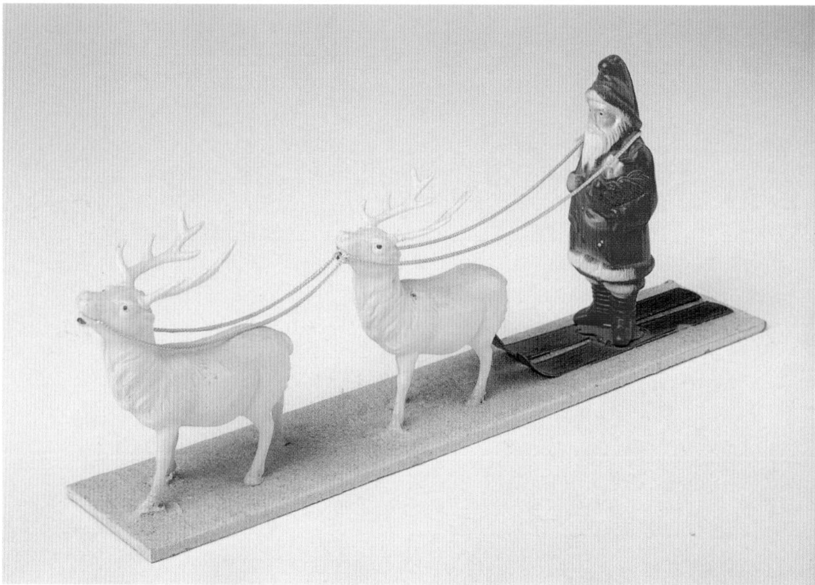

Late 1940s into early 1950s celluloid Santa with two reindeer on wooden flocked base. $85-95.

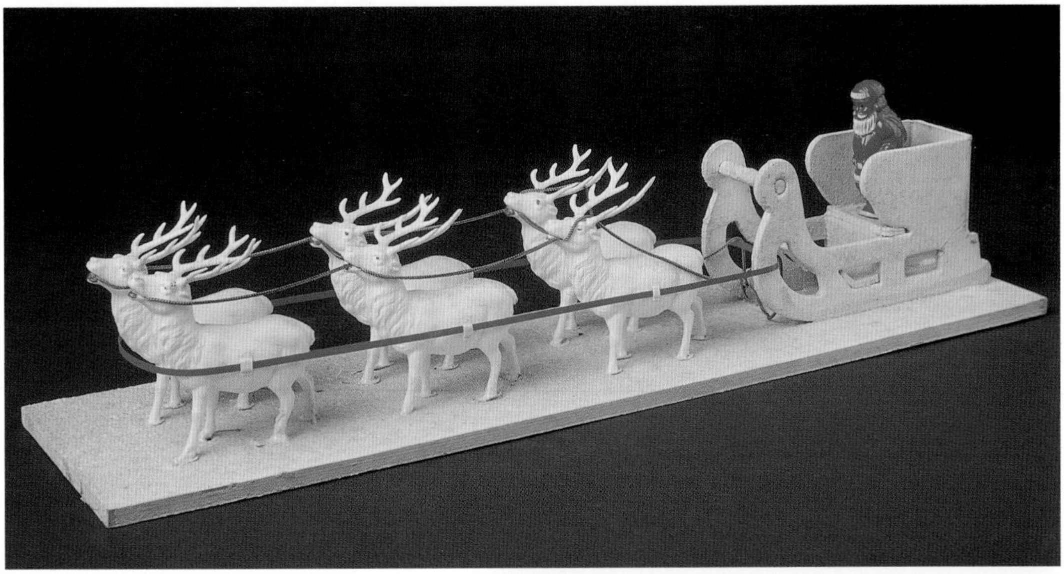

Late 1940s into early 1950s celluloid Santa with six celluloid reindeer on heavy flocked cardboard stock. $75-85.

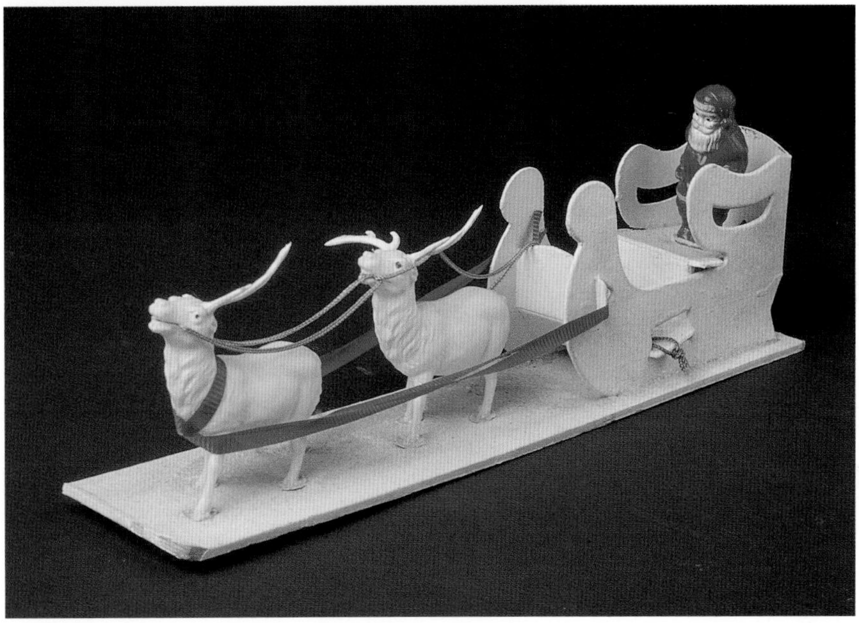

Simple late 1940s into early 1950s celluloid Santa with two reindeer on heavily flocked base and sleigh. $55-65.

Hard plastic items continued to proliferate as American manufacturers attempted to outdo each other, creating new designs for items each Christmas. Since this was the period in which European customs and traditions were shunned, these unbreakable toys and decorating items became symbols of a period in time when American pride reigned supreme.

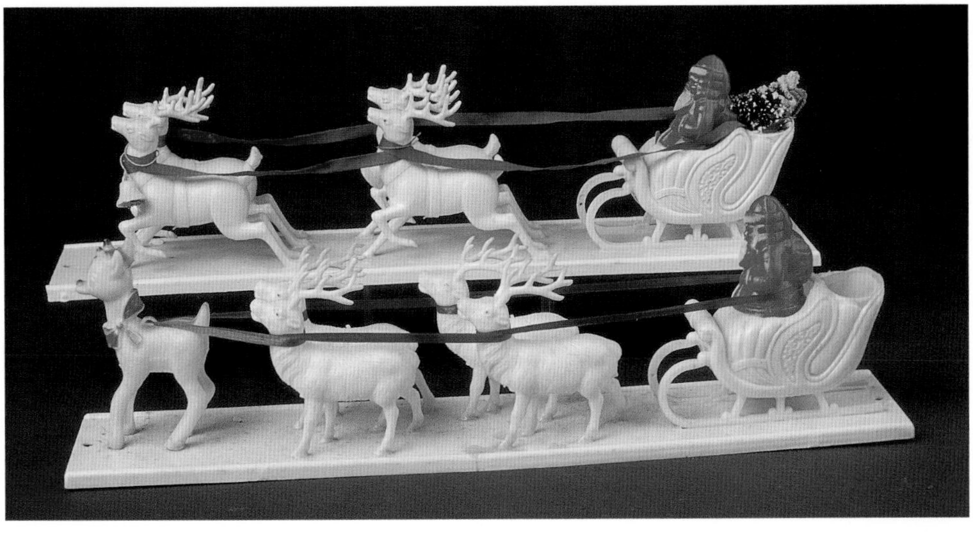

Mid-1950s plastic sleigh: the rarer example is the one with Rudolph in the front. Front sleigh, $40-50. Back sleigh, $55-65.

Hard plastic sleigh in typical colors of the late 1950s. $40-45.

Boxed set of mid-1950s reindeer and Santa sleigh set. Manufactured by Irwin Corporation, USA. $30-35; $60-70 with box.

Bradford Novelty USA marketed hard plastic sleigh with Santa and reindeer. Mid-1950s. $25-30; $55-65 with box.

Mid to late 1950s silver coated plastic sleigh and reindeer sets. Larger, $40-45. Smaller, $25-30.

Two Santa toys in hard plastic on wheels from the mid-1950s. Car, $75-85. Santa pull toy, $90-100.

Very large 12" Santa toy. Originally a candy container. $225-250.

Santa pull toy, hard plastic. Originally a candy container. $90-110.

Large 8" hard plastic car with movable wheels. $250-300.

Hard plastic Santa on reindeer with movable wheels. $140-150.

Hard plastic Jack-in-the-box. $75-85.

Plaster and bisque items continued to be sold, but were not as popular as their unbreakable plastic counterparts. Most of these items were manufactured in Japan, a few made in West Germany, and even a few were manufactured in the United States, such as the plaster and vermiculite banks.

Plaster items, all manufactured in Japan. Left to right, Santa, $45-55; Santa (fairly common), $10-15; Snow Baby-type Santa in a boat, $90-100; Snow Baby-type Santa on a house, $100-110.

Assortment of more common sleigh and reindeer sets. $20-30 each.

Smaller ceramic items. All from Japan. Left to right: Santa match holder, $50-60; miniature Santa ornament, $8-10; Santa figure, $25-30; choir trio, $50-60.

Hard plastic nodder.
Rare. $60-70.

Larger 6" bisque Santa which was marketed as a candy container. Japan. $60-70.

Large 24" plush Santa with rubber face, hands, and boots. USA manufactured. $40-50.

Plush Santa figures. While many were sold in stores as presents for children, even more were given as premiums by gas stations and other stores at holiday time. Left to right: Santa pajama holder (with pajamas still inside), $50-60; plush doll with fat body, $25-30; Santa with thinner body, $35-45.

A 1954 plush Santa wind-up musical toy. USA manufactured. FAO Schwarz marketed product. $75-85.

Early 1950s Santa baby dolls. Note the baby face with the beard. Sold by Sears Roebuck. $50-55 for non-musical dolls. $70-80 for dolls with a wind-up key in the back. "Jingle Bells" is the melody.

Santa in chair with list. USA. Plaster and vermiculite bank. $75-85.

Plaster and vermiculite banks continued in popularity in this decade. Very inexpensive (often no more than 25 cents), these banks were very popular with children, who often used them as a Christmas savings program. With no hole in the bottom for coin removal, they were broken with a hammer, the money removed, and the money spent on Christmas presents for family members. Whereas thousands upon thousands of these banks were produced, not many survived because "they were used and broken."

Plaster and vermiculite banks. USA. Santa head, 13", $45-55; large 22" bank, $50-60.

Santa in easy chair bank, USA, plaster and vermiculite bank, $60-70. It is shown here with a standing Santa bank of the same composition and era, $45-50.

Made in Japan cardboard snow-flocked Snowmen. $50-60 each.

Japanese-manufactured Santa figures from cardboard, with paper faces and cotton beards. $55-70 for larger sizes. $30-40 for smaller sizes.

USA cardboard papier-mâché Santa figures. Left to right: $40-50; $50-60; $25-35.

More elaborate "Made in Japan" Santa figures with composition faces. $55-65.

USA cardboard papier-mâché Santa figures. Left: $45-55. Right two (white): $45-55.

Also very popular in this decade were those Japanese-manufactured battery operated and wind-up toys made from metal and celluloid. While some were used as toys and as table and mantle decorations, many of them found their way to the bottom of the tree in the Christmas Putz or Snow Village scene, finding renewed popularity in this decade. While the items were not so much European in nature, these Santa figures and toys from Japan and the United States were revered and placed on cotton batting sheets under the tree.

Wind-up celluloid headed Santa with metal body on metal deer covered with brown hide-type fabric. Japan. When wound, he hops along the floor or table. $180-190.

"Occupied Japan" wind-up celluloid toy. Reindeer heads bob up and down as the Santa top with celluloid toys goes round and round. $200-210.

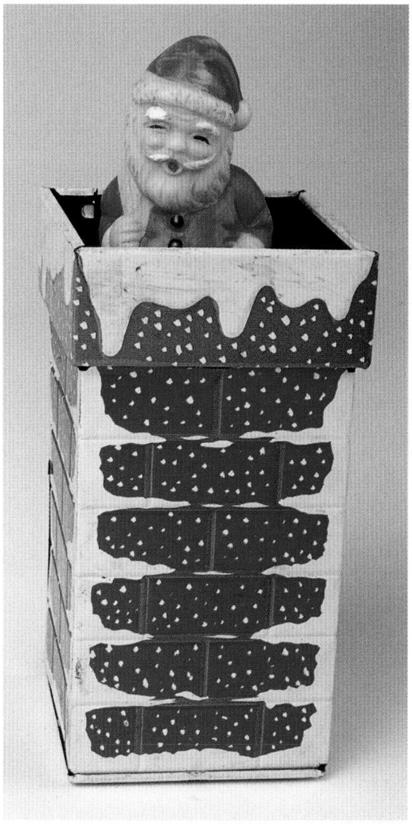

Wind-up celluloid full-bodied Santa in metal chimney. Santa goes up and down when toy is wound. Japan. $135-145.

Wind-up celluloid faced metal Santa toys from Japan. Left to right: Santa with bell and sign, $100-110; Santa with bell, $90-100; Santa with plastic balloons and bell, $140-150.

Wind-up toys from Japan. Left toy is entirely made of metal. Toy skis across flat surface and Santa moves ski poles when wound, $165-185. Celluloid-faced Santa with cotton beard. When wound, he turns pages of his story book and nods his head. $130-140.

Wind-up Santa and sleigh from Japan. Early 1950s. He sleighs across flat areas and rings his bell when wound. $145-165 with original box.

Battery operated Santa toys from Japan. Left: Santa rings bells, moves head from side to side, and eyes light up, $160-170. Right: Santa rings bell and moves head, $80-90.

Battery operated Santa toys from Japan. Left to right: Santa on house doubles as a bank. As money is inserted, he rings a bell and his eyes light up. $185-200. Santa on a little wagon moves across the floor when he is operated. His eyes light up as well. $200-220. Santa drum set. When operated, his head swings back and forth, his eyes light up, and he plays the drums with his hands and foot. $225-250.

Celluloid toys, from Japan, meant for children. Late 1940s into early 1950s production. These toys doubled as rattles and teething rings. $120-140 each.

Indoor Electric Lighting of Our Trees and Homes

One of the more intriguing developments of the 1950s was lighting the tree by placing a floodlight at the base of the tree, rather than using the traditional strings of lights. This especially gained popularity in the latter part of this decade. In 1956 Americans purchased over 4,000 million domestic and imported Christmas bulbs. This number about equaled all lamps purchased for residential use. Outdoor lighting had increased 67 percent since 1947, with about 25 percent of the lighting sold being used outdoors. Almost $90 million dollars was spent each year on lights. This demand caused phenomenal growth in the Christmas tree lamp industry. One of the giants included Noma lites, who alone used 85 million lamps a year in its sets. Noma had its roots formed in 1925 and continued to grow under the guardianship of Henri Sadacca. Through diversification that took the seasonal curse off his lighting business, Sadacca headed toward an integrated, full-line appliance company. But that, too, seemed doomed and he arranged a spin-off in January 1953, whereby the former Decorative Lighting Division became Noma Lites, Inc. Sadacca became board chairman, and Joseph Ward was appointed as president.

Noma introduced 10 to 15 new specialty lighting items every year, with electric lights in each one of them. The official sales season opened with the Toy Show in March. Flurried activity continued into June with sales beginning to pick up, and finished on December 25th. "You work all year for just one day," stated Joseph H. Ward, president of Noma Lites, Inc. in 1957. On December 26, the company started its annual check of inventory left in dealers' and jobbers' hands. Inventories were high at times. On June 30, 1952, Noma had an inventory of $6.3 million—a figure that rose steadily for the rest of the year. In 1952 they did a business of $11.5 million with $16.5 million in 1953, a gain of 32 percent. Noma controlled 35 percent of the total U.S. market for Christmas lighting. Noma was both an assembler of parts and a manufacturer. It bought the wire, bulbs (from General Electric and Westinghouse), and other parts for the outfits while producing its own plastic items. Each year it had almost 200 different lighting items for sale.

Items in a 1954 catalog included a multiple indoor outfit set of 7-light fancy figure which included angel, dog, cat, bird, rabbit, Santa, and snowman plastic figures that fit over independently burning replaceable candelabra base bulbs. Both series and multiple bubble-lite sets of seven and eight, along with replacement lamps, were sold. Also sold that year were illuminated wreaths with nine red translucent plastic bells that spelled out "Merry Xmas." The traditional red cellophane and chenille wreaths with a lighted candle or Santa figure in the center were still offered. Multiple candoliers in three, five, eight, and nine lights in ivory-finished plastic appeared with their traditional tree top angel lite. Outdoor weatherproof specialties including snowman, Santa, candy cane, reindeer, star, and candle shapes finished out the pages of this very extensive catalog.

One of their most popular products included small Visca trees, electric candle tipped. Available in green or white, this 16-inch tree had a star top and 16 multi-colored "candles" glowing from a bulb inside. It sold for about $3.29. A 17-inch size in white or green Visca was wired with nine sockets for 15-volt miniature lamps. This same type of tree was available in 25-inches, wired with 18 lights. The largest size was 33-inches and was wired for 28 lights. Instead of regular lamps, many individuals used plastic wonder stars or other novelty lights.

But most elaborate were bubble light trees. Pitted with sockets, these green or white Visca trees were perfect apartment trees or perfect trees to place indoors for all to enjoy. Sizes ranged from 16-inches (9 bubble-lites) to 26-inches (18 bubble-lites).

Bubble lights enjoyed increased popularity as different varieties, including shooting stars and oil filled tubes, were produced. Multitudes of colors appeared in the clear glass tubes. In all, approximately thirty plus different styles and brands of bubble lights were manufactured. As stated before, the word "Lite" was used by Noma for their Glo-Lite (a "generic" brand of Noma), Reliance, and Renown brands. "Light" was used by Paramount for the company's Sterling (a "generic" brand of Paramount), Holly, and Grant sets. Of the many styles available, Noma's and Paramount's are the most common. The Polly, Peerless Shooting Star, Yule Glow, Amico, candelabra Rocket Ships, the candelabra oil Paramounts, and the candelabra Shooting Stars are the most difficult to find. A most unusual bubble light is the Peerless Shooting Star. Peerless Shooting Star lights have a small amount of heavier liquid that does not mix with the regular liquid. The bubbles form in this thick liquid, then spring up into the thin liquid, but because of their weight, cascade back down, similar to a 4th of July fireworks fountain or a juggling effect. The way to distinguish an unlit Shooting Star from another type of unlit bubble light is to turn it upside down and study the fluid in the tube. If it separates into two obvious types, the larger section being the lighter fluid, you probably have a Shooting Star.

In the late 1950s, the Tinkle Toy Company of Youngstown, Ohio, updated the revolving paper shade by forming shades of plastic, with a small aluminum pinwheel balanced on a pin inside. Many Americans remember these shades since they were extremely popular at that time. These shades were intended to be hung over or near the bulbs, but not actually on them as, by this date, the majority of electric lights used 120-volts instead of 15 and generated a great deal of heat. The new shades looked more like birdcages, and finding one without the original box to identify its use could easily confuse the younger Christmas collector.

Predominant colors in miniature and candelabra bulbs included red, blue, green, and orange, all in varied hues and shades. In 1951 General Electric switched to the use of aluminum for their lamp bases, with other manufacturers soon following suit. In 1955 General Electric produced a pink color bulb, opening the door to some experimentation with the basic colors previously used. New colors introduced included yellow, fuchsia, peacock blue, and turquoise green. In 1959, two-color pear-shaped bulbs were introduced with bright swirls of color-red on white, green on white, red on yellow, blue on white, or orange on white. Meant for indoor use only, they cost 17 cents each or 85 cents for a package of five.

In the 1950s, ceramic enamel coatings were sprayed on both indoor and outdoor lamps. Since the flutes on outdoor intermediate-screw-bases were indistinguishable from a distance and caused an uneven distribution of color, smooth bulbs were adopted.

It was reported by *Consumer Bulletin* in December 1958 that in the series-wired sets Japanese bulbs had a relatively short life—only a fraction of that of American-made bulbs. In the multiple-wired indoor candelabra-base sets, the average life of American-made and Japanese-made bulbs was about the same. Of the outdoor lights, the Japanese bulbs were found to be superior to those made in the United States.

There were still milk glass figural lights available from Japan, the primary figurals being houses, churches, Santas, lanterns, and snowmen. However, their popularity waned as Americans turned to Italian miniature lights. But Paramount (the same producers of bubble lites) still produced an eight-lamp set of Mickey Mouse characters in the late 1950s. Each candelabra lamp burned independently. In 1959, Continental Products of Chicago, Illinois, advertised a set of Mickey Mouse Christmas Tree Lights in a set of eight. The imported multi-colored bulbs were shaped like Walt Disney characters. Each bulb burned independently. However, this was an unauthorized production item and the sets quickly disappeared from the market, making them quite rare today.

Several different companies in the late 1950s produced special sets of twinkle lights operating on transformers. The lamps (either cone or tube shaped) were C-6 miniature based, 6-8 volt, used on a special cord, wired in multiple, and connected to a transformer. The transformer, though, was too heavy and impractical for extensive decorating.

The rising technology of the 1950s created a desire for something new, and out of Italy came the "midget" lights—tiny 1/2" bright lights. These midget lights came, not in the usual eight on a string, but with up to 35, 50, or even 100 bulbs per string. First marketed in 1950, they were equipped with shunt devices so if one burned out, the others would remain lit. And most of them were designed in straight-line construction. The first midget lamps were wired directly onto the cord. Replacing a burned out lamp was sometimes impossible. Later, American and Japanese sets used lamps with tiny screw bases.

Some popular sets included 20-light poinsettia sets created of snow-white flowers, the center of each which contained a replaceable independently burning lamp. If one went out, the others stayed lit as long as no bulbs were removed. Another set employed multi-petaled red rose buds.

Twinkle lamps in a candelabra and intermediate size also made an appearance in sets of seven and fifteen. Each translucent colored lamp blinked and burned independently. To accompany lights such as this, Noma created translucent colored plastic reflectors in red, green, amber, blue, and clear. Twinkle lights gained popularity in the 1950s for use on candelabra and intermediate sets. These cone-shaped lamps, painted in bright transparent colors, were pleasing when mixed with steady burning lamps, especially in outdoor decorating.

However, the lamps were still wired on the intermediate series basis and sets were not foolproof. The wires were thin and broke easily, and it was more frustrating going through 35 or 50 lamps to find the problem instead of the old-fashioned eight. Consequently, consumers who did not have the time, patience, or knowledge to check for the problem trashed thousands of these sets each year.

Strings of Italian midget lights introduced in the 1950s were also manufactured outside of Italy in Germany, Holland, and Japan. General Electric added twinkle lamps in four translucent colors—red, yellow, green, and blue—as well as clear glass in 1956. The 6-volt twinkle lamp incorporated a new bulb shape resembling that of a tight rose bud. The development of this lamp with a built-in flasher turns indirectly from similar lamps produced by the Ontario Lamp Works of the Canadian General Electric Company for the Royal Air Force during World War II. They flash because of built-in bi-metal trips similar to those used in thermostats. When the lamp lights, heat from the filament causes the bi-metal strip to bend away from the lead-in wire. This breaks the circuit and the lamp goes out. As the bi-metal strip cools, it bends back to its original position against the lead-in wire and lights the lamp. These first 6-volt midget lights had a screw base and a 3/4" diameter bulb. A set of 20 with cord sold for $5.50. A card of four replacement bulbs ran about 50 cents.

Another innovation in 1957 was the lighted ice lamp. Offered in pearl, topaz, emerald, turquoise, garnet, and ruby, the crystal coating on the lamps diffused yet transmitted the sparkle of the filament located near the center of a spherical bulb about 2-3/4" high. Designed for 120-volt service, either indoor or out, these bulbs could be used base up, base down, or base horizontal. This first year they were manufactured in limited quantities to test consumer strength regarding this innovation. In 1959, they were priced at 29 cents each or $4 for a string of seven.

Quite similar were snowballs coated with white Styrofoam when unlighted. Their colors included blue, red, green, violet, white, or yellow. They were priced at 39 cents each or $5 for a string of seven in 1959.

One popular item was a plastic Santa figure that came in a variety of sizes. Illuminated by a candelabra-based bulb, this freestanding figure was made of lightweight durable plastic. Often the year of manufacturing is stamped right onto the base of the figure. Commencing in 1949, Royal introduced a snowman and a Santa Claus made of hard plastic, holding a bubble light in the left hand of each. The first figures held Royal "Crown" lights; many figures are found by collectors holding different bubble lights, the original lights having been replaced over the years. The snowman and Santa were advertised as children's night-lights and as holiday decorations. While the Santa figure is easier to locate, the snowman is often quite elusive to collectors.

One marvelous musical device was created in the 1950s. This set of 12 tarnish-proof metal bells is connected by cord and was attached anywhere on the tree. A motor inside a metal house with Santa on the roof near the chimney set his hand in motion, pulling the cord, and tinkling the bells on the tree. The cord was created for a six-foot tree and sold for $3.89.

One of the most familiar figures of the 1950s was the Noma Santa with outstretched arms which served as a tree top, table decoration, or wall plaque. Made of unbreakable translucent plastic, he glowed with sparkly color and was the tree top for many youngsters growing up in the 1950s. Retailing at one dollar, his affordability explains his wide-spread appearance on so many American trees during this decade.

Another musical piece in the early 1950s was an illuminated nativity set. A small turntable revolved as a Swiss music box in the base played "Silent Night," creating a moving procession of wise men and shepherds to worship at the manger. An inside bulb illuminated the brilliant star. The stable was made of heavy fiberboard; the 10 figures were delicately airbrushed, hand-painted, and glued on the base. On the back can be found the story of the first Christmas along with the manufacturer's name, Clemco. Numerous musical crèche scenes and illuminated altars were sold in this decade.

The tree of the 1950s was lit electrically as before, but bubble lights were the rage of the day and they were used on many trees. Miniature lights were introduced but were not used to a large extent, since Americans became captivated in the late 1950s with artificial trees and floodlights for lighting them.

Floodlighting of trees became popular in the 1950s with the appearance of flocked trees and aluminum trees since electrically lighting these trees could be extremely dangerous. Due to aluminum's reflective quality, revolving multi-color floodlights slowly bathed trees in arrays of red, blue, green, and amber. Retailing for about $10, the floods almost went hand-in-hand with sales of aluminum trees. Ball-type floodlight holders in ivory and gold housings held a 150 watt light which was either used in clear or blue to light white flocked trees in picture windows across America.

Some decorators suggested that electrically lit trees be highlighted with floodlights for a more natural appearance. While red or orange lamps alone tended to make foliage look unnatural, adding floodlightings in blue or green could remedy that look. White floodlighting on a tree with all green or all blue bulbs defined its shape more clearly.

Boxed sets of tree lights were marketed under numerous brand names by different stores over this decade. "King-O-Lites" was the marketing label for those sold by Gambles in 1959 while GLOLITE was marketed in the early to mid-1950s. Western Auto Stores marketed "XMAS-LITE," fitted with General Electric lamps.

Multi-painted color round bulbs were an alternative to the regular cone-shaped lamps ordinarily used. One such set was marketed by Paramount, employing G14 (120-volt) lamps in a set of seven. Another set was marketed by Glo-Ray in bright holiday colors and had a line with berry beads for holding lights in position.

Lighted Ice lights (multi-colored glass balls with coated clear plastic crystals) were sold in sets of seven. Light colors included green red, orange, blue and white.

The terms used in the 1950s to describe the sizes of bubble lights produced were "Candelabra" and "Miniature" base. These lights usually sold for 25 cents each. Noma bubble-lites were a popular choice in the 1950s in sets of eight or nine, each lamp having a spring clip for attachment to the branches. There was an eighteen inch spacing between the sockets and three or four feet of lead with an add-on plug.

However, among the most exciting innovations of this decade were those midget lights, often advertised as "Starlight" Miniatures. With American-made green or white cords, these early sets were equipped with imported bulbs with "permanent contact" shunt-devices so that as long as the bulbs were secured tightly in their sockets, the entire set would remain lit if one bulb burned out. Montgomery Ward sold candles, roses, and simple midget sets in 1958. These first sets had bulbs that were wired directly into the strings.

Italian rosebud lights concealed midget lights in the middle of red plastic roses. These were not only for use on trees, but also on mantles, on tables, and in wreaths. Paramount "twinkling" lites, in sets of 20 6-8 volt bulbs in assorted colors, came complete with a transformer and safety fuse device.

Bubble-lite trees continued with immense popularity in the early 1950s. Available in the popular 18-inch and 26-inch sizes, these trees were available in white or green. The larger varieties had independent burning candelabra lamps. These larger 36-inch trees came equipped with a toggle type line switch. Santa, nativity-themed, and snowmen plastic decorations in multitudes of designs and sizes were sold to be hung on walls and in windows. When lit, all of them were bright and cheery.

1954 *NOMA Lite* catalog cover.

REPLACEMENT LAMPS

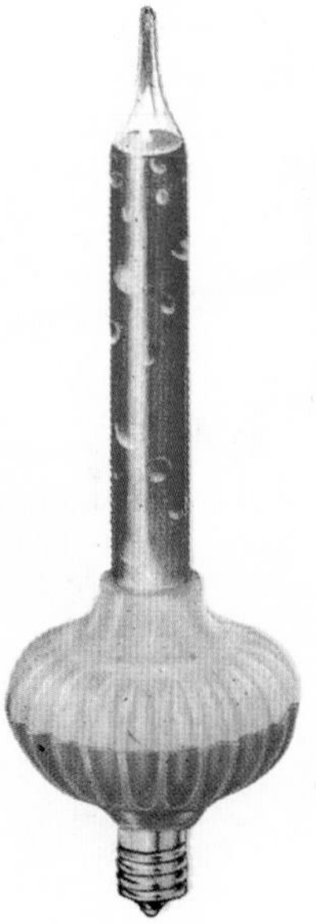

No. 420 — SERIES BUBBLE-LITE REPLACEMENT LAMPS. 15 volt miniature base lamp. Flame resistant plastic housing. Assorted colors. 10 to individual display box with 10 spring clips. 200 to carton. Weight 16 lbs.

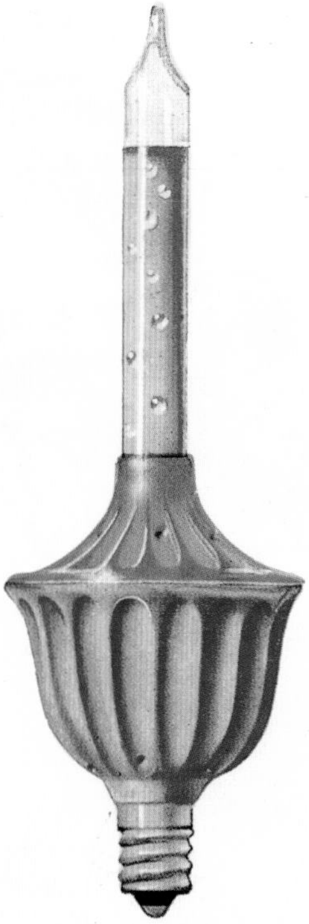

No. 520 — MULTIPLE BUBBLE-LITE REPLACEMENT LAMPS. 120 volt candelabra base lamp. Assorted colors. 10 to display box with 10 spring clips. 100 to carton. Weight 11 lbs.

G6 LAMPS. 15 volt ball shaped miniature base series type. Packed 10 assorted to box. 1000 to carton. Weight 6 lbs.

C6 LAMPS. 15 volt cone-shaped miniature base series type. Packed 10 of one color or 10 assorted to box. 1000 to carton. Weight 10 lbs.

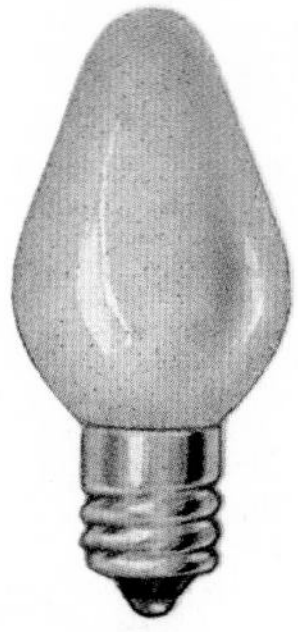

C7½ LAMPS. 120 volt candelabra base multiple type. Weatherproof, scratchproof, nonfading colors. Packed 10 assorted or 10 of a color to box, 500 to carton. Weight 9 lbs.

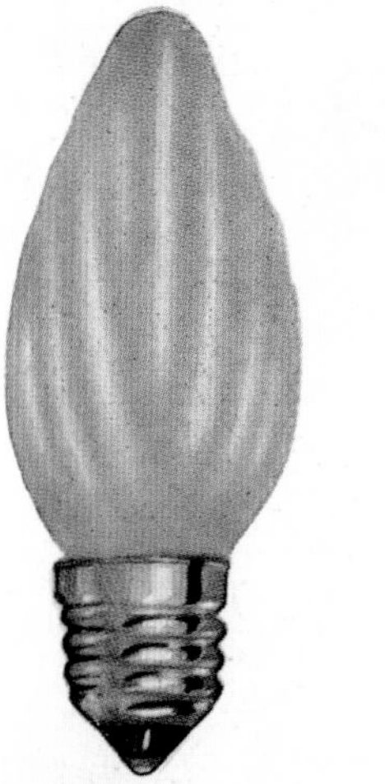

C9½ LAMPS. 120 volt, 10 watt intermediate base. Inside color coated to protect finish. For outdoor sets. Packed 10 assorted or 10 of a color to box, 500 to carton. Weight 21 lbs.

Page from 1954 NOMA *Lite* catalog.

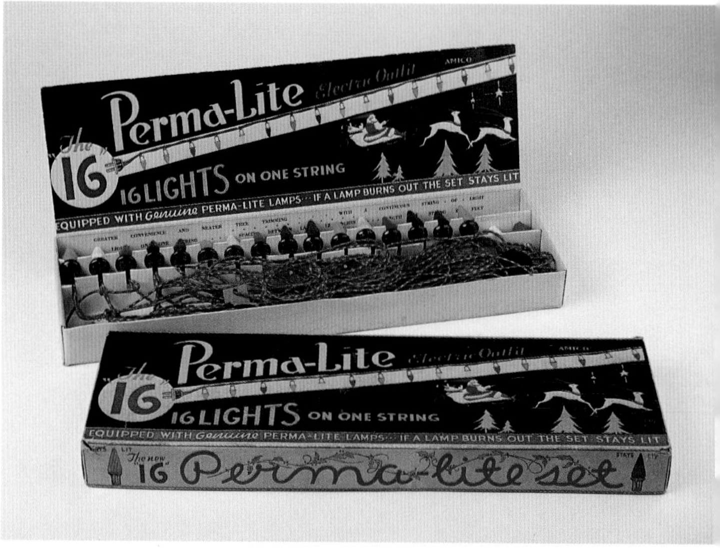

Perma-Lite brand light set with sixteen lamps. Mid-1950s. $15-20.

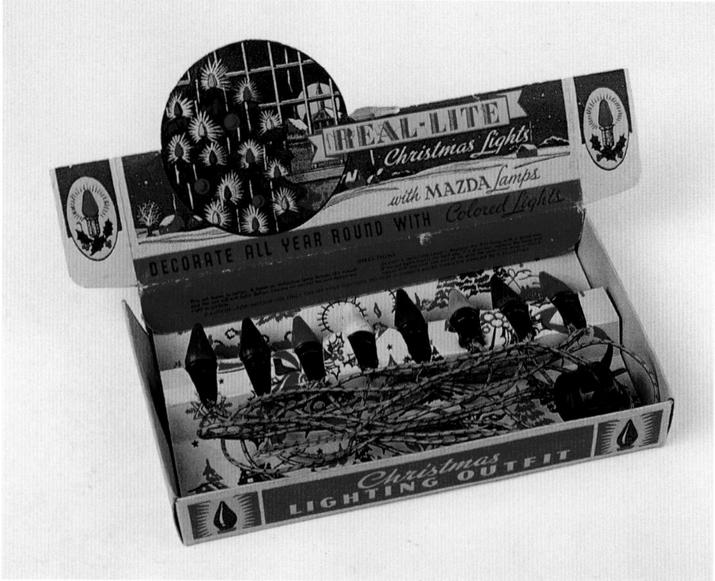

"Real-lite" brand of miniature-based lamps sold in the early 1950s. Series lighting, so if one went out, they all went out. But these were the most inexpensive lights available on the market. $35-45 boxed set.

Santa Lites brand light set with fifteen lamps. One of the more inexpensive sets available at that time. $20-25.

Paramount candelabra-based lamps sold in the early 1950s. Parallel lighting, so if one bulb burned out, the others stayed lit. $15-20.

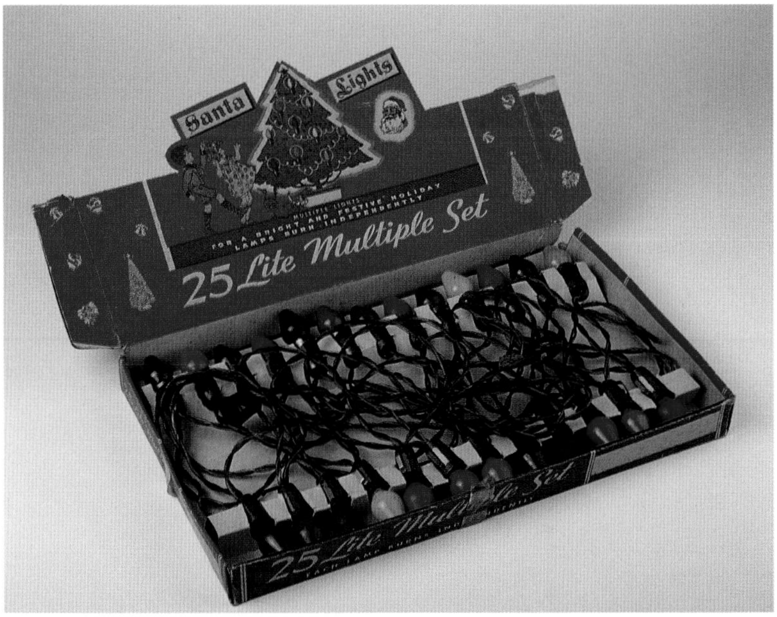

Santa Lites brand light set with twenty-five lamps. Note the variations of 1950s colors available. $30-35.

NOMA brand light set with twenty lamps. Each burned independently in parallel wiring. More common. $15-20.

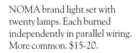

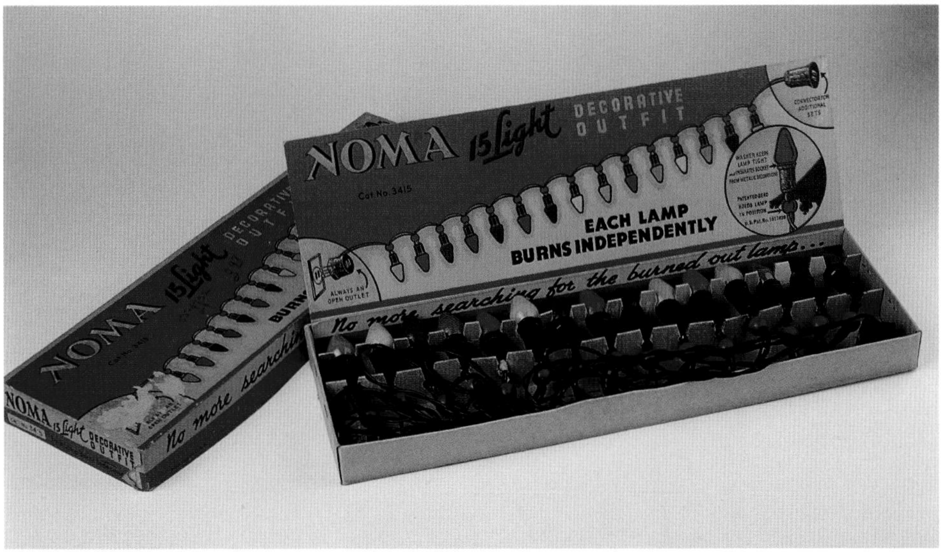

NOMA brand light set with 15 lamps. Each burned independently in parallel wiring. More common. $10-15.

Holly-Lite brand set with fifteen lamps. Mid-1950s. Note the pink colored lamp. $20-25.

Glo-lite brand set with seven lamps. Mid-1950s. $5-10.

Happy-Time brand set with fifteen lamps. Mid-1950s. Simple set with seven lamps. $10-15.

Boxed set of Miller outdoor lights. These were extremely inexpensive and among the most popular choice for outdoor decorating. $8-12 for boxed set.

Assorted boxes of miniature-based lamps sold as replacement lights. $5-8 for boxed set.

Assorted boxes of candelabra-based lamps sold as replacement lamps. (Note that the exception is the Westinghouse Mazda lamp box from the 1940s.) $3-5 for boxed set.

Boxed set of NOMA intermediate-based bulbs for outdoor decorating. Bulbs were painted on the inside so snow and the elements could not lift the paint from the bulbs. $8-10 for boxed set.

Assorted plastic reflectors from the early 1950s in a variety of shapes. There is a shallow curve to the cup shape. $3-5 each.

Plastic reflectors from the mid-1950s manufactured by NOMA for placement behind the lights. $10-15 each.

Assorted larger plastic reflectors from early 1950s in star shapes. Deep curve to cup shape. $3-5 each.

Original boxed sales set of NOMA halos for use with candelabra and tree lights. Plastic. $3-4 each. $100-125 for boxed set.

USALITE twinkling lights from the mid-1950s, complete with a heavy transformer which acted as a shunt to twinkle the lights on the tree. $85-95 for boxed set.

Fancy set of USALITE twinkling lights from 1954. Boxed set complete with transformer. $100-120 for boxed set.

NOMA's twinkling lights from the mid-1950s. Boxed set complete with transformer. $80-90.

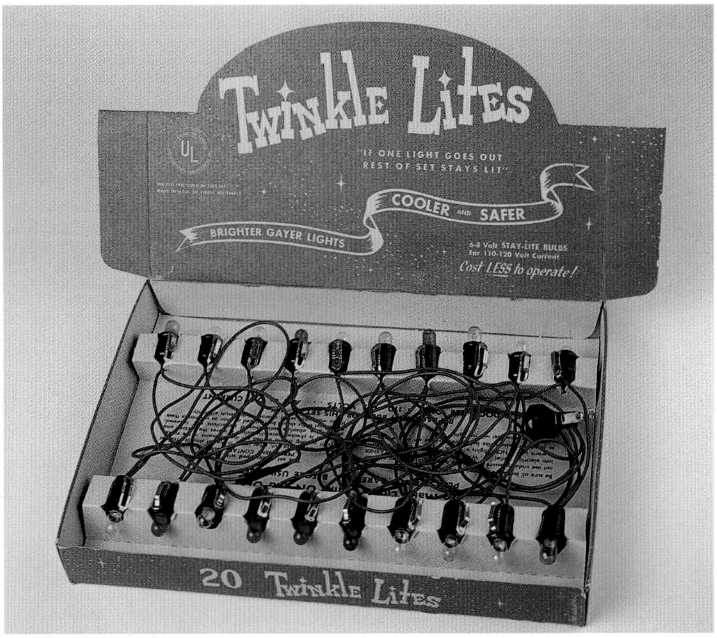

Later set of twinkling lights from the late 1950s without the large, heavy, black transformer box. $65-75.

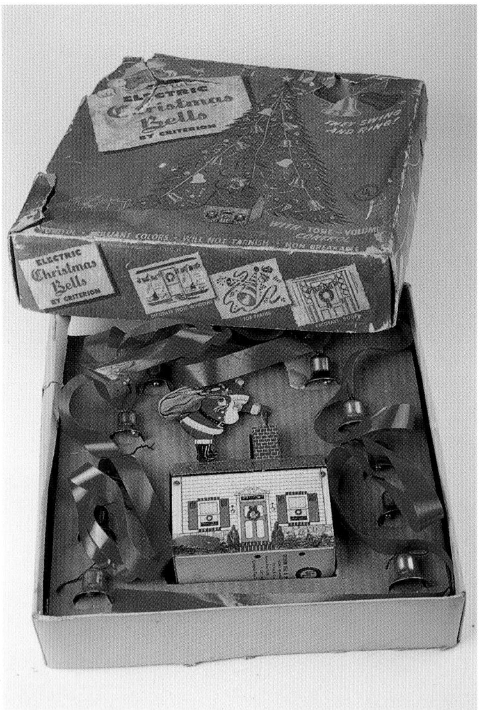

Electric Christmas bells for the tree. The metal house with metal Santa hid the electrical device which would ring the metal bells on wires by means of electric current. Mid-1950s. $120-130 for boxed set.

Assorted cellulose-acetate light covers from NOMA, dating from 1947 into the mid-1950s. Top to bottom, left to right: Dog, $25-30; yellow bird, $15-20; red cardinal, $35-40; Santa Claus, $40-50; snowman, $25-30; angel, $30-35; blue bird, $15-20; and red bird, $15-20.

1950s era imported figural milk glass light bulbs from Japan. Candelabra-sized lamps. Birds, $3-5 each; houses, $4-5 each; Santa Claus figures, $15-20 each; lanterns, $1-2 each; Santa head, $35-45 each; bells, $3-5 each; snowmen, $8-10 each.

Boxed set of 1950s Royal bubble lights, $100-125 for a boxed set with two typical simple candelabra-based lights sets from this decade. $40-45 each.

Candelabra-sized Japanese milk glass figural bulbs in unauthorized Walt Disney character shapes, 1959. $50-60 each.

Paramount bubble light boxed set with miniature-based bulbs from the mid-1950s. $100-110 for boxed set. $8-10 each.

Paramount bubble light boxed replacement set with candelabra-based bulbs from the mid to late 1950s. $120-135.

Close-up of Paramount candelabra-based bulbs. $8-10 each.

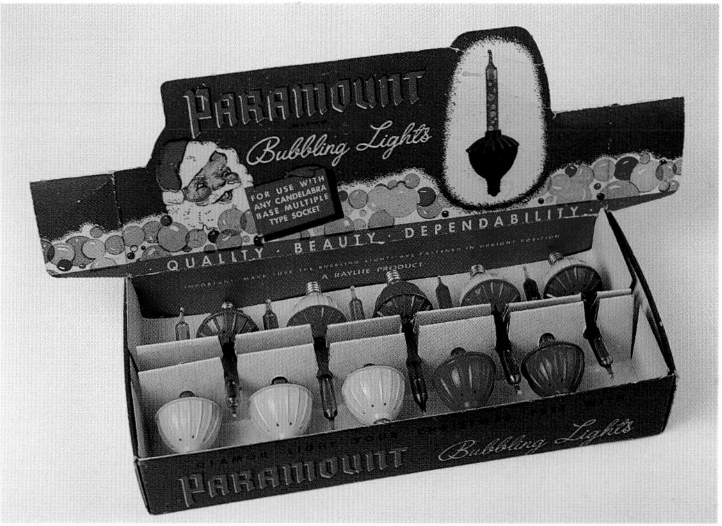

Boxed set of candelabra-based bulbs from Paramount. Late 1950s. $85-95.

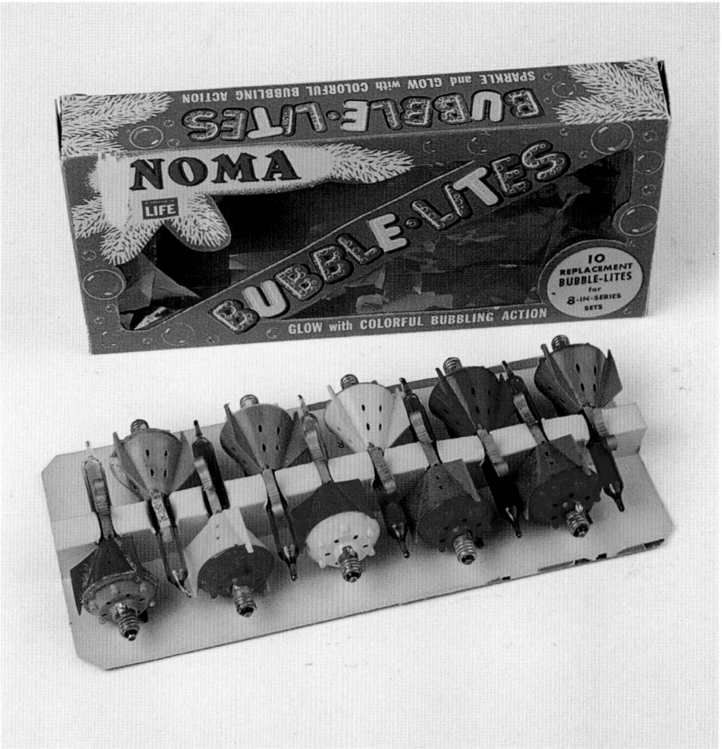

Box of NOMA rocket ship bubble lights. 1961-62. Boxed set of 10 candelabra-based bulbs. $400-450.

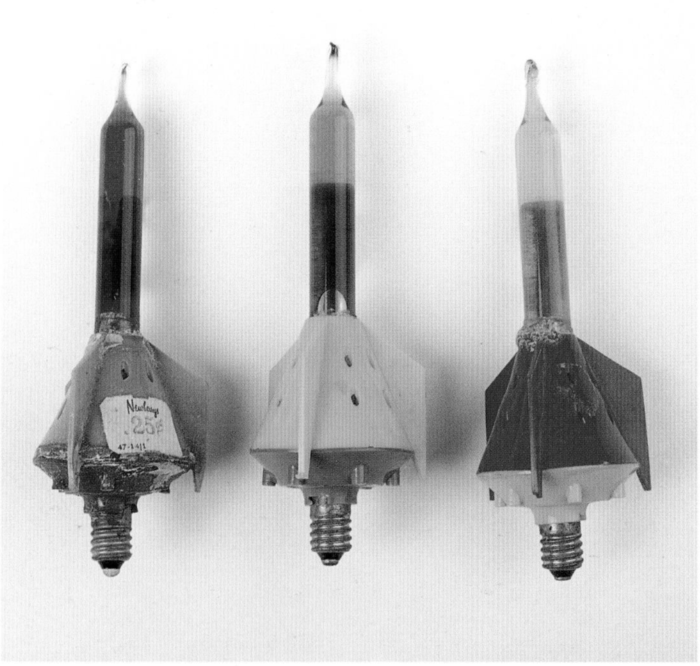

Close-up of rocket ship bubble lights. $45-55 each.

NOMA replacement bubble light boxed set with candelabra-based bulbs. $90-110 for boxed set. $5-7 each.

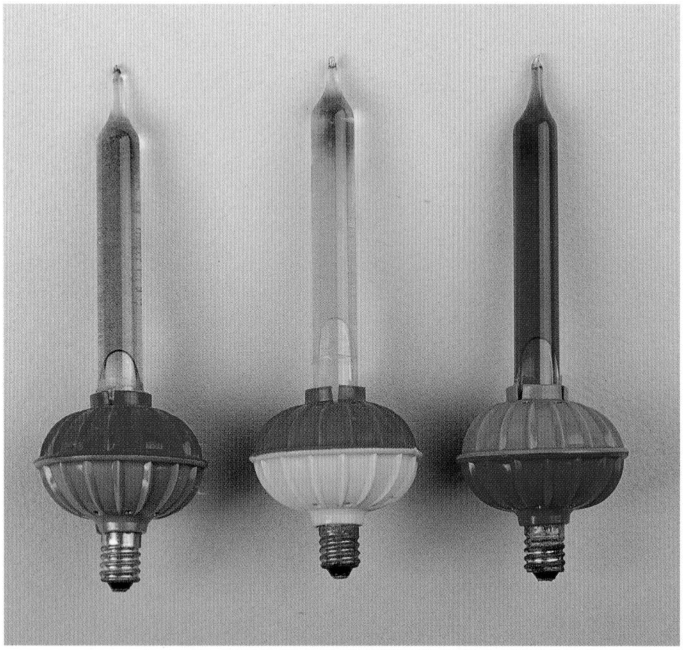

Three Renown Biscuit bubble lights. $30-40 each.

NOMA replacement boxed set of ten miniature-based bulbs. $85-110 for boxed set.

NOMA replacement boxed set of ten candelabra-based bulbs. $85-110 for boxed set.

GLOLITE chenille-wrapped cardboard wreath with NOMA bubble light in candelabra-base size. $45-50.

Large 36" bubble light tree for candelabra-based bulbs. $275-325 without bulbs.

Eighteen-inch Visca tree with plaster base. Glass tubes at the ends appear to be candles at the tips of the branches. Lit by standard-based bulb inside. Late 1940s into early 1950s. $85-95.

Twelve-inch Visca tree with a metal base. Glass tubes at the ends appear to be candles at the tips of the branches. Lit by standard-based bulb inside. Mid to late 1950s. $65-75.

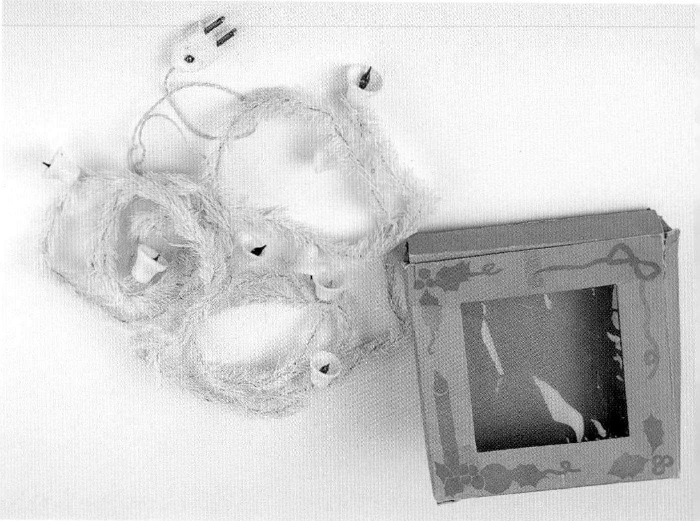

Very early set of Italian midget lights where the bulbs were directly wired into the cord. White plastic bells cover the bulbs on a garland-type cord for draping on the Christmas tree. $55-65 for boxed set.

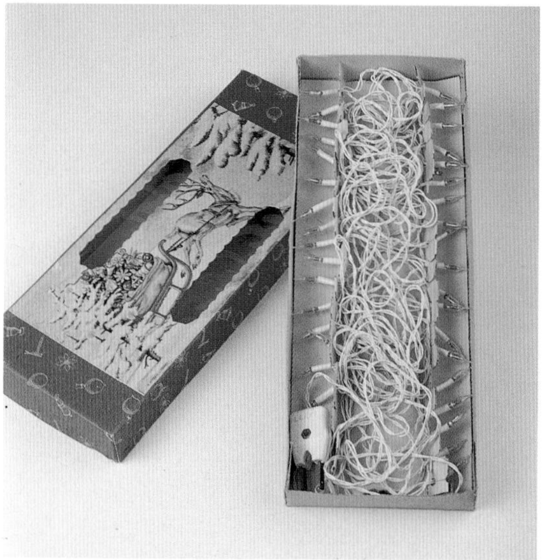

Early set of Italian midget lights where bulbs were wired directly into the cords. $20-25 for boxed set.

Early set of Italian ornament-lighted midget lights. Bulb was placed behind plastic shield which caused silver interior to glow when lit. Bulbs were directly wired into the cord. To be replaced, the bulb was unwired and a new bulb was wired into place. $120-130 for boxed set.

Early set of Italian purple plastic midget lights. Bulbs directly wired into cords. $45-55 for light set.

Early set of Italian red plastic midget lights. Bulbs directly wired into cords. $65-75 boxed set.

Fancy Italian cellophane tree complete with bulbs directly wired into the cords hidden in the tree branches. Early 1950s. $110-120.

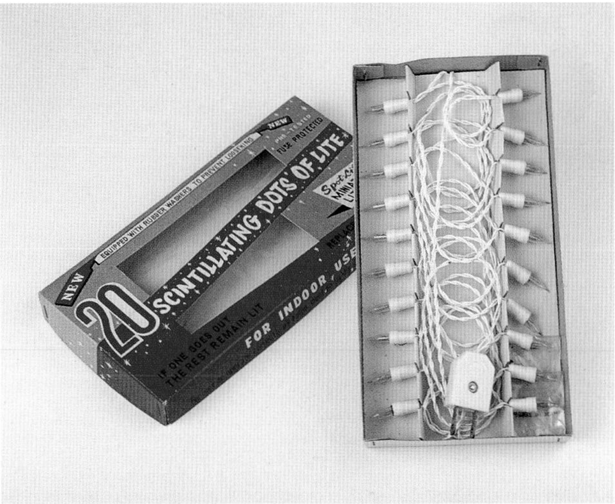

Simple set of Italian midget lights where bulbs screwed into the socket. These lights followed the sets where the lights were wired to cords. $25-35 for boxed set.

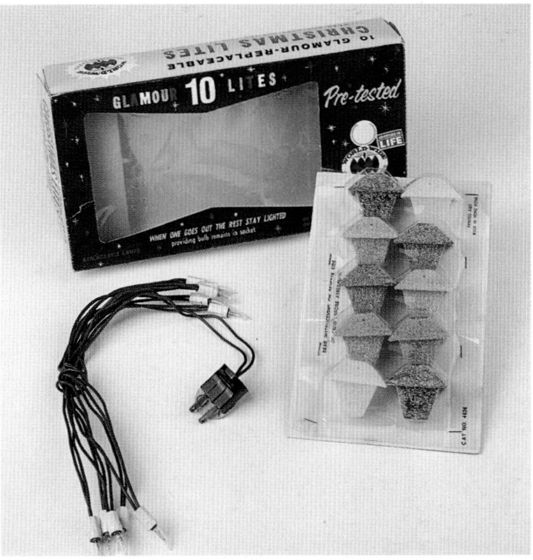

More elaborate set of Italian figural midget lights where the bulbs screwed into the sockets. These lights followed the wired-into cords sets. $100-110 for boxed set.

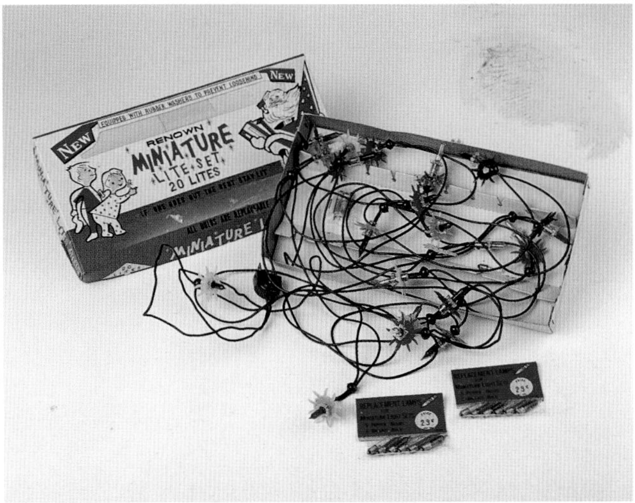

Simple set of Italian figural midget lights where the bulbs screwed into the sockets. These lights followed the wired-into cords sets. $45-55 for set.

A more elaborate set of Italian figural midget lights where the bulbs screwed into the sockets. These lights followed the wired-into cords sets. $55-60 for set.

Fancy lanterns with mirrored backs. Italian midget light set. Late 1950s. $50-60.

A more elaborate set of Italian figural midget lights where the bulbs screwed into the sockets. This set is unusual in that the plastic figural scenes hid the bulbs that illuminated the white plastic half-circles. These lights followed the wired-into cords sets. $110-115 for set.

Italian midget light set. Fancy set of bird cages. Late 1950s. Bulbs push into sockets. $80-90 for boxed set.

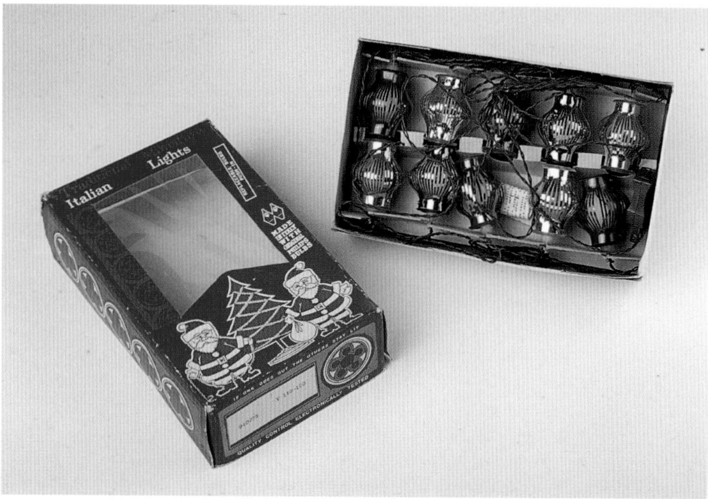

A more elaborate set of Italian figural midget lights with lantern shapes where the bulbs were pushed into the sockets. These lights followed the screwed-into-sockets cords sets. $65-75 for boxed set.

Italian midget light set. Clear geometric plastic globes over bulbs. Late 1950s. Bulbs push into sockets. $50-60 for boxed set.

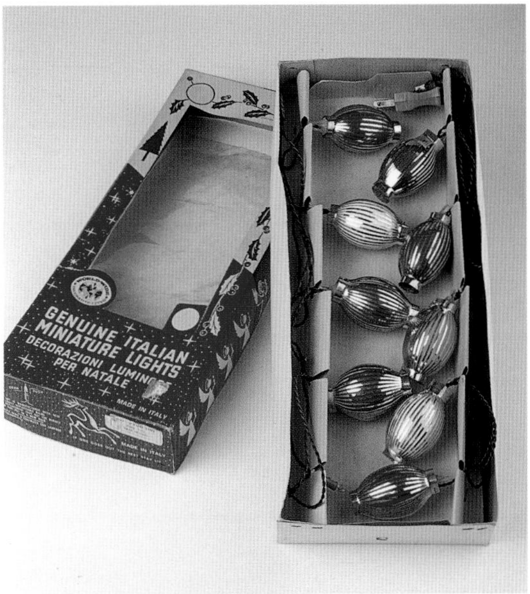

Italian midget light set. Egg-shaped foil shapes. Late 1950s bulbs push into sockets. $55-65 for boxed set.

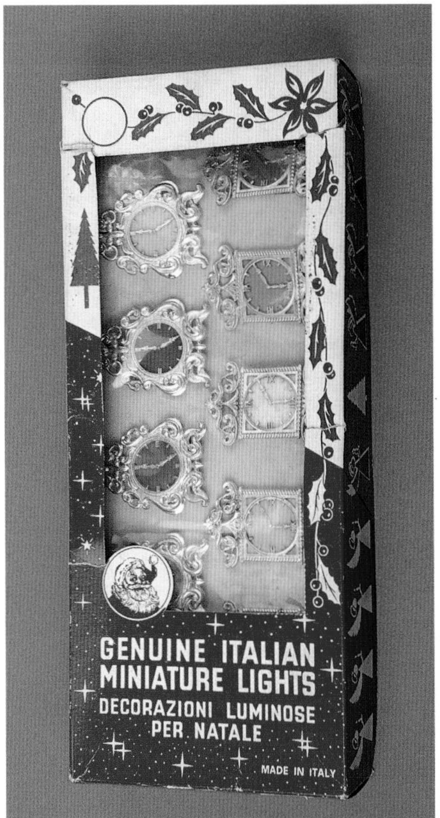

Italian midget light set. Elaborate clock faces into which bulbs were placed. Late 1950s. Bulbs push into sockets. $110-120 for boxed set.

Outdoor Electric Lighting

Outside decorations grew in scale and quantity in the 1950s. No longer satisfied with lighting houses, bushes, and other ornamental features, homeowners turned to plastic life-size figures of the Nativity and carolers as well as hundreds of thousands of snowmen and Santas on their lawns. On one end were nativity scenes consisting of painted hollow figures 48-inches high to candy canes 24-inches in length. All were lit by an intermediate-sized light bulb inserted into the back center of the plastic decoration. Other elaborate, large figures lithographed on card-stock paper were glued onto Masonite and came equipped with wooden spikes for easy erection on lawns. One of the largest advertised was a life-size Santa supported by a wooden frame, with lengths of stiff wire being used to hold the arms in position. The jacket and trousers were made of red oilcloth fitted over the frame and stuffed with old clothing or papers. A Santa Claus mask and hat, gloves, belt, and cotton trim completed the outfit. He was a popular decoration in the early years of this decade.

Our fascination for aluminum trees, wreaths, and branches inside our homes led to the outside, for we used aluminum outside our homes as well. Perforated aluminum "trees" made of three by three-foot sheets of aluminum were lit by the means of a bulb placed inside. *Popular Mechanics* provided patterns for these trees and other outside decorations made with aluminum sheeting.

In 1954, a record two billion lights made America's trees brighter than ever. The use of outdoor lights was up 67 percent since 1947. This demand led to improvements in the lights themselves. Fused-on enamels gave smoother, clear, longer-lasting colors. Novel new shapes inspired trimming ideas. Even an adjustable timer to set the blinker interval was created as well as a lamp, which flickered deceptively, like a burning candle.

Municipalities continued to expand their community decorating every season. One of the most elaborate in the nation was at Nela Park, in East Cleveland, where General Electric Lamp Division created fantasies in light which drew an average of 500,000 motorists each year. Towering, stylized trees rising steeply from the Nela hilltop cast muted echoes of color for miles around.

Outdoor display items were sold by the thousands during this decade. Molded of heavyweight translucent vinyl-plastic, with raised figures for a three-dimensional effect, these appeared as Santa in a sleigh being drawn by reindeer, Santa with a pack of goodies on his back, a caroling snowman, and trios of carolers holding a book of songs and a lantern. Even large plaques portraying the Nativity were sold in a 47" x 28-½" size.

Large wooden plywood figures covered with lithographed scenes of Christmas were popular choices for outdoor lighting. Thus this stimulated sales of outdoor floodlights for night viewing of Santa and Sleigh and countless other figures placed on the lawn or even on top of roofs.

Animated Christmas displays began to gain popularity as Americans saw their neighbors ingeniously animating displays. Animated musicians, choirboys, and nodding Santa figures appeared on lawns. One of the most novel was a design suggested by *Popular Mechanics* in November 1937. Santa spoke through a hidden microphone and speaker. A peephole in the garage allowed the operator to observe passersby and extend friendly personal greetings. Another designed featured Christmas carols via a hidden record player played while entranced cherubs flew back and forth overhead, moved by long loops of clothesline wire, which traveled around two large wheels mounted on short posts on the roof. Still another allowed Santa to appear in a jet plane, flying over the roof, also animated by clothesline wire mounted on a pulley and operated by a small motor. Neighbors attempted to outdo each other in subsequent years with sound and animated displays on their property.

NOMA Santa tree top manufactured through this entire decade. This decoration was used as a tree top, a decoration on the wall, a decoration in the window, and even as a decoration outside. Candelabra-based bulb slipped inside metal Santa with red and white flocked exterior. $45-55 in original box. $15-20 without box.

Paramount plastic Santa going down the chimney with an intermediate-based bulb providing light. Large 28" size. $55-65.

Paramount Santa for indoor and outdoor use. 12" in height. $90-100 with original box. $65-75 alone.

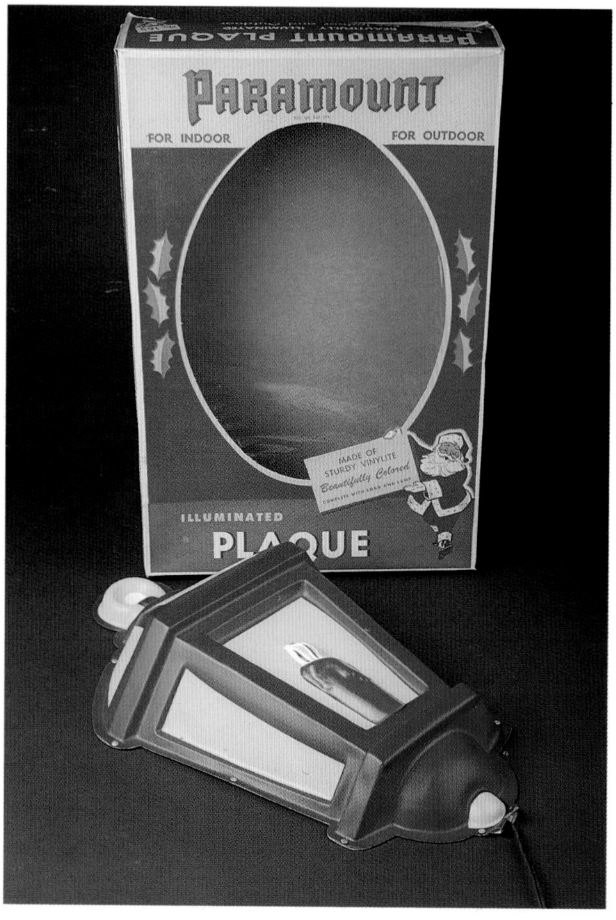

Paramount plastic lantern light-up decoration for use outdoors. Made of a very light plastic, it glowed brightly in the dark. $30-40 complete with box. $15-20 alone.

Assortment of candelabra-based "Candoliers," very popular in this decade. Earlier models from the 1940s were made of wood. Later models from the late 1940s through the 1950s were made of plastic. $6-12 each.

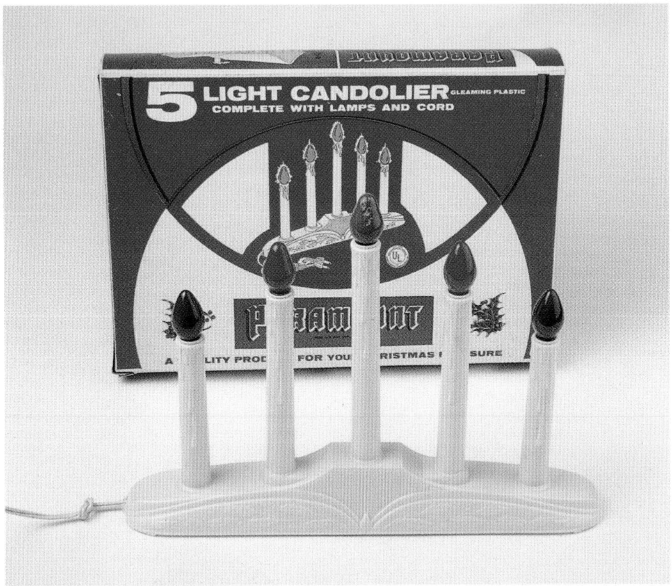

"Candolier" with original box. Typical of the type made in the 1950s. $8-12 with box.

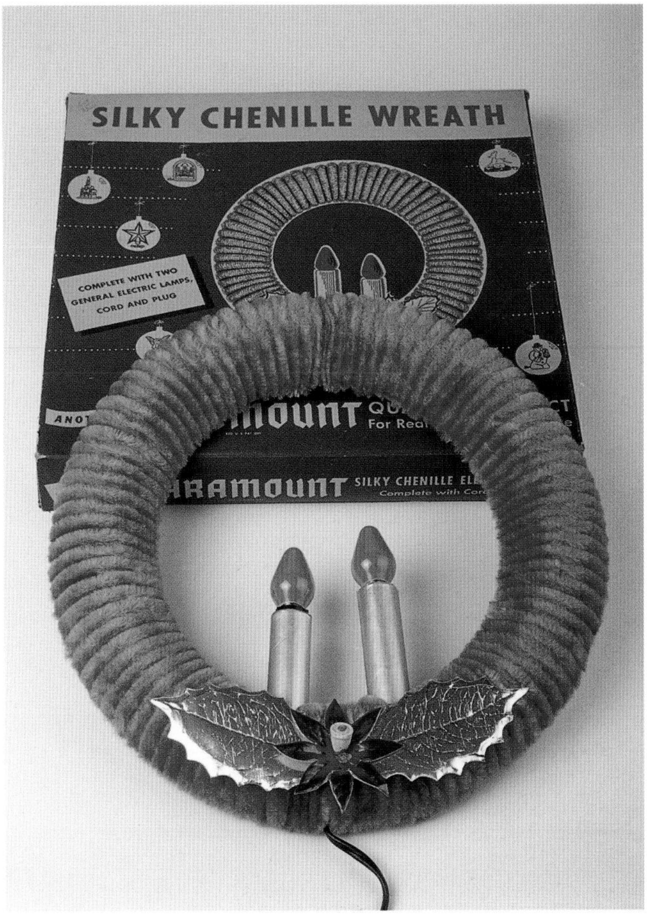

Paramount chenille wrapped wreath. More unusual with two candles. $15-20 with box. $8-15 alone.

The USALITE "Christmas candle" was designed for use inside on tables, but was most often used in windows. The Christmas candle used a candelabra-based bulb. $5-7 with box.

The Paramount chenille wrapped wreath was typical of those wreaths made from the late 1940s to the mid-1950s. $15-20 with box. $10-15 alone.

Cellophane wreath from the early 1950s. Note the NOMA halo around the candelabra-based bulb. $8-15.

References Cited

Brenner, Robert. *Christmas Past.* (3rd edition) Atglen, Pennsylvania: Schiffer Publishing, 1996.

_____. *Christmas Revisited.* (values updated) Atglen, Pennsylvania: Schiffer Publishing, 1998.

_____. *Christmas Through the Decades.* (values updated) Atglen, Pennsylvania: Schiffer Publishing, 2000.

"Christmas hasn't changed—It's just more Plastic." *Oil, Paint and Drug Reporter.* 19 December 1960: 3+.

Country Home: An old-fashioned Christmas. Des Moines, Iowa: Meredith Books, 1992.

Dezso, Douglas M., J. Leon Poirier, and Rose D. Poirier. *Collector's Guide to Candy Containers.* Paducah, Kentucky: Collector Books, 1998.

Early, Ray and Eilene. *Snow Babies.* Ohio: Newark Leader Printing Co., 1983.

Ehernberger, Jerry. *Keeping Christmas, Collecting Memories.* Chicago, Illinois: Jerry Ehernberger, 1997.

Hillier, Bevis. *Greetings from CHRISTMAS PAST.* Great Britain: The Herbert Press, 1982.

Iwamasa, Robert. *Antique Christmas Figural Light Bulbs.* York, Pennsylvania: Shuman Heritage Printing Co., 1996.

Johnson, George. *CHRISTMAS Ornaments, Lights, and Decorations* (values updated). Paducah, Kentucky: Collector Books, 1995.

_____. *CHRISTMAS, Ornaments, Lights, and Decorations Volume II.* Paducah, Kentucky: Collector Books, 1997.

_____. *CHRISTMAS, Ornaments, Lights, and Decorations Volume III.* Paducah, Kentucky: Collector Books, 1997.

Kaufman, J. G. and Jerry Ehernberger. *THE HISTORY AND CATALOG OF ELECTRIC CHRISTMAS LIGHT BULBS.* Prospect, Kentucky: Christmas Antiques, Inc., 1978.

Lasansky, Jeanette. *HOLIDAY PAPER HONEYCOMB.* Lewisburg, Pennsylvania: Oral Traditions Project, 1993.

Moore, Connie A. and Harry L. Rinker. *SNOW GLOBES.* Pennsylvania: Running Press, 1993.

Neuwirth, Waltraud. *Glasperlen Christbaumschmuck.* Vienna, Austria: Selbstverlag, 1995.

Pinkerton, Charlene. *Holiday Plastic Novelties: The Styrene Toys.* Atglen, Pennsylvania: Schiffer Publishing Ltd., 1999.

Rinker, Harry L. "Let it snow, let it snow, let it snow." *Antique Week (Central Edition).* 20 December 1993: 1+.

Rintz, Don. "Christmas Greetings from Racine." *The Golden Glow of Christmas Past Newsletter.* August 1995: 61-62.

Rittenhouse, Judith A. *ORNAMENTAL AND FIGURAL NUTCRACKERS.* Paducah, Kentucky: Collector Books, 1993.

Snyder, Phillip V. *The Christmas Tree Book.* New York: Viking Press, 1976.

Segeth, Uwe-Volker. *Nostalgischer Weihnachtsschmuck.* Augsburg, Germany: Battenberg, 1994.

Stille, Eva. *Christbaumschmuck.* Nuremberg, West Germany: Rinehardt & Company, 1979.

_____. *Christbaumschmuck des 20. Jahrhunderts.* Munich, Germany: Klinkhardt & Bierman, 1993.

_____. *Ulter Christbaumschmuck.* Nuremberg, West Germany: Rinehardt & Company, 1972.

Whitmyer, Margaret and Ken. *CHRISTMAS COLLECTIBLES.* Paducah, Kentucky: Collector Books, 1994.

Index

Advertising blotters, 15
Advertising Calendars, 1950s, 84
Advertising greeting cards, 81
Advertising matches, 15
Advertising, 1940s, 14-7
Advertising, 1950s, 84,87
Aerosol snow, 89
Aluminum tree top, 117
Aluminum trees, 92
Amer. Brake Shoe Co., 115
Amer. Indian, Italian ornament (orn.), 112
American orn., 1950s, 115
American sphere orn., 116
Angel hair, 43
Angel, Italian orn., 114
Angel, orn. Glass, 107
Angel, plastic, 130
Angels, wax, 42
Animals, celluloid, 46-7
Artificial snow, 1940s, 43
Artificial snow, 1950s, 90
Augsburg annuals, 85
Autry, Gene, 10
B. Schackman Co., 115
Ballerina, Italian orn., 112
Banks, plaster, 147,149
Banks, Santa, 51-2
Banks, vermiculite, 147, 149
Beading, glass, 120
Beading, Japanese, 120
Bear orn., glass, 107
Becker, Karl, 112
Beistle decorations, 22
Bells of St. Nicholas, 64
Bells, Japanese, 33
Bing Crosby, 69
Bird orn., glass, 107
Books, 1940s, 16-17
Books, 1950s, 85-6
Books, mechanical, 86
Books, pop-ups, 1950s, 85
Boots, plastic, 135
Bradford Novelty Co., 129-30
Bradford Novelty Santa, 144
Brush trees, 1940s, 45-6
Brush trees, 1950s, 139-40
Bubble light tree, large, 167
Bubble lights, 1940s, 58-61
Bubble lights, oil, 59-60
Bubble lite trees, 1940s, 22
Business, 1940s, 9
Business, 1940s, 9
Calendars, 1940s, 16-7
Cambridge Plastics Co., 38
Candelabra lamps, 53
Candle holders, 97
Candles, 1940s, 41-2
Candles, 1950s, 127-8
Candles, Santa, 42
Candoliers, 1950s, 172-3
Candy box place settings, 122
Candy canes, plastic, 129
Candy containers, 1940s, 35-8
Candy containers, 1950s, 121-3
Candy containers, Austria, 121
Candy containers, glass, 35, 121
Candy containers, metal, 123
Candy containers, paper, 36-7,123
Candy containers, plastic, 36-7,122
Candy ornaments, 124
Captain Kid, Italian orn., 114
Car, plastic, 146
Cardboard orn., 1950s, 124
Cardboard ornaments, 33
Cards, 1940s, 14-5
Caroler candles, 127
Cat head, Italian orn., 114
Cellophane decorations, 21
Cellophane tree, 169
Cellophane wreath, 1950s, 173
Cellophane wreaths, 21
Celluloid animals, 46-7,140-1
Celluloid deer, silver, 140
Celluloid nodders, 141
Celluloid ornaments, 1940s, 21
Celluloid Santa Claus, 48-9
Celluloid Santa/sleigh, 47-9
Celluloid, 1950s, 140
Cellulose acetate, 141
Cellulose-acetate lights, 164
Ceramic decorations, 128
Ceramics, 93-7
Chandelier, plastic, 132
Cheerbrite boxed set, 57
Chenille cross, 22
Chenille wreath, 1950s, 173
Choir boy, plastic, 130
Choir trio, 147
Christmas crackers, 1940s, 10
Christmas crackers, 1950s, 69
Church candy boxes, 123
Church, plastic, 130
Circus crackers, 124
Clock faced Italian lites, 171
Clown orn., glass, 107
Clown, Italian orn., 114
Cohn, Irwin, 39
Cole, Helen, 93
Color wheel floodlight, 93
Coloring books, 86
Comic books, 86
Corning Glass Co. 1940s, 24-5
Corning glass, 1950s, 115
Cotton ornaments, 99
Cowboy, Italian orn., 114
Crackers, Christmas, 10, 69
Crèche, Amer. Cardboard, 137
Crèche, Italian, 138
Crèche, Japanese, 138
Crosby, Bing, 69
Czech bead orn., 1940s, 28-9
Czech bead orn., 1950s, 111
Czech. Customs, 111
Czechoslovakia, 110-11
Deer, plastic, 130
Dennison Manufact. Co., 22
Display Santa, 87
Dittman, Paul, 55
Double-Glo, 124
Dow Chemical Co., 124
Dresden ornaments, 124
East German cooperatives, 100-2
East German orn., 98-106
Eckardt, Ernst Paul, 99
Eckardt, Max, 24,115
Egg shaped Italian lites, 171
Eisenhower, President, 69
Elastolin, 136
Electric bulbs, candelabra, 52
Electric bulbs, intermediate, 52
Electric bulbs, miniature, 52
Electric Christmas Bells, 164
Elf w/skis, Italian orn., 114
Elf w/snowball, Italian orn., 114
Elf, Italian orn., 114
Elves, plastic, 135
English candy containers, 123
Ernstthal, 98-9
Ethic trees, 98
Fences, 1940s, 44
Fences, 1950s, 139
Fleischer, Max, 10
Flocked trees, 89
Floodlighting trees, 155
FLORIDA, 112
Fluorescent lights, 62
Fluorescent orn., 1940s, 38
Fluorescent orn., 1950s, 131
Football player, Italian orn., 114
Frank Paper Products, 129
French sold., Italian orn., 114
French trees, 98
Frog orn., glass, 107
Garland Tinsel boxes, 125
Garland, foil, 124
Garland, foil fiber, 125
Garlands, cellophane, 34, 125
Garlands, chenille, 34, 125
Garlands, tinsel, 124
Geometric Italian lites, 171
Gift boxes, 1950s, 83
Gift tags, 1940s, 19
Gildemeister, Carl, 80
Glass beading, 120
Glass orn., World War II, 22-4
Glass orn. Catalogs, 102-6
Glass orn., American, 24-6
Glass orn., Europe, 1950s, 98-114
Glass orn., Europe, 1940s, 26-9
Glass, wire-wrapped, 27
Glo-lite boxed sets, 160
Glolite bubble lights, 59
Glolite trees, 22
Glowlite Cross, 68
Greeting Card Assoc., 15
Greeting cards, 1940s, 14-7
Greeting cards, 1950s, 80-2
Gurley Company, 41-2
Halvorson, Roy, 89
Happy-Time boxed sets, 160
Heartland Plastic, 136
Heim, Harry Sr., 24,115
Holt-Howard china, 93
Home-crafted, 1940s, 30
Home-crafted, 1950s, 93-4
Houses, Japan, 1940s, 45
Houses, Japan, 1950s, 139
Howard, Charles W., 9
Icicles, plastic, 136
Imports, 1940s, 23
INARCO, 96
Indents, Amer. Orn., 116
Indents, Italian orn., 112
Indian, Italian orn., 112
Indoor lighting, 1950s, 154-6
Inge-Glas, 110
Intermediate lamps, 53
Irwin Corporation, 39-40, 141
Italian lights, early, 168
Italian lights, mirror, 171
Italian lights, purple, 168
Italian lights, red plastic, 169
Italian lites, 1950s, 168-71
Italian ornaments, 112-14
Italian tree, cellophane, 169
Italy, 112-14
Jablonec, 110
JABLONEX, 110
Japanese bead orn., 111
Japanese china, 93-7
Japanese ornaments, 29
K & W Glass Works, 25
Kirk, Paul, 89
Kiss L Toe Advertising, 84
Kitten in shoe orn., glass, 107
Korean War, 69
Krebs & Sohn, 99, 109
Krebs, Erika, 109
Krebs, Helmut, 109-10
Krebs, Wilma, 110
Kristolite reflectors, 54-5

Kurt S. Adler, Inc., 25
Lauscha, 1940s, 26-7
Lauscha, 1950s, 98-102
Lawson, Myron O., 80
Lead tinsel, 1950s, 126
Lefton china, 93
Lighted ice lamp, 155
Lineol, 136
Magic-Glow Corp., 40
Maietta, Frank J., 115
Marks, Johnny, 10
Marolin, 136
Marzipan orn., 124
Matchless stars, 55-6
Matison, John, 69
May & Scofield, 60
May, Robert L, 8
Mechanical books, 86
Metal decorations, 128
Mexican, Italian orn., 114
Mica, 43
Midget lights, Italy, 155
Midget lights, Japan, 155
Midwest Importers, 128
Milk glass lights, 1940s, 65
Milk glass lights, 1950s, 154
Miller outdoor lights, 160
Milwaukee Pulp Products, 50
Miniature lamps, 53
Mirrored ornaments, 30
Muller-Blech Heinz, 26-7, 110
Municipal displays, 1950s, 171
Musical centerpieces, 66-7
Musical instr., plastic, 131
Musketeer, Italian orn., 114
Musser, Fred, 20
Napco creamer, 95
National Christmas Tree, 8
National Tinsel Co., 124
Nativities, American, 44
Nativities, West German, 44
Nativity scenes, 1940s, 44
Nativity scenes, 1950s, 136-8
Nodder, hard plastic, 147
Nodders, celluloid, 141
NOMA biscuit bubble lites, 60
NOMA bubble lites, 166
Noma Electric Corp., 56-60,154
NOMA halo reflectors, 63
NOMA halos, 162
NOMA Santa tree top, 172
NOMA twinkling set, 163
Nutcrackers, 128
Oberfrankische Glas, 99
Occupied Japan, 27-8
Occupied Japan nodder, 49
Occupied Japan toy, 151
Office of Civil Defense, 54,67
Office of Precious Metals, 38
Oil bubble lights, 60
Otis, Charles, 58-9
Outdoor lighting, 1940s, 67-8
Paper ornaments, 33
Paper ornaments, 1950s, 124
Papier-mâché, 50-1
Papier-mâché, 1950s, 140
Paramount boxed set, 57
Paramount Santa lite, 172
Paramount tree top, 117
Paramount wall plaques, 66
Peerless boxed set, 56
Pencil sharpeners, 52
Perma-Lite boxed set, 158
Plaster figures, 93
Plaster of Paris banks, 51-2
Plastic figural lights, 63
Plastic icicles, 129
Plastic ornaments, 1940s, 21-2
Plastic rosette lights, 65
Plastic, 1940s, 38-41
Plastic, 1950s, 129-36
Plax Corporation, 40
Plush Santa figures, 148
Poland, 27-8
Polish ornaments, 1950s, 108
Polystyrene, 129
Pulpco, 140
Puzzles, 87
Rauch, Marshall, 129
Records, 1940s, 18
Reflectors, 1940s, 55-6
Reflectors, 1950s, 162
Reindeer, celluloid, 46
Reindeer/Santa boxed set, 144
Relpo Ceramics, 95
Rempel, Fritz, 99
Renown Biscuit bubbles, 168
Renown bubble lights, 166
Revolving color light, 93
Reynold's Aluminum, 92
Ribbon, 1940s, 18-9
Ribbon, 1950s, 84
Rockefeller Plaza, 9-10
Rocket bubble lights, 165-6
Roosevelt, President, 8
Rosbro Plastics, 39
Rosen Plastic Co., 36-39
Ross, Gerd, 98-9
Royal biscuit bubble lites, 60
Royal Bubble lights, 164
Royal electric items, 155
Rudolph beverage tray, 87
Rudolph cake mold, 87
Rudolph candles, 127
Rudolph night light, 87
Rudolph reindeer, 1940s, 8
Rudolph sleigh, plastic, 143
Rudolph tin board, 87
Rudolph top-45, 133
Rudolph, plastic, 133
Russia, 114
Sadacca, Henri, 56-7,154
Sal Puleo Co., 89
Salt/pepper shakers, 96
Samurai man, Italian orn., 114
San Puleo, 89
Santa,
Santa baby dolls, 149
Santa candles, 42
Santa candy box, 122
Santa celluloid toys, 153
Santa Claus school, 9
Santa Claus shortage, 9
Santa Claus, hard plastic, 144
Santa Claus, silver-coated, 144
Santa Heim, 115
Santa in boat, plaster, 147
Santa in chimney toy, 151
Santa in easy chair, 149
Santa in sleigh, plastic, 134
Santa Lite boxed set, 158
Santa match holder, 147
Santa on deer toy, 151
Santa on deer, plastic, 146
Santa on house, bisque, 147
Santa on skis, plastic, 134
Santa orn., glass, 107
Santa ornaments, plastic, 133
Santa pull toy, plastic, 145
Santa tool set, plastic, 134
Santa toys, plastic, 145-6
Santa w/bell toy, 152
Santa w/book toy, 152
Santa w/sign toy, 152
Santa w/skis toy, 152
Santa wind-up toy, 148
Santa, battery toys, 153
Santa, bisque, 147
Santa, bisque candy cont., 148
Santa, Japanese, 150
Santa, papier-mâché, 150
Santa, plush, 148
Santa/sleigh celluloid, 143
Santa/sleigh plastic, 143
Santa/sleigh, cardboard, 52
School candy boxes, 123
Schwab & Frank, 129
Seahorse, Italian orn., 114
Seiffen, East Germany, 35
Series boxed set, 158
Sheet music, 1940s, 17
Shooting star bubble lites, 61
Shopping displays, 69
Sleigh-O-Lights, 66
Sleighs, silver-coated, 144
Snap-on orn., plastic, 135
Snow domes, 129
Snow flocking, 92
Soldier, Italian orn., 112
Song birds, plastic, 131
Sorcerer, Italian orn., 112
Spun glass angel hair, 90
Spun glass manuf., 98-9
Star Band Co., 92
Stars, plastic, 132
Steinach, 99-102
Steinbach, 128
Steuben, 24
Stockings, 121
Styrofoam ornaments, 129
Symbolism, ornaments, 108
Table decorations, 1940s, 51
Tavern Candle Co., 128
Thompson, Bill, 24
Tinkle Toy Co., 154
Tins, 37-8
Tinsel ornaments, 126
Tinsel, lead, 1940s, 34-5
Toys, battery operated, 151-3
Tree hooks, 90
Tree stands, 136
Tree top, aluminum, 117
Tree top, Paramount, 117
Tree top, plastic, 117
Tree top, Polish, 117
Tree tops, 1940s, 31-2
Tree tops, 1950s, 117-19
Tree tops, American, 117
Tree tops, West German, 117
Tree, feather, 20
Tree, viscose, 20
Trees, aluminum, 92
Trees, artificial, 1950s, 20
Trees, brush, 1940s, 45-6
Trees, brush, 1950s, 139-40
Trees, feather, 1950s, 89
Trees, flocked, 89
Trees, live, 1940s, 19-20
Trees, live, 1950s, 89
Trees, Visca, 1950s, 89
Turbaned Indian, Italian orn., 112
Twinkle lamps, 155
U.S. Zone ornaments, 109
Ulbricht, Otto, 128
USALITE electric candle, 173
USALITE set, 163
VEB, 98-100
Village houses, 1940s, 44-5
Village houses, 1950s, 139
Village houses, Japanese, 139
Village houses, wooden, 44-5
Visca bubble trees, 154,156
Visca trees, 89-90
War Production Board, 14
Ward, Joseph, 154
War-time lighting, 54-5
Wax angels, 42
Wax boots, 41
Wax figural orn., 41
Wax ornaments, 1940s, 41-2
Wax ornaments, 1950s, 127
Wax Santa heads, 123
Waxed paper stars, 41
Wegner Family, 110
Welk, Lawrence cards, 82
West German orn., 107-10
West Germany, 107
White visca trees, 93
Whitehurst, Olga and Carl, 27
Whitman Publishing Co., 80
Whitman story books, 85
Whitman's cards, 80
Wicked step sisters, 113
Winslow, Helen, 98
Winter Olympic orn., 113
Wire-wrapped orn., 1950s, 109
Wisconsin Delux Co., 121
Wise men, plastic, 134
Wonder stars, 56
Wooden ornaments, 1940s, 35
Wooden ornaments, 1950s, 128
Wrapping paper, 1940s, 18-9
Wrapping paper, 1950s, 82-3
Wreath, cellophane, 1950s, 173
Wreath, chenille, 1950s, 173